ART IN CONTEXT

THIRD EDITION

ART IN
CONTEXT
THIRD EDITION

Jack A. Hobbs
Illinois State University

Harcourt Brace Jovanovich, Publishers

San Diego   New York   Chicago   Atlanta   Washington, D.C.

London   Sydney   Toronto

To
  Marge
  Amy
  Martin—
  And to the memory of
  Ethel Hobbs

Preface

The basic approach of *Art in Context* has not changed since the publication of the first edition in 1975. The tendency then to emphasize the formal aspects of art was still relatively strong; an introductory textbook that stressed the cultural and psychological aspects was something of a novelty. Today, however, the importance of these latter considerations in the interpretation and appreciation of works of art is widely recognized: The word *context* now plays its proper role in contemporary critical vocabulary.

While not changing the basic approach, the Second Edition underwent major revisions: an expansion and rearrangement of some of the material in Part I, the deletion of two chapters and the addition of a new chapter in Part II, and the enlargement of each chapter in Part III. These changes were the result of my personal observations while teaching art appreciation at Illinois State University.

Revisions in the text of this, the Third Edition, are relatively modest: increasing the vocabulary related to the analysis of art in Chapter 1; expanding, together with identifying the antiquity of, the various media reviewed in Chapter 3; adding examples of architecture in Chapter 4; rewriting Chapter 6 to effect a more consistent survey of the development of the nude; and updating Chapter 11 in view of the latest developments in art. Wherever possible, relevant material and examples covered in earlier parts of the book are referred to in the later parts so the student may better integrate the total presentation.

The most significant change in this edition consists of providing chronologies for Parts II and III and a 240-term glossary. The Part II chronology lists all of the works reviewed in Chapters 5, 6, 7, and 8 (plus related works in Parts I and III) in chronological order so the student can see quickly and easily how one particular work relates temporally to others. The Part III chronology lists all the artworks in Parts I and II that relate to the development of the modern movement as presented in Chapters 9, 10, and 11.

As in the previous editions, each of the three parts deals with a basic context of art. Part I examines the perceptual context: the influence of artists' and viewers' cultural backgrounds on what they see, the visual elements, and the various media. Part II presents the human context and is organized around several major themes of art. It demonstrates the reciprocal relationship between art and life by analyzing why artists of different cultures depict nature in markedly different ways and how artists of different eras express their beliefs and ideas in images instead of words. Finally there is the historical context, Part III, in which the process of change in art is examined and the major developments of the modern era are traced by focusing on the evolution of new forms of visual expression.

Organization according to the major contexts and themes of art permits a freer treatment of each topic and a broader range of examples than does the traditional historical approach. Works from different periods, places, and media are compared and contrasted in ways that provide readers with a vivid sense of the purposes of art. Accordingly, wherever feasible, works have been selected that serve not only to illustrate a particular point but to offer striking juxtapositions—encouraging students to experience the pleasure of making their own connections and drawing their own conclusions.

Once again I thank the professors and doctoral students at Illinois State University whose advice I sought while writing the First Edition—and whose ideas are preserved in this Third Edition. I also wish to recognize members of the Caucus on Social Theory and Art Education—especially Robert Bersson of James Madison University and Lanny Milbrandt of Wichita State University—for their encouragement and for their contributions to the development of my ideas.

Finally, I thank Robert C. Miller, my house editor at Harcourt Brace Jovanovich, for his diligence and high standards in editing. My thanks also go to Amy Krammes, art editor, and Cheryl Solheid, designer, for their efforts during the critical stages of completing the book.

Jack A. Hobbs

Contents

ART IN
CONTEXT
THIRD EDITION

I Perceptual Context

What we see depends in large part on *how* we see. Our perception of even such an ordinary object as a hamburger is affected not only by the visual data of its shape and color but also by our knowledge of hamburgers—which includes such things as their taste, smell, feel, and ability to satisfy hunger.

What we see in a work of art also depends on a combination of visual information and past experience. The ability to perceive images in the lines and shapes that artists put on a piece of paper or canvas is not automatic. We need practice and experience simply to interpret the kinds of pictures that are widely familiar in our own society.

The aesthetic horizons of today are broader than those of the past. Art museums and art books gererally show art not only from our own society but from those of the past and those of other parts of the world. Furthermore, the artists around us are constantly trying to develop new forms of art, which further increases the variety of art that we may encounter. The knowledge and perceptual habits we have developed for looking at art in the past may therefore be inadequate for the present.

Part I consists of four chapters that focus on the perceptual context of the visual arts. Here we will deal first with the effects of differences in cultural backgrounds on how art is perceived; then with the visual elements that artists manipulate, and how these elements can be used to affect our perception of artworks; and finally, with the diverse materials and techniques that artists use to create their works—media that can range from pencil and paper to the materials needed to construct a skyscraper.

1 Context

When we speak of *language,* we ordinarily think of a system of communicating with words and sounds. But language, taken in a larger sense, can mean any system of communicating. For example, one *nonverbal* language that we are all familiar with is the one that has been popularly dubbed "body language." We all use body language every day. Indeed, we use it almost every moment of every day, for we say few things that we do not accompany with a gesture or change in facial expression—consciously or unconsciously—that says the same thing. Very often we can figure out what people are talking about without even hearing their voices. And sometimes we can tell what they *really* mean even though what they say is just the opposite.

Most of the body-language signals people make are conventions that have developed within their particular culture or subculture. The gesture that a Spaniard makes to indicate "come here" is almost the opposite of the gesture that an American makes. Some Asians, it has been observed, are likely to be expressing anger if their eyes open wider, whereas Occidentals usually express surprise that way. So perhaps it would be more accurate to say body *languages,* since they seem as numerous as spoken languages.

**Art as
Language**

The visual arts are also nonverbal languages, but in more ways than one might expect. We all know that paintings communicate, and that we are able to derive some information from them

4

more effectively than we can from words. A great many words would be needed to describe a miracle performed by a saint or what the Rocky Mountains looked like in 1848 with the same degree of detail found in a painted image of such a subject. But few of us are aware of the fact that obtaining information from an image is not automatic—not even from the most realistic picture of a familiar subject. We have to be able to "read" a particular system of distortions that has been used to translate the original three-dimensional scene into a two-dimensional reproduction.

In some ways, learning a visual language is like learning a spoken language. For example, most Americans learn to read the language of cartoons and photographs in very much the same manner they learn English. Their parents explain the vocabulary and the grammar of comic strips by reading the text and translating the pictures for them ("The little boy is unhappy. See the tears?") and tell them what to look for and how to identify it in home snapshots ("This is your birthday party. See Grandma?"). Learning to read a photograph may not sound like much of a challenge, but in fact there are many people who have never learned to do this. In *The Shape of Time,* art historian George Kubler describes an experience with a Peruvian shepherd who had never seen a photograph before.

> . . . when I produced a photograph of him . . . he was unable to orient the flat, spotty paper or to read it as a self-portrait, for want of those complicated habits of translation which the rest of us perform from two to three dimensions without effort.

The Peruvian shepherd, because of a lack of experience with these particular pictorial conventions, could not even identify his own image. But we who have grown up with photography and movies take these things so much for granted that it is hard for us to imagine anyone in the world not being able to grasp their meaning immediately. In order to understand this, let us turn the situation around and look at an image that is not familiar to our own culture.

An Alaskan Mask

We would not say that this Alaskan Indian mask (fig. 1-1) has no meaning at all for us. We recognize the image of a face, which immediately generates several associations and ideas. But how well do we actually understand it? Before going any further, let us try to decide exactly what it is we see here. The following

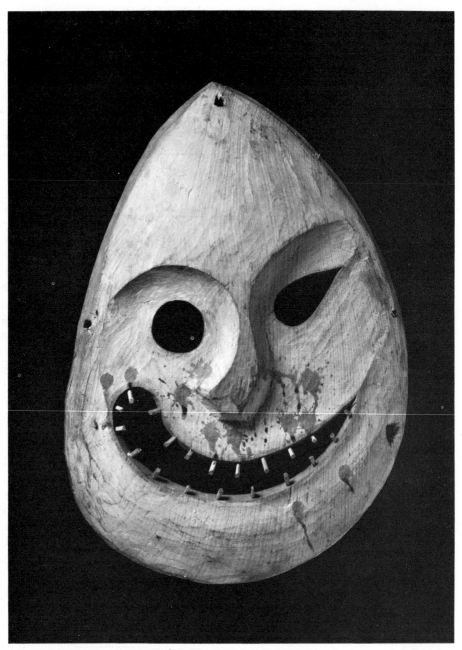

1-1　Alaskan Indian mask. Museum für Volkerkunde, Berlin.

description will be simple and objective—that is, limited to statements about the appearance of the mask that all of us could agree with.

To begin with, it is obviously not a realistic image of a face. Consequently, we may say that it is a "stylized" image. The shape of the head and the arrangement of the features are asymmetrical and do not seem very precise or detailed. Most of the mask is convex, but there is a concave area surrounding the main features. One eye is circular, the other almond-shaped. A spiral movement starts along the edge of the scroll-shaped nose, moves around the circular eye, and is carried by the mouth to the other side of the face. There it almost joins with the S-shaped line that forms the eyebrow and the other edge of the nose. The surface of the mask reveals the marks of the carver's tool, and there is a spattering of color around the mouth.

We would probably try to interpret this mask in the same way that we interpret images of faces in our own art. Characteristically, we read an upturned mouth as smiling or laughing. The almond-shaped eye suggests a wink, which reinforces the idea of smiling. Still, there is so little information yet so many unusual features that this face is not very easy to understand. For example, we are not accustomed to asymmetry in the representation of a face. Why are the eyes different shapes? Why is the nose twisted and the mouth off to the side? Does the mask represent someone who has been frightened? Or does it represent a simple-minded person, or a madman?

We soon become aware that our cultural background is inadequate for helping us to interpret the mask. And even if we were told that it represents a man-eating mountain demon with a bloodstained face, many things would remain unclear. We still would not know how those people regarded demons. Were all demons alike? Was this one to be feared or pitied? Did the Alaskan Indians represent both their benevolent and malevolent spirits with lopsided faces? Obviously there are many questions that need to be answered before we can begin to understand this particular artwork. We can enjoy looking at it, but we are not able to fully interpret it.

Peanuts   Americans looking at a comic strip of Charlie Brown and his dog Snoopy (fig. 1-2) can understand what is going on and relate it to their own experience, even though it is an improbable situation. If they had never seen the *Peanuts* comic strip before but were reasonably well-informed and three years old or more,

1-2 Charles M. Schulz, Charlie Brown and Snoopy.
© 1973 United Feature Syndicate, Inc.

they would still understand that this is a picture of a little boy and his pet dog. But if we look at Charlie Brown's face as closely as we did at the Alaskan mask, we will realize that it actually has less detail and is less realistic than the mask. Everything is expressed with extreme economy. When he speaks, Charlie Brown's mouth, like that of the mask, is a simple void. In the final frame, however, it is downturned, which we interpret as unhappiness. The eyes are no more than a pair of dots bounded by curved lines, but they help us to define his reaction. Charlie Brown's hair is an abstract scrawl above his eyes, and Snoopy's nose is a black dot stuck to the side of his face. But because we are so familiar with these conventions of drawing, we grasp their meaning at a glance.

There is more meaning in *Peanuts* than just the depictions of a boy and a dog. At times it reveals a great many things about the anxieties of growing up in suburban America, public schools, and peer relationships. In order to understand these themes in *Peanuts*, one has to have some familiarity with twentieth-century American culture. And it also helps if one is familiar with the ways in which these themes have been treated not only by the cartoon but by movies, television, and novels. People who lack this knowledge are at a disadvantage in understanding *Peanuts*—just as we are in understanding the image of a mountain demon when we know so little about Alaskan culture.

Picasso People who are unfamiliar with the work of Pablo Picasso or who are unwilling to accept his personal artistic language often do not care for paintings like *First Steps* (fig. 1-3). They are apt to criticize such things as the gross hands and feet, the lopsided faces and bodies, the simple eyes, and the abnormally foreshortened head of the mother. Oddly enough, these same people are rarely aware of the radical distortions of anatomy that are committed daily in *Peanuts* and other comic strips. However, the difference between the painting by Picasso and the cartoon by Schulz does not rest only on the fact that the latter uses more familiar conventions. A Picasso painting is not meant to be as easily understood as a frame of a Schulz cartoon.

Describing *First Steps* is a rather formidable task compared to that of describing the mask or the picture of Charlie Brown, so we will have to concentrate on only its more conspicuous aspects. The dominant feature in the painting is the child's face, especially the eyes, which are wide ellipses staring straight at us. Like the Alaskan mask, the shape of the head and the ar-

1-3   Pablo Picasso, *First Steps,* 1943. Oil on canvas, 51¼″ × 38¼″.
Yale University Art Gallery, New Haven, Connecticut (gift of Stephen C.
Clark, B.A. 1903).

rangement of facial features are asymmetrical. But unlike the mask, which was dominated by a spiral form, the face of the infant is made up of lines and shapes that come and go in many directions. The mother's face, which appears smaller than the child's, seems to be looking downward. Her head, neck, and body arch around the infant, while her elongated hand on the right side seems to be both prodding and supporting his hand. Although we recognize the forms of two different people, the many shapes and lines within the picture tend to confuse their separateness so that, in places, the bodies of mother and child and the space around them become a single shape. This effect can be seen at the top of the painting, where the arched lines of the mother's head, eyes, and breasts complement the lines in the child's head; at the right and left sides, where the stubbier lines of hands interpenetrate; and at the bottom, where legs, feet, and ground are all warped in similar ways.

We can identify the subject of Picasso's painting because it is close enough to forms of representation that we already understand—in particular to the forms of *Peanuts*. (And this is largely because Picasso's art influenced artists who draw cartoons, not the other way around.) We can also appreciate some things about the way *First Steps* is presented because elements of it— the archlike protective shape of the mother, for example—are simple and direct enough for us to grasp. But most people run into problems if they try to go beyond the subject matter and these few elements. Why, for instance, does the child's face look the way it does? Someone unfamiliar with art might rightly guess that there is some relationship between these distortions and those of children's paintings. But *First Steps* also contains references to such things as Christian Madonnas of the Renaissance, African masks, and Picasso's own Cubist experiments (figs. 1-4 and 1-5). The fact is that without some knowledge of the language of Western art and the themes that have been important in the past, we cannot appreciate the richness of this painting or grasp much of its meaning.

The meaning of Picasso's *First Steps* is more than the simple act that the title helps us discover in these shapes and colors—a mother helping her infant son take his first steps. So to stop at this level of meaning is to seriously impoverish an exceptional work of art. First steps are, after all, a major moment in the life of any human being—"a moment of crisis in which eagerness, determination, insecurity, and triumph are mingled," as museum director Alfred Barr once wrote of this painting. Picasso

1-4   Fra Lippo Lippi,
Madonna and Child (detail),
1437. Galleria Nazionale
d'Arte antica, Rome.

1-5   African Negro Mask,
c. 1775. Wood, 14″ high.
Itumba region, Africa.
Collection, The Museum of
Modern Art, New York
(given anonymously).

used a particular artistic language to express this deeper meaning, and we can find it there if we know how to read his work. It is in the way the child's face is distorted, in the radiating lines of his clothing, the awkward balance of his body, the protective domelike shape of the mother, and at least a dozen other details. All of these help to convey the emotions of this extraordinary moment.

Art as Abstract Form

Meaning is not the only thing we can get from a work of art. We can also derive satisfaction from an appreciation of its *form*: its abstract colors, its lines and textures, and the ways in which these things are combined. For example, looking at the Alaskan mask we might spend less time trying to determine its meaning and more time considering such things as its unusual texture, the random spatters of color, and the relationship of the openings to its overall shape. Looking at the Picasso, we could spend an enjoyable time observing and appreciating its bold contrasts of light and dark, its complex patterns, and the solid construction of its composition. In fact, there are many who place an enormous value on responding to art in this way. And some art—especially certain kinds of twentieth-century abstract art—seems intended to be appreciated only in this way.

Most, however, believe that a full appreciation of an artwork, even a very abstract one, involves not only responding to its form but also seeking its meaning—the unique way in which it contributes to our understanding of the world. To accomplish this degree of appreciation and to derive the most from art requires knowledge, patience, and—most importantly—an open mind.

Some Basic Terminology

The terms "medium," "subject matter," "form," and "content" refer to different aspects of a work of art and constitute a systematic way of thinking about it.

Medium refers to the materials and methods employed in creating a work. The medium of the mask is carved wood, that of the comic strip is pen and ink on paper, and that of *First Steps* is oil paints applied to canvas. "Medium" and "media" (plural) also refer to general categories of art such as "popular art," "sculpture," and "painting."

Subject (subject matter) refers to people, objects, or places represented in a work: the face in the mask; the boy, dog, and doghouse in the comic strip; the woman and child in the painting. Like "medium," "subject" can also refer to general categories (themes) such as "childhood" or "religion."

Form, as defined earlier, refers to the lines, colors, and textures—and how these are combined in a work.

Content refers to the meaning of a work. And meaning, as we learn from the examples in this chapter, is based on response to a combination of medium, subject, and form.

Some of the following chapters emphasize only one or two of these aspects of artworks. For example, Chapter 2 emphasizes form, specifically the "visual elements," while Chapters 3 and 4 focus on medium. Similarly, Chapters 5, 6, 7, and 8 (Part II) focus primarily on subject matter and content. Each chapter deals with a different "theme"—another word for subject matter. In Chapters 9, 10, and 11 (Part III), once again the issue is primarily form. But this time, instead of explaining the visual elements, these chapters chronicle the changes and varieties of styles that have sprung up since the beginning of the modern movement.

Summary

When confronting an artwork, one does not ordinarily stop to consider it as a language and then as an abstract form, or deal with each of the aspects one by one. The natural thing to do is to respond to it as a whole. Indeed some critics insist that to do otherwise—to "dissect" a work in terms of the various approaches discussed thus far—does more harm than good. Interestingly, these same critics are often extremely articulate about an artwork and its various aspects.

The most important benefit of art may be its capacity for capturing our undivided attention, a kind of unconditional involvement often described as the *aesthetic experience*. However, this does not mean we should not pause to reflect, to take stock of what we see as well as our reactions to it. To do so in an honest and systematic way helps us not only to know more about art (and ourselves), but also to enjoy more fulfilling experiences in our future encounters with art.

2
The Visual Elements

A painting like Georges Seurat's *Bathing at Asnières* (colorplate 1) is—to us—obviously a picture of boys gathered along a riverbank on a summer day. But let us imagine for a moment how it might appear to the Peruvian shepherd of Chapter 1. If he were to describe what *he* saw as precisely as he could, he might tell us that it is a flat, rectangular surface covered with patches of color.

What is interesting about this is that Seurat himself would probably have described this painting in very much the same way. For the fact is that he was more concerned with arranging the *visual elements* of the painting—colors, shapes, lines, textures, and space—than he was with the recreation of a particular scene. Artists of any sort, whether they make paintings, design buildings, or weld scraps of iron into sculptures, are always basically concerned with the visual elements. This is true whether the work is intended to look like a group of swimmers on a riverbank or an abstract collection of shapes and colors.

By the same token, the viewer must understand something of the visual elements—the form of a work—in order to fully appreciate and enjoy a work of art. To be unaware of the ways that Seurat meticulously organized the visual elements in *Bathing at Asnières* is to miss a great deal of what the painting has to offer. In the following pages, therefore, we will examine these elements in some detail and try to establish a fairly precise and useful set of definitions for them.

Color　The problems of definition begin almost with the first sentence one writes. So many writers on art have approached the visual elements in so many different ways that there is often great disagreement over exactly what the elements are and how they should be dealt with. For example, many people consider _light and dark_ to be a separate element. Others use it, as we will do here, to refer to one property of color.

If we accept the idea of black, white, and gray as being part of color, then we may say that color is basic to all things. Not only that: color is basic to the other visual elements. It is through variations of color that we distinguish shapes, lines, textures, and space.

In order to understand the role of color in art and vision, we must analyze it in terms of three basic properties: _hue, value,_ and _saturation._ Although all three are continually and inseparably present in normal vision, they can be separated in theory and isolated for purposes of this analysis.

Hue　Words like _red_ or _green_ refer to hues, the qualities that differentiate one color from another. Our perception of them is affected by the frequency of the light waves reflected to our eyes from the surface of an object, whether it be a green leaf, a poster printed with red ink, or particles in the atmosphere that deflect the sun's rays and make the sky seem blue. Hue can be established with great precision by measuring light waves with scientific instruments, but for everyday purposes this is certainly not necessary. The words for color that everyone learns in childhood are quite sufficient for communicating to other people what we mean. Yellow, red, blue, green, purple, and orange are rarely confused by Americans with normal vision.

Three of these hues—yellow, red and blue—are called _primary colors_ because they can be combined to create any of the others, except black or white. (Technically the three primaries are _yellow, magenta_—a slightly purplish red—and _cyan_, a turquoise blue. Printers often refer to these as "process yellow," "process red," and "process blue.") Yellow combined with red produces orange, yellow combined with blue produces green, and red combined with blue produces purple. The three new colors—green, purple, and orange—are called _secondary colors_. These relationships can be illustrated with the use of a _color wheel_—or color circle as it was called by Isaac Newton, the man who originally designed it—a circular chart on which each secondary color is placed between the two primary colors of which it is composed (colorplate 2). Most color charts also include *terti-ary colors,* those that lie between the primaries and secondaries and are created by making unequal mixtures of any two of the primaries; many variations are possible. The names of these colors are somewhat arbitrary and often exotic—such as cerulean, aqua, and peacock to name but a few of those that lie between blue and green. Finally, combining all three primaries (or a primary with the secondary color opposite it on the color wheel) produces dull versions of the hues, or browns and grays.

Hues that are situated alongside one another on the color wheel are called *analogous;* those that are directly opposite each other are called *complementary.* The former tend to relate to each other; the latter tend to contrast with each other. Seurat made use of this characteristic of complementaries in *Bathing at Asnières.* He painted many of the surfaces that received the direct light of the sun in variations of orange and the shadows in variations of the complement of orange—blue or blue-violet. He further employed complementaries to make figures stand out from the background—a combination of adjacent colors sometimes referred to as *hue contrast.* The orange cap of the bather on the far right contrasts sharply with the background blue of the water. Less vivid are the variations of the mahogany red of the dog and those objects on the bank that are roughly complementary to the green grass.

Seurat often used an unusual method for producing different color effects. Rather than blending hues before applying them to the canvas, he would apply them unmixed in separate little strokes, allowing them to blend in the viewer's vision— provided the viewer is standing at a normal distance from the canvas. This effect is known as *optical mixing,* and it is the opposite of hue contrast (in which relatively large areas of color are made to appear more separate). We can see the principle at work in the blue-green of the water, which Seurat painted by daubing several hues—mostly blues, greens, and whites—directly on the canvas rather than physically mixing them beforehand. (The same principle was later applied to color printing, with only the three primaries and black ink used to recreate even as complex a subject as this painting.)

Value   The range of light and dark in color is called *value* (colorplate 2). Had Seurat chosen to paint *Bathing at Asnières* with just a single hue—say, red—we would still be able to distinguish the riverbank and the boys and the water because of the different values

2-1
Example of color constancy.

of red. We could easily make out the shapes of figures and details on the basis of their differences in light and dark, for we could read the all-red visual field essentially the same way that we would read a black-and-white photograph.

The range of light and dark we experience in everyday vision is much more relative than we often realize. We tend to think that a white sheet of paper is always the same white, whether it is in bright light or shadow. This effect is referred to as *color constancy*. Normally, we see the color of an egg (fig. 2-1) as a uniform off-white over all of its curved surface. Yet if we look at the image in this photograph as a pattern of lights and darks, we can easily see a great difference in color—specifically the values of the color—between the top and bottom of the egg. Color constancy, then, points up one of the discrepancies between optical data and the mind's interpretation of those data in the everyday business of viewing our world.

Artists, aware of the factor of color constancy, use different values to make an image of something appear three-dimensional. The method for picturing the effect of reflected light as it plays across a surface—whether that of an egg or a human body—was developed several centuries before the time of Seurat. Called shading (technically, *chiaroscuro* from the combined Italian words for light and dark), the method is admirably demonstrated in a study of the boy wearing a straw hat that Seurat drew in preparation for his painting (fig. 2-2). Using broad strokes of crayon on rough-grained paper, the artist skillfully manipulated light and dark values to suggest the volumes of the boy's body and clothing.

2-2 Georges Seurat, *Seated Boy with Straw Hat,* 1883–84. Conté crayon on paper, 9½″ × 11⅞″. Yale University Art Gallery (Everett V. Meeks, B.A. 1901, Fund).

Like hue contrasts, *value contrasts* were used in *Bathing at Asnières* to help set off the figures from their surroundings. We can see the adjustments of color in the river where it forms the background of the central figure. The values of blue touching the shaded parts of the boy—his face, neck, and back—are lighter; those touching the sunlit portions are darker. The artist also adjusted the values around the figures in the water. By so doing, Seurat helped to make these figures stand out from their surroundings.

As is the case with hue, values are subject to optical mixing. Side-by-side black and white lines or brushwork can appear to be shades of gray. In the woodcut *The Four Horsemen of the Apoca-*

2-3
Albrecht Dürer, *The Riders
on the Four Horses from the
Apocalypse*, c. 1496.
Woodcut, 15¼″ × 11″.
Metropolitan Museum of
Art, New York (gift of
Junius S. Morgan, 1919).

lypse (fig. 2-3) we see a masterful use of chiaroscuro: The sixteenth-century German artist Albrecht Dürer used only black ink and the white of the paper, yet the work appears to have a wide range of *middle values,* or grays. If we look carefully, we can see that any of these middle values is actually the result of optical mixing caused by the closely spaced black lines.

Similar to optical mixing is an effect referred to as the *assimilation effect,* in which a pattern of small units of one color superimposed over a different background color seems to cause the color underneath to shift its value and hue somewhat toward that of the pattern. The red of the background in *All Things Do Live in the Three* (colorplate 3) is actually the same throughout, but it appears to be two or three different reds forming subtle but clearly distinguishable diamond-shaped patterns across the canvas. The artist, Richard Anuskiewicz, accomplished this illusion by overlaying the red with a system of uniform dots of blue, green, and yellow.

Saturation   Saturation refers to the the relative purity of a color on a scale from bright to dull (colorplate 2). Most paints are intense to start with; thus an artist who desires a strong blue uses the paint straight from the tube. A less intense, or "muted," blue can be made by mixing blue with brown or with its complement, orange. Some colors are so muted—such as most browns and grays—that they are sometimes called *neutrals*. Typically, most colors in a painting are intermixed and, as a result, tend to be neutrals and/or varieties of muted hues, such as "olive green," "brick red," "burnt orange," and "goldenrod yellow." Seurat, however, did not always mix his pigments; he preferred to use bright colors applied in individual strokes. In colorplate 1, the river, in addition to blues and blue-greens, contains dots of orange that, had they been mixed with the other paint, would have produced a dull, grayish blue. Instead, the orange interacts in our vision without sacrificing the intensity of either. We see a vibration of color, an appropriate equivalent of sparkling water.

Expressive   Although some knowledge of color theory is helpful in under-
Use   standing works of art, the effect of color on human feelings is no
of Color   doubt more important. Color does affect us emotionally, but questions remain as to exactly why and in what ways. Without attempting to deal with these questions in detail, we can summarize some general tendencies of human response to color.

People probably do not respond in a particular way to a particular color by itself. Yet when comparing two or more colors with each other they will respond differently to each one. Yellow compared to purple is cheerful, black compared to white is somber, a bright color compared to a dull color is exciting—and so forth.

Color qualities are often identified with thermal qualities—they are said to be "warm" or "cool." Reds, yellows, and oranges are considered warm; blues, greens, and violets are considered cool. Correspondingly, we usually regard warm colors as stimulating and cool colors as relaxing. There are probably associations between thinking of color this way and the colors of such things as fire, blood, and water. But there may also be a physiological reason for human responses to the different hues. Light consists of energy waves of different lengths, and warm colors have longer wavelengths than cool colors.

Warm colors give the impression of advancing toward the viewer, while cool colors seem retiring. This effect is also achieved by the other properties of color—darker values seem closer than lighter values; brighter intensities seem closer than duller intensities. Reasoning from this, one might assume that a red—the warmest hue—with a dark value and high intensity would advance the most. And indeed, this seems to be true. When one looks at a crowd of people in a stadium, for instance, one is invariably more aware of those who are wearing bright reds.

It must be remembered that colors in art (or life) do not function in isolation from one another or from the shapes to which they belong. They are part of a context. For example, what we perceive as green in the Seurat painting is influenced by the fact that it is the color of the grassy bank and the distant trees—and the only green in the picture. But if Seurat's green were placed beside a truly bright green, it might not appear particularly green at all. Compare this to the abstract painting by Anuskiewicz where there is no subject matter to influence our perception of the colors and where our perception of each color is affected by the others in the picture. As we have seen, if the colors are patterned in a particular way, the effects can be surprising.

Shape

It was pointed out earlier that technically we cannot perceive shapes or anything else without color (in the case of black-and-white photography or of one who is colorblind, the value aspect of color). But we certainly can *conceive* of shapes independent of their color, and we tend to see ourselves and the objects we live with in terms of their characteristic shapes. Indeed, in our everyday commerce, shape may be more important than color.

Two-Dimensional Shapes

We live in a three-dimensional world, surrounded by infinite space in every direction and filled with three-dimensional objects. Originally, human beings did not think in two-dimensional terms. Indeed, it took at least a million years for them to begin drawing images of any kind on cave walls. But after that, making marks on a flat surface—whether they functioned as images, symbols, or patterns—became one of the most common types of communication.

In order to survey the nature of shape perception in two dimensions, it would be helpful to review two principles developed by Gestalt psychologists. The first of these, the *figure-ground principle,* has to do with our tendency to divide a visual pattern into two kinds of shapes—figure and ground. A figure appears to stand out, to be "on top of" a ground; a ground, on the other hand, appears to be underneath and surrounding a figure. For example, printed letters usually are figures while the white page is the ground. As a general rule, smaller and darker shapes are figures while larger and lighter ones are grounds. (Artists sometimes use the terms "positive shapes" and "negative shapes"; designers sometimes use the term "counterchange" for an alternating pattern of black and white) Figures, however, do not have to have solid colors. The outlined shapes of Charlie Brown and Snoopy (fig. 1-2) function as figures.

When we look at the world around us, we normally see objects and people as figures and their surroundings as the ground ("background," as we usually say). This habit of perception applies as well to the way we perceive Seurat's riverbank scene; indeed, realistic pictures like this can be likened to windows. But whether something is figure or ground can also depend on its circumstances and how we attend to it. The reclining man in Seurat's picture usually functions as a figure, but if we concentrate on just his ear, then he becomes the ground and the ear alone becomes the figure.

Although abstract paintings lack the familiar visual cues of realistic paintings, we tend to perceive their patterns as figure-ground relationships. However, these relationships may not always be so obvious or stable. At first view, one is likely to see the white shape—the single, unbroken form—of Ellsworth Kelly's painting (fig. 2-4) as the figure and the black shapes around it as the ground. In other words, it looks like a black canvas with a large white shape painted on it. Yet, with little effort, one can also see this painting in exactly the opposite way— a white canvas with four separate black shapes painted on it. This reversal of figure and ground—a flip-flop one can almost feel when changing from one way of looking at it to the other— is virtually impossible to accomplish with a realistic work such as Seurat's. On the other hand, with one of M.C. Escher's fantastic illustrations (fig. 2-5), figure-ground reversal is not only possible but nearly impossible to avoid and is an essential part of the work.

The second principle of perception that is helpful for us to understand is *closure*, the tendency for incomplete figures to be perceived as complete. Closure occurs, for example, when a person sees a square in an arrangement of four dots—the mind's eye fills in and completes the latent connections along the sides of the figure (fig. 2-6). Gestaltists reason that the human mind

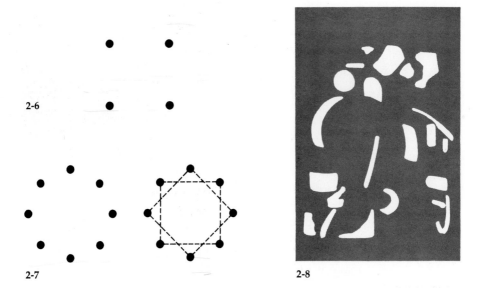

2-6

2-7

2-8

searches for the simplest and most stable form in a complex optical structure. A square, therefore, is more satisfactory than four separate dots; similarly, a circle (fig. 2-7) is a more satisfactory form than two overlapping squares.

But there is also reason to believe that experience plays an equal if not a more important role in the process of closure. This can be demonstrated through the use of "completion figures" that are designed to confuse the beholder. The white patches on a black background in figure 2-8 seem to resist any particular arrangement other than that of an abstract pattern. If, however, the viewer is told that the picture represents a train, the image of an approaching steam locomotive is apt to surface. Once it does, this interpretation of the completion figure becomes virtually irresistible.

Representing Three-Dimensional Shapes

The constancy of perception is an important factor in any discussion of three-dimensional—solid—shapes. If we perform the simple act of turning the cover of a book, we can witness the paradox of *shape constancy*. As the cover turns, its rectangular shape goes through a series of distortions (fig. 2-9). It changes to a trapezoid that grows progressively thinner, until at one point it becomes nothing more than a line that is the thickness of the cover material—its ultrathin shape contrasting with that of the remainder of the unopened book. But what we actually perceive

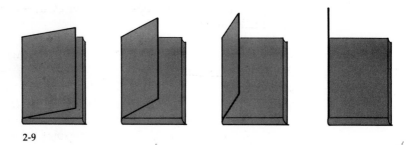

2-9

is an unchanging rectangular book cover swinging on the hinges of its binding.

The phenomenon of shape constancy, like color constancy, must be dealt with by artists who try to represent the third dimension in a flat picture. In a sense they must distort a form to make it appear undistorted. The drawings in figure 2-9 are a good example. The artist radically shortened the width of the cover in those drawings where it was necessary to make it appear to be a tilted plane in three-dimensional space. This is called *foreshortening*. In a natural-looking scene the use of foreshortening is much more complicated. In Seurat's painting of the bathers it is manifested in numerous places—for example, in the bodies of the dog and the man lying in the foreground. Actually, foreshortening is present wherever any object—a forearm, a finger, or the brim of a hat—has to be represented in depth.

A related phenomenon artists must deal with is *size constancy*, the tendancy to perceive objects as being a certain size no matter how far away they are. A striking demonstration of this phenomenon is seen in a photograph of a row of posts that stretches away from the camera (fig 2-10). The last post in the row has been exactly duplicated alongside the nearest one, but the contrast between them appears so obvious that we are tempted to measure and compare the two. Were it not for the duplicated image, we would assume that the last post is more or less the same size as the first one.

As proof of the power of this phenomenon and the difficulty that artists have in dealing with it, one might cite the fact that it was not until a few hundred years ago that painters began to represent the world of three dimensions on a two-dimensional surface with any real success. Apparently it was difficult for them to understand that by making something smaller in a picture, they could make it appear farther away—rather than simply smaller in size.

Three-Dimensional Shapes

Three-dimensional shapes, those with width, height, and depth, are the bases of the sculptor's art (The term "mass" is sometimes used to refer to such a shape, particularly if it is thick and solid.) The crucial difference, visually, between a painting and a piece of sculpture is that the latter offers more than a single point of view. Each vantage point reveals a different shape. Yet, as was pointed out earlier, the factors of shape constancy and size constancy tend to fuse the viewer's different perceptions into a single perception. This is ordinarily true of realistic sculpture. But in the case of more abstract work that employs unfamiliar shapes in novel compositions, these factors are likely to play a less important role. Picasso's concrete *Bust of Sylvette* (fig. 2-11) does not allow itself to be easily understood because of the difficulty of establishing in the mind's eye a single configuration for the entire work.

Expressive Use of Shapes

Just as colors are spoken of as warm and cool, shapes are habitually grouped by artists into "organic" and "geometric" categories. Organic shapes, those with irregular contours, are usually found in nature; geometric shapes, those with perfectly straight or curved contours (or combinations thereof), are generally associated with objects made by human beings. This division of shapes is accompanied by sets of associations such as natural versus made, soft versus hard, feminine versus masculine, or even warm versus cool.

2-10

But again, human feelings toward particular shapes cannot be isolated from the other elements present in a work of art. As with colors, the expressiveness of shapes is a function of complex interrelationships. Jean Arp frequently expressed the theme of a life force in the undulating and organic shapes of his abstract sculptures. *Growth* (fig. 2-12), a blend of plant and human anatomy, suggests life and procreation. But because of the sleek, unbroken envelope of its surface, it seems to be a self-contained and reticent type of life. Moreover, its twisting form and shiny surface tend to project coldblooded rather than warmblooded growth.

Line   In a sense, lines can be considered another species of the category of shapes—very thin shapes. Practically speaking, however, lines are normally distinguished from shapes and can be

2-12
Jean Arp, *Growth*, 1938.
Bronze, 31½" high,
Philadelphia Museum of Art
(gift of Curt Valentin).

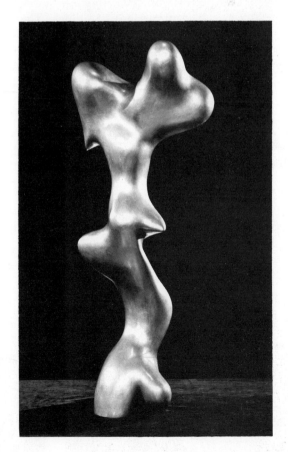

◀ 2-11
Pablo Picasso,
Bust of Sylvette, 1967.
Concrete and black
Norwegian basalt aggregate,
36' high. Courtesy of New
York University.

perceived virtually anywhere: the wrinkles of a person's face, the veins of a leaf, the spiny ridges on a seashell, or the wind-etched surface of a sand dune.

But we probably come across lines most often on paper in the form of drawings, diagrams, printed words, notations, doo-dles, and so on. People begin early in life looking at drawings made with lines, such as those in storybooks and comic strips. People also begin making lines themselves at early ages—first in the form of random scribbles inspired by the pride of being able to leave personal marks on paper (or walls) and later in the form of rudimentary images or symbols, when children begin to name the scribbles (fig. 2-13).

In art, lines can be used to represent objects in a simple, direct way—by describing their outer contours. The cartoon characters Charlie Brown and Snoopy (fig 1-2) and the opening book cover (fig. 2-9) are two examples in which lines function primarily as outlines. The images are flat, having little more depth than that afforded by the most basic kind of figure-ground relationship. But lines can also be employed to represent a subject in far more complicated ways, even going so far as to suggest texture and three-dimensional shapes. In the drawing

2-13
Martin Hobbs, *Mommy and Daddy,* 1973.

2-14
Albrecht Dürer,
Barbara Dürer, 1514.
Charcoal drawing, 22″ × 23″.
Kupferstichkabinett, Berlin.

of his mother (fig 2-14), Albrecht Dürer described the bony
structure of the brow, nose, cheeks, mouth, and chin of the face,
and the tendons of the neck as these are both revealed and concealed by leathery, sagging flesh. He also showed the heavy-lid-
ded protruding eyes, the wrinkled forehead, and a few strands
of hair as well as the folds and gatherings of the veil. In places
the artist employed fine, closely spaced lines to indicate shadows or touches of chiaroscuro. But he accomplished the effects
of depth—the numerous bumps and hollows—mostly by
means of single lines that are light or dark, thick or thin.

Unlike the drawing of Barbara Dürer, *Bathing at Asnières* con-
veys the sense of depth by use of chiaroscuro rather than line.
Indeed, following the definition of lines being very thin shapes,
one might have a hard time locating any lines at all in Seurat's

paintings. But many "invisible" lines are implied by the boundaries that separate objects from one another or from their surroundings—such as the edge of the riverbank and the contour of the man lying down. Such a line is also implied at the horizon. Although far from being a single, unbroken line, the horizon extends from one side to the other—both because of and in spite of trees, a bridge, and buildings. Closure helps us complete the horizon just as it does the square and circle in figures 2-6 and 2-7.

Expressive Use of Line

Lines do not have to be used descriptively. In the twentieth century, abstract art liberated line from the need to represent things. In *No. 3* by Jackson Pollock (fig. 2-15), the convoluted lines suggest movement and energy rather than describing the shapes of objects; the lines' alternating thickness and thinness are qualities in their own right rather than means of conveying

2-15
Jackson Pollock, *No. 3,*
1951. Oil on canvas,
56⅛" × 24". Collection
of Robert U. Ossorio.

2-16
Käthe Kollwitz, *Death
Seizing a Woman*, 1934.
Lithograph, 20" × 14½". The
Museum of Modern Art,
New York (purchase).

2-17
Pablo Picasso, *Portrait of Igor Stravinsky*, 1920. Private collection.

an impression of depth. Compare these lines with the thin nervous lines of the painting by the same artist in colorplate 15 and with the rigid architectural lines of the painting in colorplate 24.

Whether intentionally used for expression or for description, lines are, in one sense, inescapably expressive. This claim is based on the belief that gestures such as the drawing of lines reveal something about personal behavior. Like handwriting, they are a fairly direct reflection of an artist's thinking and feelings.

Käthe Kollwitz made a number of works dealing with suffering, death, and human vulnerability. In *Death Seizing A Woman* (fig. 2-16), the intensity of feeling is evoked by the starkness of the lines and their abrupt shifts in direction as well as by the familiar symbol of death, the struggling woman, and the look of terror in the mother's face. Compare Kollwitz's bold and forceful strokes with Picasso's flowing, leisurely lines in the portrait of the composer Igor Stravinsky (fig. 2-17). The vast difference between the two works is due to the different personalities of their lines as much as it is to their different subjects.

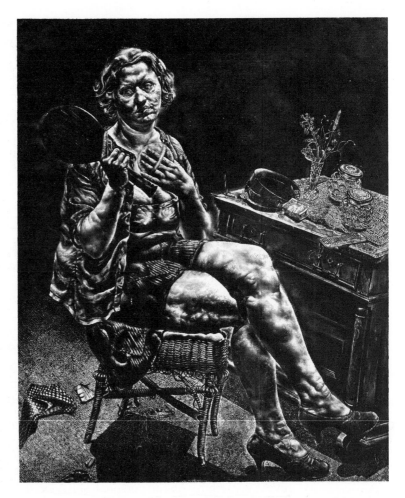

Texture

The term *texture* is used to refer to the surface qualities of things— for example, the hard smooth feeling of an egg or the soft smooth feeling of velvet. The best way to experience the texture of anything is to touch it. Yet most of our day-to-day information about texture comes from simply looking at things.

Visually, information about texture is transmitted by the way in which different materials affect the light that falls on their surfaces. A surface rough with bumps or pores will cast many little shadows. A matte surface will absorb light; a glossy one will reflect it. In other words, these textures can be perceived by the eyes in essentially the same way that color and shape are perceived.

In painting, texture actually can take two different forms. In

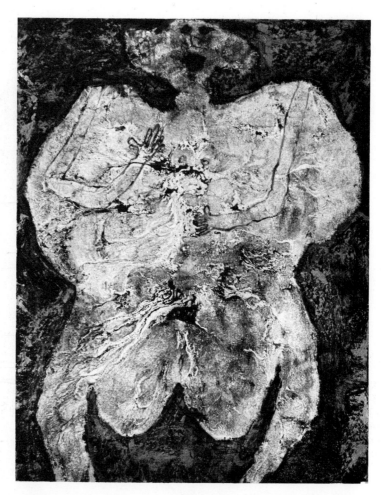

representational works it can be simulated with patterns of light
and dark. It can also be a characteristic of the materials themselves—the paint, the canvas, or some substance that is attached to the surface or mixed with the paint. Usually one or the
other of these forms predominates. In Ivan Albright's *Into the
World There Came a Soul Called Ida* (fig. 2-18), the simulated textures of a wicker chair, a vanity, cosmetic jars, clothing, and,
especially, middle-aged flesh do much of the work in suggesting
the process of human aging and deterioration. In Jean Dubuffet's *Tree of Fluids* (fig. 2-19), it is the paint itself that seems to be
deteriorating. Here the material existence of the art object parti-
cipates symbolically in a statement about the universal fate of
biological and spiritual decay.

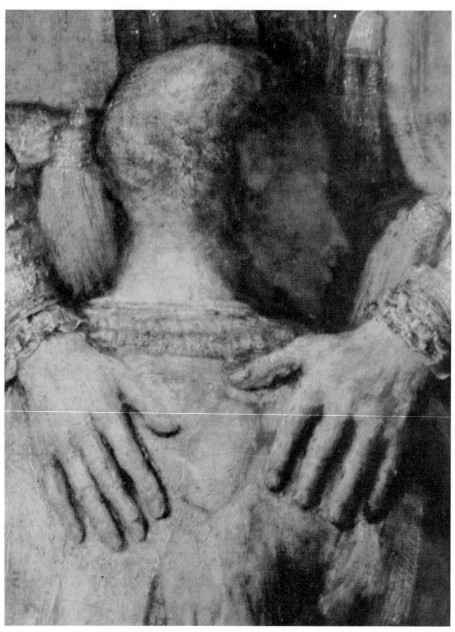

2-20   Rembrandt van Rijn,
detail of *The Return of the Prodigal Son* (fig. 7-11) *c.* 1665. Oil on Canvas.
Hermitage Museum, Leningrad.

Some paintings can exhibit both kinds of texture. From a normal viewing distance, the textures in _The Return of the Prodigal Son_ (fig. 7-11) by Rembrandt are simulated ones: the brocaded sleeves and hands of the older man; the back of the shaved head and the coarse, wrinkled clothing of the younger man. But close up (fig. 2-20) these things reveal themselves as simply brushmarks and ridges of oil paint.

Texture is even more fundamental in sculpture than it is in painting. The Alaskan mask (fig. 1-1), the Picasso sculpture (fig. 2-11), and the Arp sculpture (fig. 2-12) differ vividly from one another in several ways. But chief among those ways is the texture of their respective materials.

For centuries, many of the best sculptures have emphasized the textures of both the materials used in them and the materials of the objects they represent. As the art historian Herbert Read pointed out:

> For the sculptor, tactile values are not an illusion to be created on a two-dimensional plane: They constitute a reality to be conveyed directly, as existent mass. Sculpture is an art of _palpation_—an art that gives satisfaction in the touching and handling of objects. That, indeed, is the only way in which we can have direct sensations of the three-dimensional shape of an object.

Read went on to lament the fact that visitors to museums are not allowed to touch the artworks. But he would no doubt concede that human visual perception, assisted by past experience and a little imagination, is enormously capable of appreciating the tactile values of a piece of sculpture without actually touching it. It would certainly be a pleasant experience to pick up the Barbara Hepworth carving (fig. 2-21) and experience its surfaces directly. But though we cannot touch the object depicted here, the photograph provides enough cues for us to compare the sculpture with our memories of other wooden objects and to imagine its smooth surfaces, subtle contours, weight, and perhaps even its smell.

Space

Space can be thought of as the "empty shape" that exists around solid shapes (masses). Can we see space? To the extent that air, or atmosphere, is not really empty, space can be seen under certain conditions—and painters are able to depict it. (More will

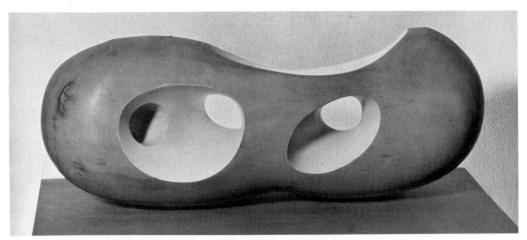

2-21   Barbara Hepworth, *Pendour*, 1947. Painted wood, 10¼" × 27¼" × 9".
Hirshhorn Museum and Sculpture Garden, Smithsonian Institution,
Washington, D.C.

be said about this under the topic of aerial perspective.) Under most conditions, however, space is relatively transparent. Yet we are aware of it at all times, and, like solid shapes, it can be described and measured. Space is really seen by its boundaries— where it touches objects and other solid shapes. For example, the space of a room is defined by the ceiling, floor, walls, and objects in the room. By looking at these things we can see the space well enough to describe it (interior space is sometimes referred to as "volume"). Outdoor space is defined by the land, trees, and buildings it touches (while its outer limits may be the horizon and the dome of the sky). The complementary relationship between solid shapes and space in our perception of the three-dimensional world is similar to that between figure and ground in our perception of two-dimensional pattern.

We also experience space through *kinesthetic sense*—our feeling of the position and movement of our bodies. If we were blindfolded, the only way we could perceive and adjust to the space of a strange room would be by moving about in it— perceiving it with our kinesthetic sense (along with our tactile sense). And although we see, we still sense the space surrounding us by how it feels to move through it; and we invariably do this in our imagination when not actually moving. Like texture, for which the eyes are aided by the sense of touch, the element of space is experienced cooperatively through vision and movement.

Architecture and Sculpture

Space is a most important element for the architect, who is concerned about designing it for human use. Michelangelo, famous as a sculptor and painter, also undertook several architectural projects, including the redesigning of Rome's Capitoline Hill (fig. 2-22). His solution was to redesign the front of one of the two buildings already on the hill and add a third building to create a symmetrical, trapezoidal public square. To accent the shape of the square and to set off the statue of Marcus Aurelius in its center, Michelangelo provided a strikingly decorative oval pavement. Most squares of the time were closed on all four sides by buildings; Michelangelo chose to leave this square open on one side, with a low balustrade to define the limits of the square. Today's visitor to the Capitoline Hill experiences not only the majesty of the ancient buildings but the drama of being inside an ordered, symmetrically balanced, and partly closed space.

Another dramatic space that is entirely closed is the inside of

2-22   Michelangelo, Capitoline Hill, Rome, designed *c.* 1537.

New York's Guggenheim Museum (fig. 2-23), designed by Frank Lloyd Wright. There is little question that the spiraling, multileveled interior appeals vividly to both the visual and the kinesthetic senses. To view the artworks displayed on the outer walls of all the levels, a visitor takes an elevator to the top level and then descends a gently sloped spiral ramp on foot. The spectacular interplay between the solid shapes and spaces (masses and volumes) of the complex structure is experienced directly.

The interplay between shape and space is a primary concern of most modern sculptors, who, like Hepworth, tend to include openings in their work for space to flow through. Traditional sculpture was usually a solid, relatively uninterrupted shape with few openings. The forms of today's abstract sculpture, such as Richard Hunt's *Drawing in Space No. 1* (fig. 2-24), are usually very open, allowing for a maximum of shape-space interplay. This alternation between closed and open creates a con-

2-23 Frank Lloyd Wright, The Solomon R. Guggenheim Museum, New York, 1943–59. View of interior from dome.

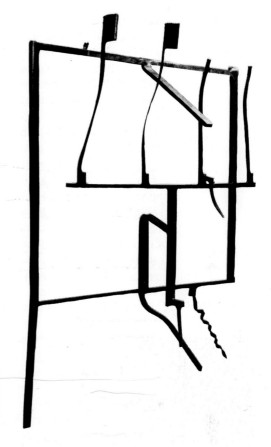

2-24
Richard Hunt, *Drawing in Space, No. 1,* 1977. Welded steel, 34" high. Collection of the artist.

tinually changing perception of shape and space relationships when viewing the piece from different vantage points.

Representing Space in Painting

In his painting of bathers, Seurat created the illusion of depth in a variety of ways. Two of them already discussed, chiaroscuro and foreshortening, were used to make individual objects and people appear three-dimensional. Seurat also employed several methods to make the people and objects appear to exist in space—nearer to or farther away from the viewer.

One of the most obvious methods is the *placement* of things higher or lower in the picture, because we tend to think of the things that are higher as being farther away. Another is *overlapping*—one thing set in front of another, such as the dog and the man—which also strengthens the impression of nearness or farness. A further set of cues is provided by the artist's use of *aerial perspective,* a method that simulates the effects of color in the atmosphere. Sometimes air contains high amounts of particulate matter—as with the smoke in the distance in Seurat's painting—which can be easily seen. But even without the presence of smoke, air is dense enough to affect the appearance of objects: The farther away they are, the softer their outlines and the more subdued their colors. We can see how Seurat imitated this effect if we compare the colors of the people and objects in the foreground with those of the buildings and bridge on the horizon. *Gradient of texture and detail* is yet another system for suggesting depth. Gradients can be seen in the grassy bank of the Seurat painting, where the blades of grass gradually turn into a generalized texture as they move farther back in the picture.

The most traditional system of spatial representation that Seurat employed is *linear perspective,* which dictates the relative sizes of things according to their distance from the viewer. This technique was not completely developed until the fifteenth century—when it became widely used in nearly all painting—but it continued to be used extensively until the twentieth century. Its basic principles can easily be demonstrated in a set of drawings of a football field. The simplest form of linear perspective is single-point perspective (fig. 2-25), in which all the lines moving away from the viewer meet (if continued) at one point—the *vanishing point*—on the horizon. Note that the yard lines and the crossbars of the goalposts, if extended, meet at the vanishing point. The same is true for the dotted lines connecting the tops of the goalpost uprights and the light poles. (Indeed, the heights of these things are established by means of lines extended to the vanishing point.) The remaining lines are either vertical, such as the light poles and uprights, or horizontal, such as the sidelines. Accustomed to this system of representation since childhood, we are able to interpret the yard lines as being at right angles to the sidelines, and, as long as the vanishing point is on the horizon, we think of them as being level with the plane of the ground.

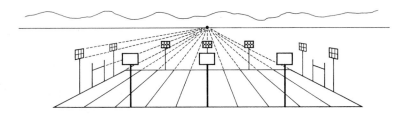

2-25
Single-point
perspective.

Pictures that use two or more vanishing points (fig. 2-26) accommodate more complicated views of things. Whereas the single-point system works only for a line of sight that is perpendicular to the horizontal lines of the things being viewed, the two-point system works for all other lines of sight, including one that might occur if the viewer were sitting at the corner of the field. Note that the sidelines are not horizontal and, if extended, would meet at their own vanishing point. And anything else, like the bandmaster's platform, that sits at an angle to the field would have its own set of points. The final illustration (fig. 2-27), showing a single-point perspective of one end of the field,

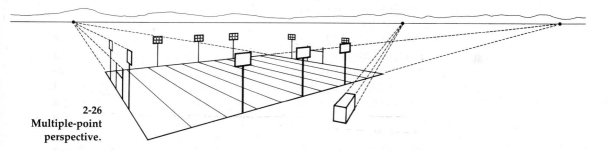

2-26
Multiple-point
perspective.

demonstrates the effect of lowering the horizon (or eye-level) line.

Although Seurat's painting presents a somewhat more complicated problem than that of a football field, we can still see that the sizes of the people in the picture are progressively reduced according to their relative distances. The eye level is on an implied line somewhere just under the distant bridge line that is intersected by the head of the central figure. Specific vanishing points are difficult to locate, because the few linear features of the picture are almost all on the horizon.

Many twentieth-century painters deliberately avoid using linear perspective, as well as some of the other methods for creating traditional illusions of depth. But this does not mean

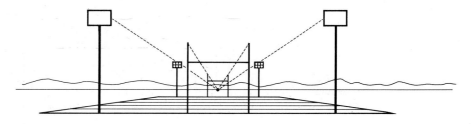

2-27
Single-point
perspective from
a low angle.

that modern paintings lack depth entirely. Recall the discussions of figure-ground relationships and of how various values and hues advance or recede. Though shallow, the depth of abstract and semiabstract art is manipulated by contemporary artists who are sensitive to the dynamics of abstract form. Picasso's *First Steps* (fig. 1-3) is a good example of a shallow, nonillusionistic depth that seems to undulate as our eyes scan the picture. This is due to the "push and pull" of the darks and lights and also to the ambiguous figure-ground relationships (such as at the bottom of the picture where it is difficult to tell if a foot is in front of or behind the background). The subtle depth of Anuskiewicz's painting (colorplate 3) depends entirely on the effects of advancing and receding hues.

Composition

So far we have discussed each visual element separately. But in order to understand how they function in a work of art we must also examine how these elements work together. *Composition* is the term used to describe the organization—the working together—of the visual elements.

Seurat composed *Bathing at Asnières* to create a convincing illusion of people and objects in spatial depth; at the same time he was concerned about composing the picture in such a way that its various parts harmonized with one another and made it pleasing and interesting to look at. Under the headings of *unity* and *balance*, the discussion that follows will present some of the principles and methods involved in creating a successful composition.

Unity

Unity refers to integrating everything in a work of art to make it a single, indivisible whole. The greater the variety of things in a work, the more difficult it is to achieve unity. *Bathing at Asnières*, for example, contains several people—all dressed differently and doing different things—together with a river, sailboats, buildings, trees, and a dog.

One way in which Seurat managed to unify this variety was by *grouping* individual things close together to form fewer units for the eye to contend with. (We do this when we "straighten" a messy desk by organizing a hodgepodge of separate papers, writing tools, books, and coffee cups into larger and tidier-looking units.) This practice can be seen in the grouping of the three boys on the right to make them seem to form a single, almost triangular shape (fig. 2-28).

Individual things—even those far apart from one another—

2-28   Georges Seurat, *Bathing at Asnières.*

can also be connected by *similarities* of shape, color, or other elements. The dome shape of the large bather's head is repeated in the head and the hat, respectively, of the boys in the water, in the hats of two of the men on the bank, and in some of the treetops. Triangular shapes can also be found throughout the composition: in the way three of the figures are sitting, the bend of a pair of legs, the upper back of the man lying down, and the way the bather at right holds his hands to his mouth. A major color similarity connecting different parts of the picture consists of the red-orange found in the hair and trunks of the large bather, the hat and trunks of the bather in the water, the dog, the pillow underneath the boy with the straw hat, and even the band of the hat itself.

Emphasizing *continuity* is another way an artist can unify a composition. Continuity has to do with a single element or a series of elements that continues relatively uninterrupted throughout a large part of the composition. The edge of the riverbank is a prime example of continuity in this painting, even though it appears to be broken by the bather. (Actually, the lighter value of his skin blends in generally with the river, while the darker value of the shadow on his legs and trunks picks up and continues the contour of the riverbank edge.)

Another example of continuity is the horizon line that extends across the entire picture and, like the riverbank, is relatively unbroken. But unlike the riverbank, this line is made up of several barely visible vertical units—trees, bridge supports, buildings, smokestacks—that comprise a *rhythm*, or repetition of similar elements. Two more obvious examples of rhythm can be seen in the repeated shapes of geese in the Escher illustration (fig. 2-5) and the repeated balconies of the Guggenheim Museum (fig. 2-23).

The last major method Seurat used to achieve unity was that of making one part of the picture the *dominant feature*—in this case, the head of the central bather. This single feature serves as a major cohesive factor and the main focal point of the entire composition. The dominance of the head is established by a number of things: its centralized location, its isolation from other well-defined shapes, the strong contrasts between its dark value and the lighter values that surround it, and the fact that it intersects the horizon. When scanning the scene our eyes tend to return to this head, and it is probably the image we will remember most when we are not looking at the work. It is extremely influential, both visually and psychologically. Its shaded stillness affects all other aspects of the painting and underscores the general quality of summer torpor.

Balance   Seurat was particularly sensitive to *balance*. Normally we think of balance as concerned with equalizing the physical weights of things supported by something—like a seesaw or balance scales. In art it is a matter of equalizing the visual and the psychological weights of things. Visual weight refers to such things as the relative size, brightness, or amount of contrast of one or more of the visual elements. Psychological weight usually refers to the relative importance of a person or object in the picture.

Among the "heaviest" things in visual weight in Seurat's composition are the following: the man lying down, because of his size and the value contrasts of his white towel and smock set against the dark colors of the hat, trousers, and dog; the central bather, because of his size and location; the central bather's white towel, because of its extreme lightness; and the bather on the right, whose orange hat in combination with the blue background provides the strongest hue contrast in the painting. Unlike actual weights, visual weights cannot be accurately measured; so it is difficult to determine exactly how a large figure with a white smock balances a small one with an orange hat. However, considering everything with visual weight (including the boy with the straw hat, whose size and color are also relatively prominent), it would seem that there is more weight on the left than on the right. But in a representational picture, one cannot overlook the importance of psychological weight. In this case, the right side prevails because, for one thing, a river has more psychological importance than a riverbank; for another, almost all of the people are facing right; and, finally, the most important figure—the large bather—is slightly to the right of center. Thus we can probably say that the slightly heavier visual weight on the left is counterbalanced by the heavier psychological weight on the right.

The general feeling when looking at *Bathing at Asnières* is that of stability (this feeling may be a better test of balance than that of trying to add up all the visual and psychological weights and to compare the two halves of the picture). Seurat was a very methodical artist; he consciously sought both unity and balance in all his work and desired to generate an impression of harmony, repose, and stability in the viewer. But unity and balance are not the only attributes that make works of art great, and harmony, repose, and stability are not the only expressive qualities that works of art are capable of producing. Indeed, many great works of art are not particularly reflective of these attributes and qualities. Seurat's paintings are, and *Bathing at Asnières* is a fine example for illustrating them.

Summary   It is said at the beginning of the chapter that while Seurat's painting is obviously a picture of boys gathered along a riverbank, it is also a rectangular surface covered with patches of color—and that Seurat had to deal with the visual elements to make his painting. The balance of the chapter is devoted to explaining the visual elements and their role in everyday seeing as well as in works of art, both two-dimensional and three-dimensional. It also presents several artistic methods—different ways of manipulating the visual elements—used to make us see works in certain ways. An artist working with the visual elements can create illusions and even evoke certain emotions in the viewer.

Much is made of the fact that it takes a lot of learning to make art; it is equally true that it requires learning to see art. This chapter is intended to give some insight into the ordering processes of the artist as these relate to what the viewer perceives: insight that will enhance appreciation and enjoyment of works of art.

3
Fine Arts Media

The materials with which a work of visual art is created affect its appearance as much as any of the visual elements discussed in the preceding chapter. A sculpture will not look the same in marble as in wood or bronze, not only because of the appearance of each material but because each material requires the artist to work in a different way.

The materials and techniques with which a particular artwork is created are known as the *medium*. Oil paint is a medium, as are marble, bronze, and photography. Traditionally the visual arts were limited to relatively few media. But in the twentieth century, new materials and techniques—as well as new concepts of art—have expanded this number, and many of the new media are not easily classified.

Painting

There are a variety of media that come under the heading of painting. All of them consist essentially of applying colors made of *pigments* mixed with a *vehicle* (a liquid such as egg yolk or oil) to a *support* (a surface of some kind, such as canvas or wood). Oftentimes a vehicle is combined, in varying degrees, with a *thinner*, such as water or turpentine. A thinner lowers the viscosity of the paint so that it can be spread more easily.

Fresco

Fresco is the art of making murals (wall pictures) by painting on wet plaster with pigments mixed with water. (Sometimes this method is termed true fresco to distinguish it from fresco *a secco*, painting on dry plaster.) Fresco was the method used by Giotto di Bondone to create a large series of murals for the Arena Chapel in Padua, Italy in the early 1300s. Because plaster dries rapidly, Giotto was forced to plan ahead to ensure that each application of fresh plaster matched the shape of a figure (or a shape within that shape) and that he could complete that part of the picture before it dried. He was unable to make corrections or repaint any area without removing the old plaster and entirely redoing the unsatisfactory portion on a new base. This meant that he had to develop not only a carefully planned composition but carefully planned working strategies for each day that he executed the mural. Because of its nature, fresco is best suited for compositions—like Giotto's *Meeting at the Golden Gate* (colorplate 4)—that stress large well-defined images. But the nature of the medium did not prevent Giotto from representing such delicate emotions as those expressed in the tender embrace of Joachim and Anna (who have just been told that Anna will give birth to Mary, the mother of Jesus).

Although practiced by the ancient Egyptians, Greeks, and Romans, fresco enjoyed its greatest popularity and highest level of development during the Renaissance—exemplified by such artists as Giotto and, much later, Michelangelo (colorplate 12). Because fresco literally becomes part of the wall, fresco paintings are as durable as the buildings to which they are attached.

Tempera For smaller movable works, such as altarpieces, artists in Giotto's time used wood for support. They painted with *egg tempera*, a medium of pigment mixed with egg yolk and water. When applied to a surface covered with a thin coat of *gesso* (a substance similar to plaster of paris), artists were able to produce works both brilliant in color and remarkably durable (fig. 3-1).

Unlike fresco, tempera allows artists to repaint an area when necessary to effect changes or corrections. Yet like fresco, tempera dries rapidly and does not blend easily. Consequently, color mixing is accomplished by painting two or more layers of paint with short fine brushstrokes, allowing lower layers to optically mix with upper layers. Working with either fresco or tempera requires careful planning and patient execution.

Oil Beginning in the early 1400s, Flemish artists began to mix pigments with oil. But they used the medium in a limited way, applying it in thin, translucent (partially transparent) films of color over a tempera "underpainting"—the initial stage of a picture in which the drawing and values were established in mono-

3-1
Giotto, *Madonna Enthroned,*
c. 1310. Tempera on wood,
10′8″ × 6′8″. Galleria degli
Uffizi, Florence.

3-2
Hubert and Jan van Eyck,
detail of *God the Father.*
From *The Ghent Altarpiece,*
1432. Tempera and oil on
panel. St. Bavo, Ghent.

chrome (one color). This combination of tempera and oil permitted Flemish artists to make altarpieces and portraits full of realistic detail and enamel-like colors—notable to this day for their delicate craftsmanship (fig. 3-2). In the late 1400s, specially treated canvas was introduced as a support to replace wood. By the early 1500s, Venetian artists began to omit the tempera underpainting stage, using the oil medium from start to finish. Thus the era of oil-on-canvas—the most popular medium in the visual arts—was born. One reason for its popularity had to do with the lighter weight of canvas. But the premiere break-through was the versatility of the oil paint itself. Unlike fresco or tempera, oil paint dries slowly enough for an artist to take up or leave off wherever and whenever convenient and to change an area at will. Paradoxically, the slow-drying medium permitted artists to work not only more freely but more quickly. Contrary to tempera, the consistency of oil paint is not relatively fixed. Oil can be as thick as peanut butter or as thin as water, it can be translucent or opaque. Thus, it allows for an unlimited range of color and textural variations. To catalog the different ways oil can be used and the effects that can be obtained from its use would be virtually to recite the history of European painting from the fifteenth century to the present. The nineteenth-century French artist Eugène Delacroix employed many effects to arouse the romantic imagination of his public. He portrayed his exotic subjects in an impetuous colorful style that at times was almost electrifying, and took great pains to keep the surface of his pictures alive with rich, thick strokes of paint (colorplate 5).

Acrylic   Today's abstract artists share with Delacroix the appreciation of paint and its expressive capabilities, but they carry this a step further by eliminating the subject matter of their pictures so the viewer may concentrate on the qualities of such elements as color and texture. Some artists are now using *acrylic paint*, a synthetic medium consisting of pigments mixed with polymer first developed following World War II. While acrylics can be used to imitate almost every effect of oils, they are even more versatile. For example, they were used to create the diverse works seen in colorplates 3, 29, and 32. To the untrained eye, acrylic paintings may be indistinguishable in appearance from oil paintings—especially if the works in question are relatively traditional. But to the artist who works with this medium, they are very distinguishable. Oil offers far more resistance to the brush. Acrylic can be mixed with water and is much faster dry-ing, traits that can be considered either advantages or disadvan-tages depending on what the artist is trying to do. Sam Gilliam turns the water-soluble characteristic of acrylic into an aesthetic advantage by soaking the paint directly into raw canvas—something he would be unable to do with oil, since oil decays cloth. (For oil paintings, canvas has to be treated by *sizing*—applying a material such as glue to seal its surface—prior to the application of the paint.) In a work like the one shown in colorplate 31, the paint permeates the canvas, staining it rather than lying on the surface in layers of varying thicknesses.

Watercolor   Watercolor consists of painting with pigments mixed with water on white paper. Like the canvas in Gilliam's work, the paper in a watercolor is stained with color—the white of the paper mixing optically with the color of the paint. A translucent film of watercolor applied with brush to an area of paper is called a *wash*. Historically, watercolors were used as studies for larger paintings or for applying washes to drawings or prints to add a bit of color. But in the nineteenth century, watercolors came to be used as a medium in their own right by such artists as Winslow Homer (fig. 3-3). Because of their convenience and fresh results, watercolors are especially effective for outdoor subjects. However, they are not easy to use. Errors are ineradicable and colors cannot be changed, except to be made darker. Inexperienced artists tend to produce "muddy" rather than fresh colors. But, in the hands of skilled artists, watercolors are quite marvelous.

3-3   Winslow Homer, *The Berry Pickers*, 1873. Watercolor, 9¼″ × 13⅛″.
The Harold T. Pulsifer Memorial Collection at Colby College.

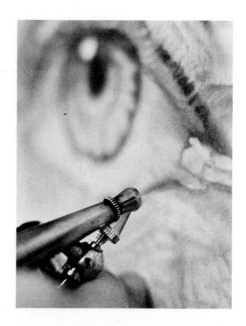

3-4
Painting with an airbrush.

Airbrush   A modern technique that has enabled artists to achieve effects previously impossible is the *airbrush*, a type of miniature spray gun that can be adjusted from a narrow, pencil-thin jet to a broad mist of paint (fig. 3-4). The instrument never touches the canvas and can be used to produce an absolutely smooth, evenly shaded surface on the painting. The first group of artists to make serious use of it was the Photo-Realists of the late 1960s— most notably Chuck Close, who adapted it to a technique similar to the color printing process. Working from photographs that separated the primary hues, Close re-created each area of the face three different times to produce a full-color picture (colorplate 32).

Drawing   Drawing consists of making marks—usually of a single color— on a support—usually paper—and including the color of the support as part of the work. Historically, drawings, like water-colors, were used for recording quick descriptions or planning larger works such as paintings or sculptures. And they are still used for these purposes. But for centuries in China, ink drawings have been highly esteemed as finished works of art and, as early as the eighteenth century in the West, artists began to create and sell drawings as works of art. Because they are the least complicated of all the media, drawings tend to be sponta-

3-5 Edgar Degas, *After the Bath,* 1890–92. Charcoal drawing on pink paper, 19¾″ × 25⅝″. Fogg Art Museum, Harvard University, Cambridge, Massachusetts (bequest of Meta and Paul J. Sachs).

neous and therefore more reflective of an artist's thinking. For this reason they are collected and highly valued whether or not they were originally intended to be works of art.

Such media as pencils and sticks of charcoal, chalk, or crayons are probably the most common and convenient tools for making drawings. The artist makes marks or lines directly on the paper. Chiaroscuro and variations of value are created by different degrees of pressure or by the close or wide spacing of small lines, and the color of the paper mixes optically with the color of the marks. The various ways in which charcoal lines have been applied to the page in Edgar Degas's *After the Bath* (fig. 3-5) serve not only to indicate the outline of the woman's body but also the volumes of her back and even the soft texture of her skin. Yet in many places the drawing is ambiguous, requiring help from the viewer's imagination. The spontaneity of the marks in those places makes them reminiscent of the brusque movements the woman would employ to dry her hair.

Ink is another common material for drawing. Typically, black or brown colors are used with pen or brush. The ink is fluid and generally opaque. But it can be made translucent by diluting it with water. A translucent film of ink applied with brush to a support is called *ink wash*. When handled skillfully, ink washes are capable of producing the subtle varieties of shades needed to suggest the misty spaciousness of a mountain landscape (colorplate 8). Diego Rivera, who was not interested in subtle variations when he made *Mother and Child* (fig. 3-6), used a brush loaded with opaque ink to create bold lines rather than delicate ink washes. Yet he skillfully varied the widths of the lines to emphasize the three-dimensional character of the stocky woman and child, and to provide accents throughout the composition.

Printmaking   *Prints* of all kinds are usually produced on paper, like drawings, but differ from them in that prints involve the production of numerous identical copies of a single work by means of partially mechanical methods. (Another difference is that the ink used in

3-6
Diego Rivera, *Mother and Child*, 1936. Ink drawing on paper, 12⅛″ × 9¼″. San Francisco Museum of Modern Art (Albert M. Bender Collection).

printmaking is thick and oil based rather than fluid and water based.) Not surprisingly, this art began to be developed at about the same time as book printing. The need to illustrate a printed text was as important then as it is today. Prints, like the illustrations in this book, were also used to reproduce famous works of art. In the days when travel was limited and photoreproduction was nonexistent, prints were the major way of spreading the knowledge of art from one country to another. Printmaking was also used by some artists as a tool for personal expression.

Woodcut

The *woodcut* is the oldest of the major techniques, a form of *relief printing* (fig. 3-7) made by drawing an image on a block of wood and cutting away the areas that are to remain white—leaving the drawn lines as ridges. After the image has been rubbed with ink, it can be printed under moderate pressure. Albrecht Dürer was well known in the sixteenth century for his extraordinary woodcuts. Today we are still awed by his mastery of the medium, by the precision and control that made possible such complex and fine-lined pictures (fig. 2-3).

3-7
Relief printing.

Intaglio

Intaglio printing (fig. 3-8) is the opposite of relief printing. The image is cut into a metal plate (usually a sheet of cold-rolled copper) and, after ink has been rubbed into the lines, transferred to a sheet of paper under extreme pressure. The metal plate may be cut with special gouges (*engraving*), scratched with a needle (*dry-point*), or dissolved with acid (*etching*). In etching, the most popular of these three methods, the plate is covered with a wax-based material and lines are drawn in this coating with a needle. When the plate is placed in acid, the exposed parts are eaten away. Shadings can be achieved by "stopping out" some lines and by allowing other lines to be "bitten" deeper by repeated immersions in the acid.

3-8
Intaglio printing.

In Rembrandt's etchings, the velvety blacks were usually the result of denser, more deeply bitten masses of lines (fig. 3-9). Gerardo Aparicio's etchings take advantage of the medium's capacity to produce incisive lines (fig. 3-10).

Lithography

Lithography is a *planographic* system of printing (fig. 3-11). It involves drawing or painting directly onto the flat surface of a special form of limestone or a zinc or aluminum plate with a greasy crayon or liquid. Of course, grease accepts oily ink and repels water. During the printing process, the surface is dampened. The exposed areas, being wet, do not accept the ink.

3-11
Planographic printing.

3-9   Rembrandt van Rijn, *Christ Healing the Sick, c.* 1649. Etching and drypoint (second state), 11″ × 15½″. The Art Institute of Chicago (The John H. Wrenn Memorial Collection, bequest of Ethel Wrenn).

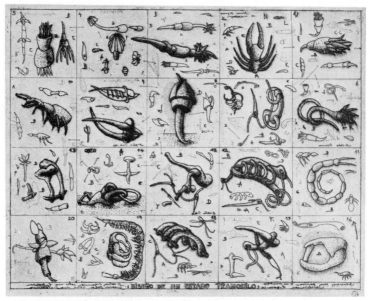

3-10   Gerardo Aparicio, *Design for a Tranquil State,* 1975. Etching, 9¾″ × 12¼″. Collection William Dyckes.

When paper is pressed against the inked surface, an almost perfect facsimile (mirror-reverse) of the drawing is produced. Not long after its invention in the late eighteenth century, it was discovered that the technique could be improved by treating the drawn surface with a solution of nitric acid and gum arabic to fix the image and integrate it with the surface. Lithography allows more freedom and directness in the drawing phase and a great variety of line, texture, and shading. Henri de Toulouse-Lautrec, who emphasized the spontaneous and witty, found lithography perfectly suited to his uninhibited talent. He also furthered the medium's potential through his technical experiments and unorthodox style (fig. 3-12).

3-12
Henri de Toulouse-Lautrec,
Jane Avril, Jardin de Paris,
1893. Color lithographic
poster, 49⅝" × 36⅛". The
Museum of Modern Art,
New York (gift of
A. Conger Goodyear).

3-13
Victor Vasarely,
Triond, 1973. Silkscreen,
31⅛″ × 31⅛″. Collection
Victor Vasarely,
Annet-sur-Marne,
France.

Silkscreen

Silkscreen, or *serigraphy,* the most recently developed of the popular forms of printmaking, consists of silk, organdy, or similar open-meshed material stretched tightly over a frame. An image or design is made by blocking out parts of the screen with glue, plastic strips, or even photographic emulsions, leaving the remainder for ink to pass through. Essentially, silkscreen is a type of stencil; any area not blocked out by the stencil will be printed. Printing is accomplished by placing the screen on the surface to be printed and pushing viscous ink across the mesh with a squeegee. The materials used in silkscreening are less expensive than wood blocks and copper plates, and the techniques used are faster and less complicated than other techniques. These are the principal reasons why silkscreen has become a popular medium. But the fact that it also lends itself nicely to precision-edged shapes has proved an important attraction to artists like Victor Vasarely (fig. 3-13).

Photography

Still photography, even more than printmaking, involves mechanical processes and chemistry, and, like printmaking, is capable of producing identical editions. A virtually unlimited number of "prints" can be made from a single film negative, an item that is to the photographer what an etched plate is to the printmaker.

Photographers, however, instead of making images largely by hand, select subjects from the environment and capture the light reflected from those subjects on chemically treated, light-sensitive film. This is achieved with a camera—essentially a dark box with a lens in the front that projects the light onto a film. Making the image visible (and permanent) requires immersing the film in certain chemicals, a process known as developing. The result is a translucent negative image in which the blacks are clear and the whites are almost opaque. A positive print, the photograph itself, is made by passing light through the film negative onto sensitized paper, again producing a latent image that must be developed. Exposing the print and then developing it—done in a darkroom—often involves such hand methods as manipulating the amounts of light exposure over different areas of the print and controlling the effects of the chemical bath.

The creative challenges involved in producing photographs concern gaining control of a mechanical process by making a series of selections each time one takes a picture. Among other things, the photographer must choose the type of film, subject, lighting, camera distance, point of view, and—depending on the type of camera—the focal length of the lens, width of the lens opening, and shutter speed. The photographer also has the option of controlling aspects of the exposure and development of the print in the darkroom. These are some—perhaps the most important—of the variables in making a photograph, but certainly not all of them.

The variables—the numerous possibilities for different results even when using the same subject—might call into question the popular notion that a photograph is a true record of something seen. Nevertheless, a photograph does have a special relationship to its subject that a painting, no matter how realistic it may be, can never attain. As critic Susan Sontag explained, a photograph "is not only an image . . . it is a trace, something directly stenciled off the real, like a footprint or a death mask." It is doubtful that Dorothea Lange's *Migrant Mother* (fig. 3-14) would convey the same sense of a real person

3-14
Dorothea Lange *Migrant Mother, Nipomo, California,* 1936. Photograph. Dorothea Lange Collection, The Oakland Museum.

existing at a certain place and time if it had been a painting instead of a photograph. And since this picture was part of a report on California workers Lange was commissioned to do in the 1930s, authenticity was an issue. But the effectiveness of the picture in evoking a story about family life and conditions in general during the Great Depression reveals that Lange was able to use the medium's variables for expressive ends as well as reporting.

Like Lange, Cindy Sherman specializes in photographs of people (fig. 3-15). But her art is about a very different world than Lange's. She addresses our popular-culture heritage through images vaguely suggestive of movie stars, soap-opera heroines, entertainers, and so forth. Though subtle, indirect, even ambiguous, her photographs are nevertheless evocative of contemporary society—especially concerning the role of women. Sherman's methods are also very different than Lange's. Rather than

seek real situations to photograph, she creates fictitious situations by using costumes, special props, and herself as model.

Jerry Uelsmann uses darkroom technology rather than costumes and props to create his fictions. But the power of his photographs rests in large part on the medium's aura of believability. In one of his works (fig. 3-16), we see the union of a tree and a gigantic leaf—a compelling and disturbing image that violates our common-sense perception of the world. The veins of the leaf can be seen as the tree's roots (as if we were looking at an X-ray photograph). Or the leaf can be seen as the tree and the real tree as the roots, if we turn the photograph upside down. The symmetry of nature is made strikingly visible in this photograph. Uelsmann creates a print like this one by integrating the images of two or more negatives in the darkroom. (Light exposures can be controlled to make parts of the print lighter or

3-16
Jerry N. Uelsmann,
Untitled, 1964. Photograph.
Collection the artist.

darker, according to the plan of the artist.) Uelsmann calls his method "post-visualization," because the greater part of the creativity does not take place in the camera—which he uses more or less conventionally—but in the darkroom.

Sculpture

Unlike the images made with the media described earlier, images in sculpture are three-dimensional, They may be *in the round*—independent, freestanding objects—or *relief,* forms that protrude from a background. With the exception of certain sculptural media introduced in the twentieth century, the materials of sculpture have generally been of harder, more permanent substances than those found in the media reviewed so far.

Carving

Gianlorenzo Bernini's life-sized in-the-round sculpture of David (fig. 3-17), showing the hero as he is about to pivot and hurl the stone at Goliath, is carved out of a single block of marble. The use of *carving* to make images is as old as human culture itself. Sometimes referred to as the subtractive process, carving calls for removing material from a block of wood or stone with a knife, gouge, or chisel. Carving requires that the artist have a well-defined idea of how the piece is to look. Bernini probably began by making a small model in clay and then having the shape roughly cut in the marble block by an assistant. Further cutting and refinements, using progressively finer tools, were executed by the artist. Unlike oil painting, carving in stone permits little room for changes and in-process modifications. The mental anxiety and the physcial exertion of chipping away at an obstinate block no doubt discourage many artists from working in this medium. Judging from his output, it appears that Bernini was rarely discouraged; indeed, looking at individual works one gets the impression that marble carving was, for him, easy. Few other sculptors of stone have been able to imbue their works with such a degree of realism. Bernini so carefully articulated and refined the textures of the flesh, hair, and cloth that one can easily forget that this figure was carved from stone. But the most innovative aspect of the work is its suggestion of movement. *David* is not a static form that merely represents a Biblical figure, but a fascinating study in potential motion and energy. David's slender body is caught in the very act of hurling the sling; its position, balance, and violent twisting compel the viewer to move almost entirely around the sculpture to understand it.

3-17
Gianlorenzo Bernini, *David,*
1623. Marble, life-size.
Galleria Borghese, Rome.

Modeling   Not all sculptural methods are as difficult as carving, and not all materials are as hard as stone. _Modeling_—sometimes called the additive process—involves forming three-dimensional shapes out of a pliable material such as clay or wax. These materials can be manipulated with simple tools such as wooden paddles and knives or even with the hands. The art of modeling was used by Paleolithic artists as long ago as 10,000 B.C. In later periods, sculptors like Bernini used it for the same purpose that painters use drawing—to make preparatory "sketches" for their finished works. The disadvantage of the medium, of course, is that figures made in clay or wax are not permanent and therefore not satisfactory for finished works. Clay, however, can be changed into a relatively hard material called _ceramic_ by baking it at a high temperature in a special oven called a _kiln_, a process that probably goes back to the discovery of fire. Both clay and wax can be copied in more durable materials by a technique called _casting_.

Casting   Casting includes several methods for making exact copies. The artist covers the original form with plaster, which hardens and becomes a mold when it is removed. The inside of the mold is a negative shape that corresponds to the positive shape of the original. Into this cavity a substance such as molten metal or polyester is poured or pressed. After the filler hardens, the mold is removed.

The _cire perdue_ or _lost wax_ process, used for bronze casting, consists of applying a layer of wax of the same thickness desired for the metal (usually around three-eighths of an inch) to the inside of a mold. The wax-coated cavity is then filled with a plaster core and the whole mold is baked. The wax melts and runs out, leaving a thin space for the molten bronze, which hardens into a lightweight, hollow cast. This method was skillfully employed by Chinese artists eight centuries before Christ. The fifteenth century Italian artist, Lorenzo Ghiberti, used bronze casting to make a series of reliefs for the doors of the Baptistry of the Cathedral of Florence known as the Gates of Paradise. A close look at one of the reliefs, _The Meeting of Solomon and the Queen of Sheba_ (fig. 3-18), reveals that the greatest relief is in the lower portion where some figures are almost in the round, while the upper third—the most distant part of the scene—is very flat. In the flat part, Ghiberti employed one-point perspective to help suggest the depth of the background.

Casting in twentieth-century materials such as vinyl or polyester resin is popular with many sculptors today. A versatile

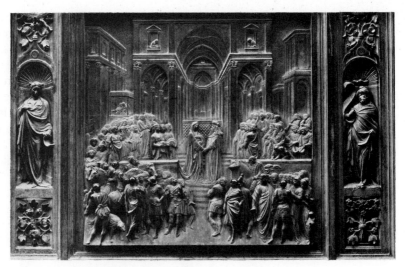

3-18
Lorenzo Ghiberti, *The Meeting of Solomon and the Queen of Sheba,*
detail of the Gates of Paradise door, Baptistry, Florence, *c.* 1435.
Gilt bronze, 31¼″ × 31¼″.

medium (far less costly than bronze casting), polyester resin is a
heavy, syrupy liquid before it is hardened by the addition of
other materials. It is extremely durable when reinforced with
flexible sheets of fiberglass. John de Andrea casts with this and
other plastics in molds made directly from bodies. After they
have been painted with oils, the images are incredibly accurate
likenesses of the actual person—right down to goosebumps (fig.
3-19). De Andrea, an exception to the general run of modern
sculptors who emphasize abstract forms, takes advantage of
new technologies and materials to focus once again on the old
problem of verisimilitude. Even Bernini, who was remarkably
successful at making marble look like flesh, would be impressed
by the possibilities now available to artists.

Other Methods   Long before de Andrea began to make his realistic sculptures
in polyester, other sculptors had experimented daringly with
new technologies. In the late 1920s, Julio González pioneered the use of *welding,* the joining of pieces of metal by heat,
as an art technique. At the time this represented a radical break
from what were considered the appropriate media for sculpture.
González made crude constructions of scrap iron, rods, and
nails. The textures, shapes, and spaces of a work like his *Head*
(fig. 3-20) are stated in a completely modern sculptural lan-

3-19
John de Andrea, *Clothed Artist and Model,* 1976. Cast vinyl, polychromed in oil, life-size cast. Collection William Jaeger.

guage. The piece is not built up from a lump of clay or cut down from a mass of stone, but pieced together around empty space— an early example of what is known as *open sculpture.*

Open sculptures can be constructed out of virtually any material. Naum Gabo used a two-piece plastic frame and nylon thread to put together *Linear Construction* (fig. 3-21). Entirely removed from traditional sculpture's attachment to human or animal forms, constructions such as Gabo's reflect the preoccupation of many twentieth-century artists with abstract shapes, lines, and spaces. Gabo, who had been trained as an engineer and mathematician, was attracted to the beauty of the forms of analytic geometry. In the early 1920s he began to translate these forms into open sculptures made from lightweight materials.

One of his later works, *Linear Construction* is a keen blend of art and mathematics as well as a gently curving, transparent image.

Lee Bontecou's untitled work (fig. 3-22) also reflects twentieth-century approaches to sculpture. Like the works of González and Gabo, it is an abstract form pieced together rather than modeled or carved. But unlike theirs, it is a closed form, highly reminiscent of relief sculpture. Bontecou made this work by building a metal armature—much like the frame of a ship or airplane—and stretching canvas and other materials over it. The relief proceeds in steplike intervals to the rim of an abyss before plunging into the black void near the center of the form. The spatial sensation is reinforced with the use of lighter and darker shadings, a chiaroscuro method that makes some intervals ap-

3-20
Julio González, *Head,* 1936. Wrought iron, welded, 17¾" high. The Museum of Modern Art, New York.

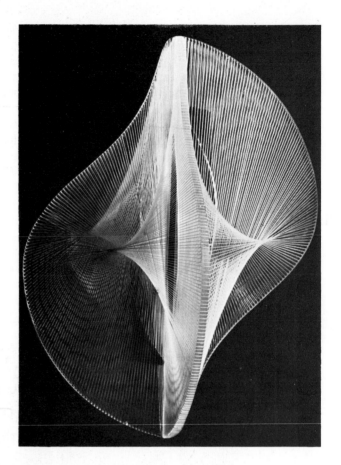

3-21
Naum Gabo, *Linear Construction,* 1950. Plastic and nylon, 15″ high. Private collection.

pear steeper than they really are. Some viewers see works like this as mysterious caverns; others find they suggest some kind of mechanical volcanoes or even the cowlings of jet engines.

Kinetic Sculpture

Sculpture's possibilities have also been expanded to include movement. *Kinetic sculpture* is the name applied to those works that—through motors, wind, or other energy sources—escape the static state of ordinary sculpture. But even though kineticism was in large part inspired by machines, the first really successful works of this kind were not motorized at all. Alexander Calder's hanging *mobiles* (fig. 3-23) depend on a system of precise balances to make their metal vanes respond to movements of the air. The drifting and dipping of the abstract color shapes continually transform the appearance of the sculpture. Motorized kinetic sculpture was revived in the late fifties. But for all the technological means it makes available to sculptors today, it has still not produced any series of outstanding works. Oddly enough, the most interesting of the artists in this area is one whose whimsical vision of the machine is anything but scientific. Jean Tinguely's sculptures are constructed of odds and ends, and have nothing of the polished discipline and sense of purpose of the machine. His most symbolic construction was the huge *Homage to New York*, the ultimate purpose of which was to destroy itself—which it did—with fire, noise, a fitting degree of confusion, and the applause of New Yorkers, in the garden of that city's Museum of Modern Art (fig. 3-24).

Mixed Media   Jean Tinguely's *Homage to New York* could as easily be included in this category as in sculpture, for the term *mixed media* covers all those works of art that break away from traditional uses of methods and materials. Typically they combine two- and three-

3-22   Lee Bontecou, *Untitled,* 1960. Welded metal, canvas, wire, 55″ × 58″. Private collection, New York.

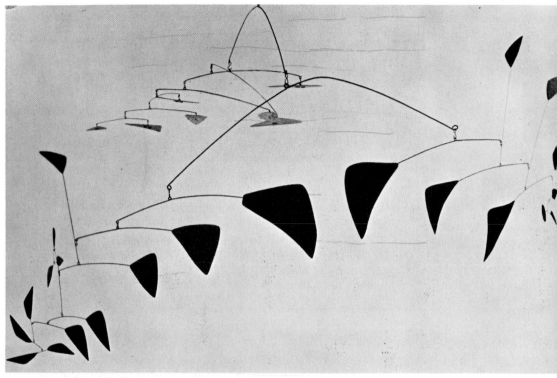

3-23   Alexander Calder, *Sumac,* 1961. Sheet metal, metal rods, wire, 49¾" × 94". Courtesy Perls Galleries, New York.

dimensional approaches or, like Tinguely's inspired conglomeration, bring together disparate, almost incompatible materials.

Collage   *Collage* consists of pasting fragments of paper or other relatively flat materials against a flat surface. Although its history goes back to around World War I, it has become popular in recent years. Romare Bearden who is noted for his collages, pieces together fragments of "found images" from photographs and other pictures. His ideas are drawn from the broad spectrum of black life in America—city and rural, North and South, old and young—and his found images include facial features, fragments of clothing, parts of buildings, and even bits of African masks. In his hands, these originally unrelated fragments magically combine to create a new whole (fig. 3-25). Although the visual patterns are interesting, it is the capacity to generate mental associations that gives Bearden's multiple images their unusual strength.

3-24
Jean Tinguely, *Homage to New York,* 1960. Kinetic assemblage of
machinery, fireworks, piano. In the sculpture garden of
The Museum of Modern Art, New York.

3-25
Romare Bearden, *Pittsburgh
Memory,* 1964. Collage,
9¼″ × 11¾″.
Private collection.

Assemblage   An outgrowth of collage, *assemblage* differs in that it is not restricted to flat materials. Typically, an assemblage employs fairly substantial three-dimensional things—oftentimes "found objects" such as stuffed birds, plaster casts, and clocks. As the name implies, this art calls for assembling these things with glue, nails, rivets, or any other means. There is no limit to the kinds of things eligible for incorporation in an assemblage or the ways they can be put together. Most assemblage makers tend to use eccentric materials or found objects as abstract forms, treating them as indifferently as individual brushstrokes. Few artists have risked using the objects for what they are, and of these only the French sculptor Arman has been consistently successful. Arman has found a perverse beauty in the refuse of the technological age. He has capitalized on this in striking compositions that often take the form of repetitions of similar items—as if imitating the assembly lines that created them (fig. 3-26).

Colo, a Puerto Rican artist, uses a simpler and more direct approach to assemblage, combining everyday objects in a provocative image. His *Artifact for Keeping Secrets* (fig. 3-27) is a sculpture that both attracts and repels the viewer: he has taken a small, chrome-plated cashbox and penetrated the coin slot with a long, sharp knifeblade that points threateningly upward. This unusual marriage of alien objects produces a variety of ambiguous connotations—sex, money, mystery, and danger.

3-26
Arman, *Brush Off,* 1978.
Accumulation of paint
brushes, 27″ × 25″ × 9″.
Courtesy Andrew Crispo
Gallery, New York.

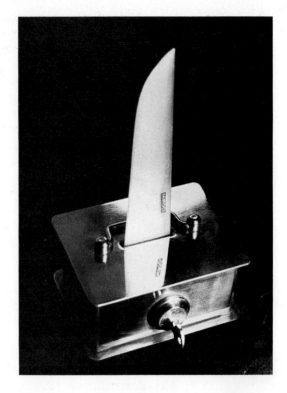

3-27
Colo, *Artifact for Keeping Secrets,* 1977. Mixed media, 17″ high. El Museo del Barrio, New York.

Environments

Environment is a relatively new term in art, created to describe experiments that began in the late 1950s and that attempted to literally bring the spectator into the artwork. Environmental works are not hung on a wall or placed on a pedestal; they surround the viewer on all, or nearly all, sides. The concept, however, is an old one, with precedents in such other areas of the arts as theater, landscaping, and architecture.

Colored Light

One of the best examples of early environmental art is the interior of the huge Gothic cathedral at Chartres, France. The thirteenth-century builders erected a structure with a masonry ceiling that spans 53 feet of the main part of the church at a height of 118 feet from the floor (fig. 3-28). This cathedral is like an enormous open sculpture, its interior spaces interrupted by massive piers and archways on the main level, and smaller arcades and columns on the upper levels. The outer walls, especially the area just below the ceiling, are penetrated by large windows of stained glass that transform the sunlight (colorplate 6). The rays of intense color, whether seen directly through the glass or indirectly as they pierce the dark interior, are a signifi-

3-28 Nave of Chartres Cathedral, 1194–1220.

cant part of the experience of being inside the cathedral.

To make stained glass, color must be added (by introducing certain minerals) when the glass is in a molten stage. Pressed into sheets and allowed to cool, the glass is then cut into smaller pieces according to a previously prepared design. Details such as facial features are usually painted on with oxides and made permanent by firing in a kiln. The fragments are then joined together with lead strips by a technique called leading.

The environmental art of Dan Flavin in our own day is related to that of the windows of Chartres Cathedral, although Flavin uses colored fluorescent light fixtures rather than stained glass (colorplate 7). The nature of the room in which the work is

3-29
Kurt Schwitters, *Merzbau,*
1924–37 (destroyed). Mixed
media. Photo Kunstmuseum
Hannover mit Sammlung
Sprengel, Hannover.

displayed obviously plays a crucial role in the appearance of the work. As the color reflects off the room's surfaces, it is affected by such factors as the size and shape of the room and the color and texture of the walls—as well as by the other light. Flavin was not the first artist to have used real rather than reflected light—but none had ever tried to actually make it the very *substance* of a work.

Merzbau   A major precedent for much twentieth-century environmental art was the *Merzbau,* a name given by the German artist Kurt Schwitters to a series of interior spaces he altered by installing constructions made of all sorts of odds and ends. The first of these, begun in 1924 in the artist's home in Hanover, was an assemblage of rusty tin cans, newspaper and pieces of broken furniture. He called it *Cathedral of Erotic Misery* and filled it with secret panels that hid other objects or tiny scenes that reflected his own erotic misery and that of his time. Eventually, however, he replaced the chaotic collection of junk with abstract forms made of wood. Although the later creation may not have been as richly suggestive as the earlier one, it did focus more attention on the spaces and their importance in an environment (fig. 3-29).

3-30
Allan Kaprow, *18 Happenings in 6 Parts,* 1959. Photo by Fred W. McDarrah.

Happenings

The *Happening*, which began as something like a cross between a temporary Merzbau and improvisational theater, attracted a number of painters and sculptors in the early sixties. The first use of the term *Happening* appears to have been in a 1959 article by Allan Kaprow, in which he included a brief script for a related series of events called *18 Happenings in 6 Parts.* He later produced a version of this work (fig. 3-30) in a New York gallery, which he outfitted with plastic partitions, Christmas lights, slide projectors, tape recorders, and assemblages of junk. "Performers" spoke doubletalk, read poetry, played musical instruments, painted on the walls, squeezed orange juice, and executed other similar acts. The gallery patrons required instructions on how to move through this potpourri, becoming in a sense performers themselves—a role that was developed in Kaprow's future works.

Happenings differ from theater in a number of important ways, although these are becoming more difficult to distinguish because of the influence that such works have had on experimental theater. The spectator-participant is involved in a work that may take place anywhere, indoors or out, and is surrounded by it rather than viewing it on a picturelike stage. Sight and hearing are not the only senses addressed. There are no actors separated from the audience by fictitous roles. Usually there is no plot and no focused structuring of sequence. Instead, there is a series of separate, often overlapping, sometimes unrelated events. Despite the apparent randomness, however, many Happenings are carefully scripted and rehearsed—though unpredictable occurrences are accepted as integral parts of the total experience.

Earth Art   For some artists a canvas, a room, or even an entire building is not enough space—they set about rearranging the landscape itself. Michael Heizer, one of the principal figures of the Earth Art movement, did a number of pieces in the desert. His *Double Negative* (fig. 3-31) is an enormous rectilinear gash in the earth at the edge of a canyon, a sculpture that consists of both real and

3-31   Michael Heizer, *Double Negative*, 1969–70. Two-hundred-thousand-ton displacement in rhyolite and sandstone, 50′ × 1500′ × 30′. Collection Virginia Dwan.

imaginary space (where the canyon eats away the earth it is cut from)—a geometric shape constructed by a human being contrasted with an organic one created by nature. Although the work may appear no more complex than any other hole in the ground, it inspires many observations. Among these are the facts that the use of a negative form makes the space itself the work and that the immense scale allows for radically different perceptions of the form of the work depending on the vantage point—including that of someone in an airplane. Another important point is that this work is far more vulnerable to the erosions of time and weather, so that it will disappear in a relatively short time. A hundred years from now all that will remain are the photographs that document it.

Summary   The complexity of today's art seems to be unlimited. In the past few decades the boundaries between the arts, which once seemed so secure, have been challenged and overrun by experimental artists bent on discovering new forms in the combination of two or more areas. Such hybrids as assemblage, environment, and Happening have gained respectability and must be considered part of art. The traditional limitations concerning the materials of art have also been challenged. One can no longer say that a sculptor is an artist who works with marble, wood, or bronze—for any substance is likely to be suitable, even water and air. Finally, the concept of the art object itself has been challenged. Performances, environments, and the use of perishable materials have raised fundamental questions about what art is and its relationship to the public.

The lack of solid definitions introduces an element of unpredictability, if not chaos, but this is the inevitable price of freedom. The advantage of this uncertainty is that it allows artists to expand the possibilities of their work and viewers to enlarge their own experience.

4
Architectural Media

Architectural objects are utilitarian—places where people live, work, and congregate. This is not to say they cannot also be aesthetic, but that is not their main purpose. Because of its utility and its intimate involvement in everyday human affairs, architecture—more than the fine arts—is closely affected by the values, needs, and technologies of the society it serves.

In this chapter we will be studying architecture from two perspectives: principles of construction and levels of architecture. The first has to do with the methods and materials, both traditional and modern; the second has to do with the ways in which we experience architecture in our daily lives.

Principles of Construction

As we saw in the previous chapter, the form of an artwork is affected very much by its medium. Similarly, the form of a building is affected by the principles of construction used to create it. Although there is an almost infinite variety of architectural forms, there are relatively few principles of construction underlying those forms.

Post and Lintel

The simplest and most ancient method of spanning a space is the *post and lintel*, in which horizontal lintels—often called beams—are supported by vertical posts or walls (fig. 4-1). This method has been used with a variety of materials throughout the world.

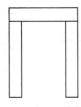

**4-1
Post and lintel.**

The oldest buildings still in existence are *masonry:* made of stone or bricks. The hall of an Egyptian temple dedicated to the god Horus employs a post-and-lintel system of carved stone (fig. 4-2). The masonry roof is carried by heavy beams which in turn are supported by massive posts (columns) and walls. The interior is dark and appropriate for its original function as a sanctuary. But this is also due to the limitation of stone as a building material. It is heavy and lacks the necessary tensile strength (the ability to withstand stress) for spanning large distances. Thus much of the floor space in a masonry building like the Temple of Horus is taken up by thick posts or walls needed to support the short, heavy lintels.

The Parthenon (fig. 4-3)—perhaps the most famous ancient temple of all—is located on a dramatic hill (the Acropolis) above the city of Athens. Dedicated to the goddess Athena, it embodies the aesthetic and philosophical ideals of the fifth-century B.C. Greeks. Like the Temple of Horus, it employs a masonry post-and-lintel system; however, in the Parthenon stone lintels are limited to spanning only the outside rows of columns and

4-2   Temple of Horus, Edfu, Egypt, 237–212 B.C.

4-3 The Parthenon, Acropolis, Athens, 448–432 B.C.

the inner rows of the porches. The ceiling (which no longer exists) was supported by wooden beams. Because wood is both lighter and stronger in tensile strength than stone, the inside of the Parthenon—though not spacious—was not crowded with a forest of heavy columns. On the other hand, wood is not permanent; it either burns or rots. All of the wood in the Parthenon, like that of other Greek temples, has disappeared. Consequently, the dilemma of post-and-lintel construction: Wood is perishable, masonry is cumbersome.

Arch

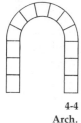

4-4
Arch.

The disadvantage of masonry can be reduced by using the *arch* (fig. 4-4), which spans a space with a number of small stones or blocks in a curve rather than with a single lintel. In an arch, the blocks are wedge shaped and press against one another to prevent falling—the force of gravity diverted outward as well as downward. The remains of a Roman aqueduct in Segovia, Spain (fig. 4-5) are an excellent example of arch construction. An aqueduct is actually a series of arches supporting a large trough through which water could flow for a great distance. Although a single arch might afford limited protection from rain, an aqueduct arch is not designed for shelter. A *barrel vault* (fig. 4-6), which is an extended arch, is the simplest form of shelter using

4-5 Roman aqueduct, Segovia, Spain, *c.* A.D. **10.**

the arch principle. Because of the downward and outward pressure of a solid masonry ceiling, a barrel vault requires heavy walls for support along its entire length. The *cross vault* (fig. 4-7), formed by two intersecting barrel vaults, is an improvement because it permits the support to be focused at just four points. Arch systems of construction were used extensively from the time of the Romans through the nineteenth century. But it was the Gothic builders of the twelfth through sixteenth centuries who carried these systems to their fullest architectural and aesthetic expression.

One of the major contributions of Gothic builders was the *pointed arch,* which proved far more versatile than the round arch in building vaults (fig. 4-8). A round arch is a semicircle; its height is strictly governed by its width. A pointed arch, which is more like a triangle, allows the ratio of width to height to vary simply by changing the angle of the arch. This in turn allows intersecting vaults of different widths to have the same height— an advantage that was very important to the Gothic builders. The sharper angle of the pointed arch also serves to divert the

Plate 1 Georges Seurat, *Bathing at Asnières*, 1883–84. Oil on canvas, 6' 7'' x 9' 11''. Reproduced by courtesy of the Trustees, The National Gallery, London.

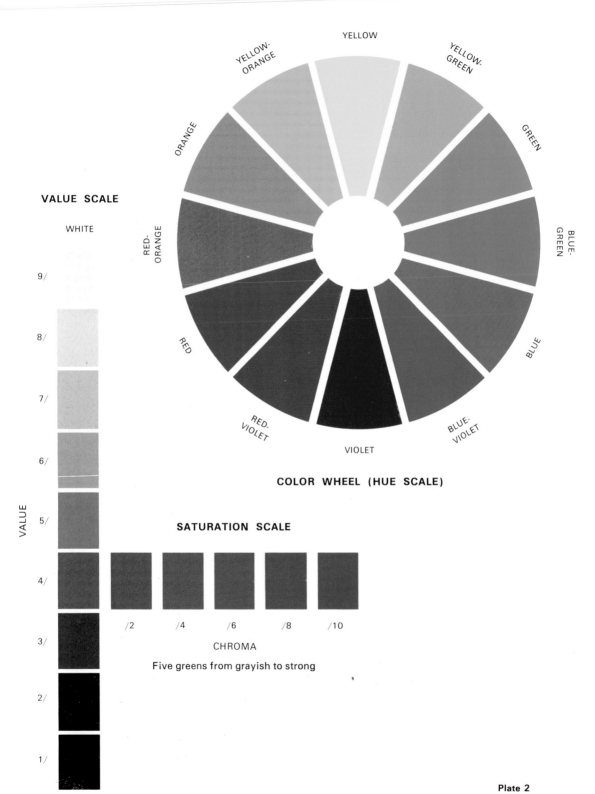

VALUE SCALE

WHITE

9/

8/

7/

6/

VALUE

5/

4/

3/

2/

1/

BLACK

COLOR WHEEL (HUE SCALE)

YELLOW

YELLOW-ORANGE

YELLOW-GREEN

ORANGE

GREEN

RED-ORANGE

BLUE-GREEN

RED

BLUE

RED-VIOLET

BLUE-VIOLET

VIOLET

SATURATION SCALE

/2   /4   /6   /8   /10

CHROMA

Five greens from grayish to strong

Plate 2

Plate 3 Richard Anuskiewicz, *All Things Do Live In the Three*, 1963. Acrylic on masonite, 21⅞'' x 35⅞''. Collection Mrs. Robert M. Benjamin, New York. © Richard Anuskiewicz, 1980.

Plate 4   Giotto di Bondone, *Meeting at the Golden Gate*, early fourteenth century.
Fresco. Arena Chapel, Padua.

Plate 5 Eugène Delacroix, *The Death Of Sardanapoulus*, 1826. Oil on canvas, 12' 1" x 16' 3". Louvre, Paris.

Plate 6 *Wine Merchant*, detail from the *Window of Saint Lubius*, *c.* 1200–20.
Stained glass, 32″ diameter Chartres Cathedral, France.

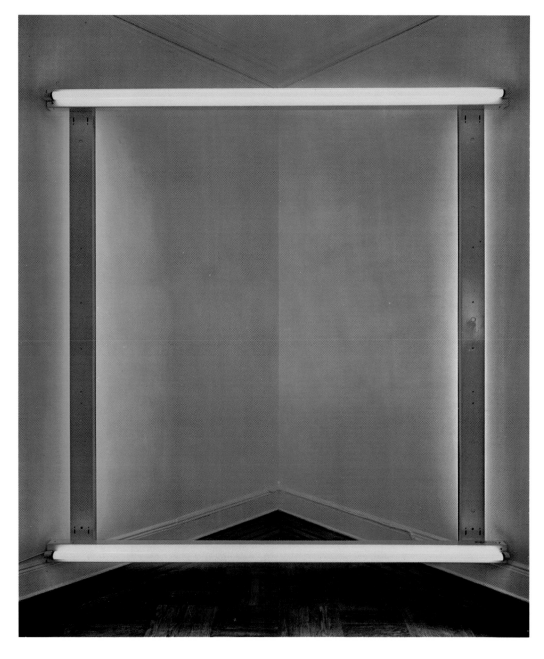

Plate 7   Dan Flavin, *Untitled (to Donna) 5A*, 1971. Yellow, blue, and pink fluorescent light,
            8′ square across a corner. Photo courtesy of Leo Castelli Gallery, New York.

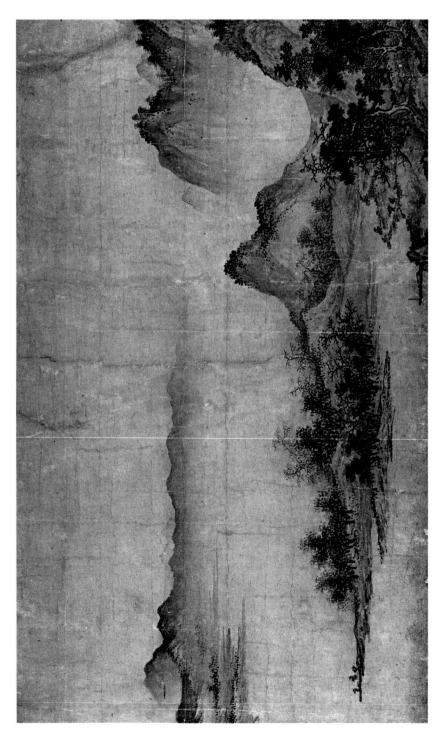

Plate 8 Tung Yuan, *Clear Day in the Valley* (detail), twelfth–thirteenth centuries. Handscroll, ink and slight colors on paper, 14¾'' x 59¼''. Museum of Fine Arts, Boston (Chinese and Japanese Special Fund, 12.903).

4-6
Barrel vault.

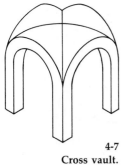

4-7
Cross vault.

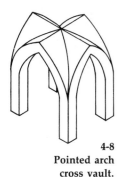

4-8
Pointed arch cross vault.

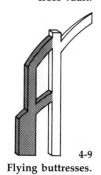

4-9
Flying buttresses.

force of gravity more directly toward the ground, thereby requiring less bracing on the sides.

The glorious effect of pointed arches and pointed cross vaults can be seen in the interior of Chartres Cathedral (fig. 3-28), a masonry building full of light and space. This effect is further facilitated by still another contribution of the Gothic builders, the *flying buttress* (fig. 4-9). This is a system of half-arches outside the walls that reinforces the vaults and walls at key points by absorbing some of the outward thrust of the ceiling. (Many vanelike flying buttresses can be seen grouped along the outside wall of Chartres Cathedral in fig. 4-10.)

A dome can be thought of as a "radial" arch. Round, semicircular domes had been used for Roman temples and later for Christian churches in Eastern Europe. The pointed dome on the cathedral of Florence (fig. 4-11)—the first of its kind—was an impressive sight when it was finished in 1436. Designed by Filippo Brunelleschi, it was a radical solution to the problem of spanning such a huge space without the use of external buttressing. Because a pointed dome, like a pointed arch, directs the force of gravity downward rather than outward, it is more stable than a round dome. Brunelleschi's design served as the basic model for domed buildings thereafter—including, among others, our nation's capitol.

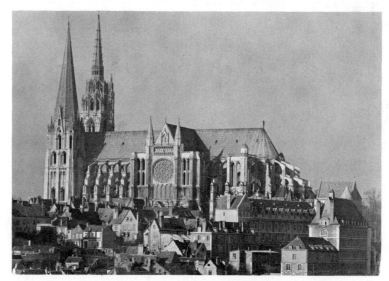

4-10   Chartres Cathedral, France, twelfth through sixteenth centuries.

4-11   The Cathedral of Florence, 1296–1436. Dome (1420–36) by Filippo Brunelleschi.

Frame   Although post-and-lintel and arch systems continued to be used into the nineteenth century, they were challenged by new technologies brought about by the needs of the Industrial Revolution. In the 1830s the wooden *balloon frame* (fig. 4-12) was developed to answer the demand for a rapid means of building houses—to keep pace with the growth of Chicago and other settlements of a rapidly developing America. Two-by-four boards were nailed together to form a lightweight framework to support the exterior siding and interior walls. This method of construction coincided with the improvement of sawmill machinery and the mass production of nails. Today it is called wood-frame construction, and is so commonplace that we have difficulty appreciating its once-revolutionary importance. Prior to the balloon frame, wooden buildings in America were either log cabins or post-and-lintel constructions—the spaces between the posts filled with such materials as stone, bricks, plaster, or earth. On the other hand, the balloon frame was not only lighter in weight, it also capitalized on the standardization of parts to speed construction. Two-by-four boards and machine-produced nails could be converted to a building in two weeks by two men who were handy with saw and hammer.

In 1851, a vast building called the Crystal Palace was erected in London. A single structure of iron and glass that allowed the light of day to flood the interior, it was the site of the Great Exhibition, a world's fair that featured industrial and agricultural products from many countries. Despite its size—a ground plan of over 800,000 square feet—the Crystal Palace was built in less than six months. To accomplish such an engineering feat, its designer, Joseph Paxton, designed structural units that could be partly prefabricated. Planned around the largest standard sheet of glass (at that time only four feet square), the wood and iron members were manufactured in Birmingham and fitted together into a framework on the site in London (fig. 4-13).

Although it was a remarkable tour de force—both as a technical accomplishment and as a spectacular sight—the Crystal Palace was not considered architecture by the architects of the time. They thought of it as a functional structure built for a particular job and suited for rapid construction (and perhaps equally rapid dismantling)—a kind of super circus tent. But the main reason it was not considered architecture was that it was made of iron and glass. Other iron buildings of the nineteenth century had more permanent uses—railroad stations, warehouses, factories—but they too were looked on merely as func-

4-12
Balloon-frame construction.

4-13   Joseph Paxton, Crystal Palace, London, 1851. Nearly 2000' long.

tional "sheds." To be considered architecture, a building had to use solid stone, not a lightweight framework of iron posts and girders bolted together. Few observers had the foresight to realize that the Crystal Palace would inspire radical changes in architecture. Its principle of construction—a metal framework that freed the walls of their load-carrying function—eventually came to be the basis of twentieth-century public and commercial building.

The revolution launched by the Crystal Palace spread to America in the last two decades of the nineteenth century when a colony of high buildings began to rise over Chicago's downtown district. These first *skyscrapers* were born of new industrial technologies including that of steel-frame construction—an outgrowth of the Crystal Palace's iron framework—and the elevator. They were also the result of a growing need for office space in a commercial hub where real-estate costs were extremely high. It was a case of simple economics: using the free space— the sky instead of the costly space on the ground. The principle of construction was the same as that of the balloon frame: a skeletal framework—this time iron and steel rather than wood— constructed prior to the walls. Of the many architects of the "Chicago School," the most outstanding was Louis Sullivan. His buildings, more than the others, are seen today as architectural masterpieces. A simple, unpretentious solid, his Guaranty Building in Buffalo exemplifies the world of business as well as metal-frame technology (fig. 4-14). The vertical lines between the windows have been stressed by means of continuous bands of relief decorations designed by Sullivan himself.

4-14   Louis Sullivan, Guaranty Building, Buffalo, 1894.

The Buffalo building, like other early skyscrapers, was covered with outer walls of masonry. Even though the practical need for masonry construction no longer existed, there seems to have been a psychological need to make a building appear heavy and solid in spite of its metal structure. Indeed, Sullivan's designs fell out of favor in the early twentieth century because they did not resemble masonry buildings enough. From then until after World War II, downtown buildings were often made to resemble Renaissance palaces or Gothic cathedrals—sometimes with phony flying buttresses.

It was not until the early 1950s that architects began to design buildings with steel skeletons covered with a nonstructural skin of glass and metal. The freedom to create a simple geometric shape and sheathe it with any material for the "curtain" was inspired in large part by the work of Mies van der Rohe. His bronze and glass Seagram Building in New York (fig. 4-15), designed with Philip Johnson, is one of the classic examples of a style that has since become commonplace in American cities.

4-15   Ludwig Mies van der Rohe and Philip Johnson, Seagram Building, New York, 1956–58.

4-16 Le Corbusier, Unité d'Habitation, Marseilles, 1947–52.

Ferroconcrete   Since the discovery of portland cement in the nineteenth century, concrete has become increasingly popular in the modern world of architecture. This material, like the methods of construction employed with it, contrasts vividly with steel. A blend of cement, water, sand, and small stones is poured into molds that correspond to the shape required by the construction. When this mixture has hardened, the molds are removed. Unlike steel, which lends itself to the geometry of sharp angles and flat surfaces, concrete can assume almost any shape. By itself, however, concrete is weak in tensile strength. But this handicap can be overcome by imbedding stretched steel rods or cables in the concrete, a combination called *ferroconcrete* or *reinforced concrete.* The dual advantage of plasticity and strength makes ferroconcrete an extremely versatile medium with its own unique qualities.

Compare Le Corbusier's high-rise apartments in Marseilles (fig. 4-16) with Mies van der Rohe's skyscraper in New York.

4-17   Jörn Utzon, Sydney Opera House, Australia, 1959–72.

Featuring massive tapered supports, deeply recessed windows, and unadorned concrete surfaces—which still bear the impressions of the casting forms—the apartments are much more rustic and sculpturesque than the sleek, austere office building. The curving vaults of the Sydney Opera House designed by Jörn Utzon are even more sculpturesque (fig. 4-17). Looking at the building, one is reminded of gull wings, swelling sails, or breaking waves—all of which are appropriate to the site on a peninsula in Sydney's harbor. The repetition of the vaults, together with their slightly varied axes, gives the whole ensemble a sense of movement. With the highest shell rising nearly 200 feet, the Sydney Opera House forms a striking landmark both for approaching ships and for residents of the city.

Geodesic Dome   Buckminster Fuller's invention, the *geodesic dome*, uses a method of assembly related to that of Paxton's Crystal Palace and the balloon frame of the previous century, but it involves a different

4-18   Buckminster Fuller, United States Pavilion, EXPO 67, Montreal, 1967.

principle of construction. Rather than a grid system, as with a wood or metal frame, the geodesic dome employs a system of hexagonal pyramids constructed of triangles; the repetition of the pyramid module eventually forms a spherical enclosure. The dome of the United States Pavilion at EXPO 67 in Montreal (fig. 4-18) employs an additional supporting system of triangles that bridges the apexes of all the pyramids. Each side of the triangle is part of a line that encircles the dome's surface. The pavilion is slightly higher than the Sydney Opera House, yet its weight is only a fraction of the weight of that building—for it was constructed of nothing more complicated than steel pipes and panels of transparent acrylic. Fuller's dome seems unlimited in its capacity for interior space, possibly capable of spans even several miles wide. It may well be the most rapid and efficient construction method presently available. It remains to be seen whether or not the geodesic shell will play as significant a role in answering future social needs as the balloon and steel frames have in the past and do in the present.

Levels of Architecture

We now consider some of the ways in which architecture affects the spaces we live in. The twin considerations of *lived space* and *architectural space* help define this topic. Lived space refers to that which we physically occupy, move through, use for various purposes, and in which we encounter and interact with objects and other people. But we also interpret this space with our minds and feelings. Architectural space consists of the solids, openings, places, and paths that shape lived space.

An architectural writer, Christian Norberg-Schulz, identified different levels of what he called "existential space." Three of these levels—landscape, urban, and house—are convenient divisions with which to classify and review some varieties of lived space and their counterparts in architectural space.

Landscape Level

The scale of space at the landscape level might be likened to that which we can see in a landscape painting or in the view from a tall building or a low-flying plane. At this level the relationship between community and site can be examined effectively.

Historically, major settlements such as San Francisco were formed on sites where favorable natural features were located, especially waterways. Because of the large bay, the fine harbor, and its location on the west coast of a developing continent, early San Francisco had the potential of becoming an international city. With a little help from historical events—such as the 1849 gold rush—the great city has lived up to the promise of its location. In addition, the Bay Area enjoys the natural endowments of rich and fertile land in a setting of sea water and foothills. It has the double blessing of harbors for trade and varied topography that provides an aesthetic identity of its own (fig. 4-19).

San Francisco's builders have both complemented and detracted from the natural beauty. The exceptional Golden Gate Bridge, which is the visual keynote of the area, and the historic personality of the waterfront and cable cars contribute to San Francisco's image. However, the regularity of the street layout—unrelated to the natural contours of the hills—and the insistence on erecting tall buildings threaten to obscure some of the very qualities that give San Francisco its unique landscape identity.

Landscape in a modern city undergoes its most visible transformation in the city's spiritual center, the commercial district. There the man-made monuments—office buildings, hotels, department stores, elevated freeways, and bridges—give the

4-19
View of Lombard Street,
San Francisco.

original site a metropolitan identity. In other times, the central
or most prominent part of a city was transformed instead by
architecture intended for religious purposes.

Probably the most venerated city landscape in the world is
the Acropolis of Athens (fig. 4-20). Crowned by the Parthenon,
this hilltop was the spiritual focus of the Athenian world—the
showplace of their artistic glory and the rallying point for their
civic and religious ceremonies. With the aid of famous artisans
from all over Greece, a great construction effort during the time
of Pericles (fifth-century B.C.) transformed the Acropolis into a
sacred marble city overlooking the *agora*, or marketplace, of the
city below. The hierarchy of sacred and profane was therefore
confirmed by landscape elevation. The landscape's potential
was further utilized in the city's ceremonies: Processions starting in the agora wound their way up the rocky slopes, through
the majestic gate of the Propylaea, and onto the exalted plateau
of the Acropolis. One of the major legacies of Greek art and

4-20   View of the Acropolis, Athens.

architecture is the concept of the heroic, and the heroic qualities of the gateways and temples on the Acropolis can best be understood in the context of their heroic landscape setting.

Less dramatic but equally important is the role of landscape in residential living, where attention is given to the selection of sites for family homes and to how the structures can be accommodated to the land. Unfortunately, the sites of many American homes—especially those in nonhilly areas—lack variety. The general criteria for developing new subdivisions consist of laying out a grid of asphalt roads, clearing the trees, and leveling each lot.

Habitat, a fascinating grouping of apartments designed by architect Moshe Safdie for EXPO 67, may be an answer to the monotony found so often in suburban developments (fig. 4-21). It provides variety of level and direction even though it is built

4-21   Safdie, David, Barott, and Boulva, Habitat, Montreal, 1967.

on a flat site. A greater variety of levels, directions, spaces, and textures is afforded by a Dogon village in Africa (fig. 4-22). This richness is due to the fact that the architecture—mostly houses and granaries—is organically related to the natural shapes and contours of the hillside.

Urban Level   The ways in which architecture accommodates social interaction are the focus at this level. The physical elements of space that define our urban world are determined by a complex network of history, beliefs, customs, and available technology.

VILLAGE AND TOWN   Bandiagara, capital of the Dogon people, is not far from the legendary city of Timbuktu in Mali. It has become, along with other settlements of the Dogon people, an object of absorbing interest to sociologists and architects.

4-22 Dogon village, Mali, West Africa.

The hand-built architecture of the Dogon has the same sensuous qualities of sculpture. And, as noted earlier, the organic arrangements of their buildings create a pleasing variety of levels. The design of the homes and the community is determined by symbol and tradition rather than geometry. A house is built in the configuration of a human being: the entrance representing the vulva, the cooking area the lungs, and the kitchen itself the head. The proportions are based on the sexual symbols of 3 (male genitals) and 4 (female labia) multiplied by 2; thus a house is always 6 by 8 paces (fig. 4-23). This anthropomorphic symbolism is extended to the village. Individual family complexes are grouped to form various parts of the total village—which represents a man's body lying in a north-south direction.

The symbolic interlocking of house parts, groups of houses, and village parts reflects a reciprocal interlocking in the social structure. Families of a village are linked by a complex patrilineal system based on marriage customs and a system of individual and collective ownership. Each person is linked emotionally to a network of houses, which in turn is linked both socially and symbolically to the village.

CITY PLANNING Perhaps the unity and togetherness of a Dogon community can only be provided in a small village of a preliterate society. The larger towns and cities of literate societies cannot always depend on inherited symbols and traditions to furnish the order needed to conduct their daily business.

The name most associated with city planning of ancient times is Hippodamus of Miletus, who allegedly introduced the gridiron scheme to the cities of Greece and Asia Minor in the fifth century B.C. (fig. 4-24). Regardless of his actual role in planning cities, the use of parallel streets intersecting at right angles in later Hellenistic and Roman communities came to be known as the Hippodamic system. Such a system not only facilitated

4-23   Plans of a Dogon house.

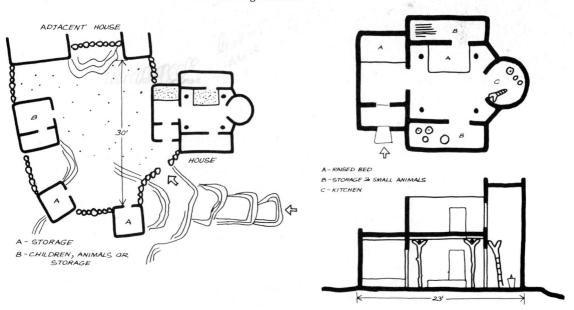

ADJACENT HOUSE

30'

HOUSE

A - STORAGE
B - CHILDREN, ANIMALS OR
        STORAGE

A - RAISED BED
B - STORAGE & SMALL ANIMALS
C - KITCHEN

23'

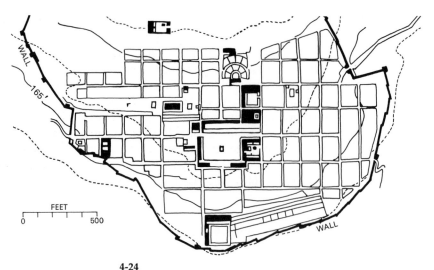

4-24
Simplified ground plan of
the city of Priene, Greece.

the flow of commerce that was essential to Greek cities; it also
provided order and regularity, in contrast to the chaos of older
cities whose streets were determined by the dictates of custom—
old footpaths and ceremonial parade routes—rather than by
people's needs.

Modern city planning is intended to satisfy the same needs;
however, the enemy of order and regularity is not the pattern of
the streets but the crowded living conditions and their attendant
social problems.

Ebenezer Howard, considered the earliest city planner of
the modern era, was not enthusiastic about modern cities. Dis-
liking what he saw, heard, and smelled in late-nineteenth-
century London, Howard proposed to halt the city's growth and
surround it with smaller cities combining the "best of town and
country." His "garden cities" would be encircled by agriculture.
Industry, schools, and housing would be grouped in planned
preserves, with culture and commerce at their centers (fig. 4-25).
In essence, his proposal was anti-city in both its rationale and
intended effects. It motivated people to think about the problems of urban living and consider decentralization—thinning
out the popoulation of the city and spreading it across the land—
as the best way to solve those problems. The concept was advanced by two men who were probably the most influential architects of the twentieth century. Both became engrossed with

their own conceptions of urban living—each of which in some way reflected Howard's garden cities.

Frank Lloyd Wright, like Howard, was no lover of cities. "To look at the plan of a great city," he said, "is to look at something like the cross-section of a fibrous tumor." Wright held this attitude despite (perhaps because of) the fact that he had learned his trade in Chicago under Louis Sullivan. A dramatic and forceful person, he promoted decentralization, equating centralization (symbolized by the evil skyscraper) with antidemocracy, the antichrist, and the gravestone of capitalism. Yet he included the automobile as an essential element of his utopian vision. The

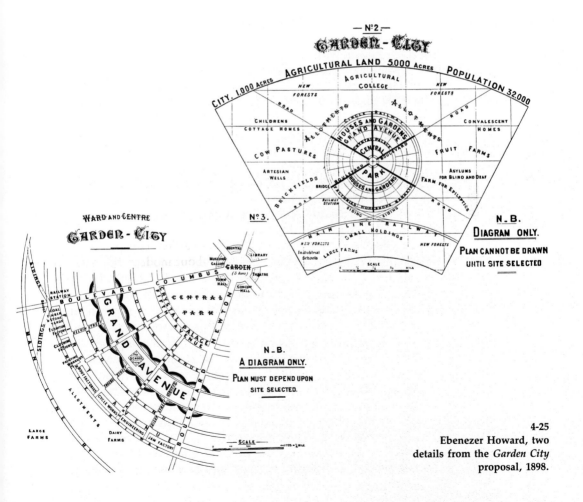

4-25
Ebenezer Howard, two
details from the *Garden City*
proposal, 1898.

4-26   Le Corbusier, sketch from the *Ideal City* proposal, 1922.

private citizen with a car, like a bird freed from a cage, could "go where he may enjoy all that the centralized City ever gave him, plus the security, freedom, and beauty of the Good ground . . ." In 1934 Wright proposed a model for this "good ground." The *Broadacre City* plan—a sort of updated version of Howard's garden city—gave recognition to and relied heavily on the automobile.

Le Corbusier, a Swiss architect based in France, was as enthusiastic about the city as Wright was opposed to it. Yet Le Corbusier did not appreciate cities in their present state, which he perceived as "bulging with human detritus, with the hordes of people who came to them to try their luck, did not succeed, and are now all huddled together in crowded slums." The *Ideal City* proposal (actually twelve years earlier than Wright's plan) consisted of wide avenues that crisscrossed to form large city blocks—the Hippodamic system on a grand scale (fig. 4-26). Many of these superblocks were to be topped with skyscraper towers—for residential or professional purposes—surrounded by large parks as well as light and air. Athough it appalled disciples of the garden city concept, it was in fact a garden city in a different form—a "vertical garden city," in Le Corbusier's own words. Although his scheme called for twelve thousand inhabitants to an acre, high-rise quarters would occupy only five percent of the surface. His ambitious idea, unlike Wright's, made extensive use of the skyscraper—but like Wright's, made ample provision for automobile thoroughfares and parking.

Le Corbusier's later versions of his *Ideal City* plan for the reconstructions of Paris and Moscow were never accepted, but his dream city has had immense influence on American city planners. The clarity, simplicity, and glamorous visibility of Le Corbusier's drawing-board city has, directly or indirectly, captured the imagination of architects, zoning officials, mayors, and even university regents. Wright's *Broadacre City*, on the other hand, has been translated (sometimes vulgarized) into the spacious spread of suburbia—the post-World War II explosion of "greenbelts" surrounding even our smaller cities.

Today many urbanologists are questioning the value of these developments that reflect the thinking of famous city planners. The solutions of Howard, Le Corbusier, and Wright are no longer viewed as answers to our problems. The vertical solution of centralizing people in high-rise housing often produces bleak skyscrapers surrounded by parking lots rather than greenery such as the Alfred E. Smith Housing Project in New York (fig. 4-27). Or worse, it destroys old neighborhoods, usually with catastrophic socioeconomic results. The horizontal solution of

4-27   Alfred E. Smith Housing Project, New York, 1948.

dispersing the population, aimed at helping families fulfill their dreams of green grass and clean air, regularly turns into expensive and inconvenient strips of housing neatly laid out with roads that go nowhere and end nowhere. The enthusiasm of both Le Corbusier and Wright for the automobile seems especially misplaced. "Our fast car," Le Corbusier exclaimed, "takes the special elevated motor track between the majestic skyscrapers." Today, however, our automobile-clogged urban and suburban streets are looked upon more as a disease of modern life than as a panacea.

PLANNING FOR PEDESTRIANS If social interaction is to take place at the urban level, cities must also provide for pedestrians.

Italy is a country famous for its public walkways, from winding medieval streets to dramatic squares like the Capitoline Hill (fig. 2-23). Even there the Galleria of Milan is unequalled in its own way (fig. 4-28). It is a covered street housing numerous shops and a permanent gallery of industrial products in one of the richest commercial cities of Europe (of all the Italian cities, the one most like an American city). But the Galleria is more than a shopping center; its arcades contain bars, cafes, restaurants, and its marble streets are for dining and leisure as well as business. It is a square for informal seminars and a promenade for strolling—a place where artists and members of the entertainment world can mix with everyday people. Add a few pickpockets and tourists, and the mixture is complete. But most of all the Galleria is a focal point for the citizens of Milan.

Precedents for the Galleria go back to Imperial Rome. Little remains today of Trajan's Forum—a large square formed by colonnades on three sides and an immense covered building called a *basilica* on the fourth—except parts of the large market on the east side of the square (fig. 4-29). But it was once an important center of the capital. In addition to being a place for shopping and leisure, like the Galleria the forum was a combination civic center, financial exchange, sacred area, and sculpture gallery. Lawsuits were tried in the basilica or in an open-air court where crowds of listeners could admire the legal eloquence.

Surprisingly, the automobile is responsible for a creation that could be considered a revival of the Forum of Trajan and a partial rival to the Galleria. Americans, who often feel compelled to drive a car even to mail a letter, are now encouraged to stroll during shopping because of a commercial solution to the

4-28   The Galleria of Vittorio Emanuele, Milan, 1865–1867.

parking problem in downtown areas of the city. Obviously serv-
ing fewer functions than a forum, an American shopping center
is, nevertheless, a unified complex of retail stores, eating places,
and malls for strolling; larger centers frequently have movie theaters, skating rinks, and sculpture courts. The Woodfield Shopping Center in Schaumburg, Illinois, even has a Greek-style
amphitheater (fig. 4-30). Some 200 attractive shopfronts face the
main courts and entryways to catch the attention of passersby.
Several balconies, crossovers, ramps, and staircases—together
with gleaming sculptures—give the shopping center the appearance of a futuristic Emerald City. These attractions were
obviously intended to inspire people to shop—and at first that
was about all. However, now that their newness has worn off,
people are beginning to use Woodfield and other malls for additional purposes: arts and crafts exhibits, music concerts, health

4-29
Vaults of Trajan's Market,
second century A.D.

fairs, fashion shows, children's theater, charity events, and even exercise programs. More significantly, teenagers and senior citizens use them as informal meeting places. Perhaps someday shopping malls will serve as many functions as Trajan's forum did.

Meanwhile, the open square is experiencing a revival in the downtowns of many cities, large and small. Prohibiting traffic for two or three blocks converts a street running through a major commerical area into a pedestrian mall. Such a practice provides more opportunities for human contact as well as some architectural variety. Also, refurbishing old stores, restaurants, and theaters—and perhaps adding some new ones along with a parking ramp—may draw some customers away from the shopping centers.

Paley Park a "vest-pocket park" in New York City, was created from empty space between buildings just off Fifth Avenue (fig. 4-31). It was not necessarily intended to attract trade, but it certainly provides some relief from an unbroken urban environment. And it is a popular place with office workers in the area, who go there at lunchtime to talk, eat, and relax.

House Level   The urban level is characterized by public places where people gather and paths where people move about. Private spaces within the urban environment are classified as the *house level*. The essence of the house level is interior space, intimately proportioned by and related to the human being. It is a center of personal activity, a place someone goes to or comes from—and most important—a place in which a man, woman, or child establishes a feeling of personal identity.

SINGLE-FAMILY DWELLING   The formal directness and material economy of Japanese art has long been an influence on some of the modern art in the West. And Western interest in Eastern art has been especially visible in the area of domestic architecture.

The basic ordering unit for a Japanese house is the *tatami*, a tightly woven rice-straw mat that is spread on the floor. Con-

4-30   Woodfield Shopping Center, Schaumburg, Illinois, 1971.

4-31   Paley Park, New York, 1967.

veying the size and function of Japanese rooms, the meaning of
these six-by-three-foot mats has so penetrated the Japanese language that the phrase "four-and-a-half-mat novel" (suggesting
an intimate nine-by-nine-foot-square room for a man and
woman) is a familiar slang expression for a romantic book.

Japanese rooms, which serve different functions depending
on the occasion, do not correspond to rooms in American homes
(fig. 4-32). For one thing, the nature and arrangement of rooms
is profoundly affected by the Japanese custom of removing

one's shoes before entering the house proper. The combined entrance hall (1) and anteroom (2) used for this purpose has thus become a very important space, which in the smallest of houses may consist of ten percent of the entire floor area. The act of taking leave of the outside world by removing one's shoes symbolizes the first stage of shedding the indifference and estrangement of the outside and assuming the peace and harmony of the

4-32
Plan of a Japanese house.

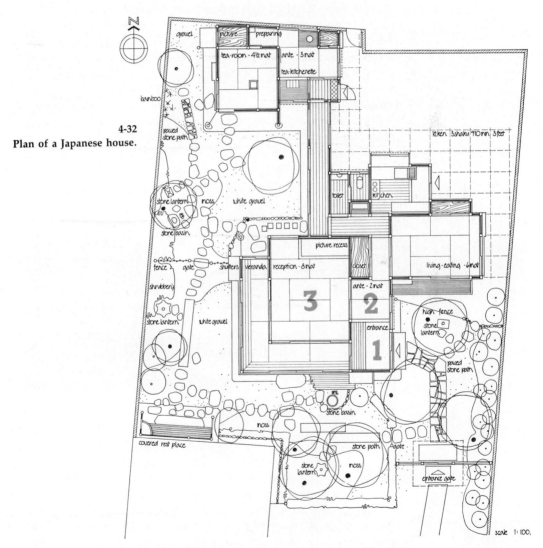

garden design for residence of 20 tsubo · 66.1 sq.m · 720 sq.ft. with tea-hut   mizusawa komuten · co

scale 1:100.

inside. The second stage of integration with the inner environment comes in the adjoining anteroom. It is here that the wife welcomes her husband, and here that the host and guest meet and bow. Now one is ready for full integration into the house. The anteroom is usually adjacent to all of the other rooms; however, a guest would be directed into the reception room (3). Roughly equivalent to an American living room, it is the most important space in a Japanese house (averaging at least eight mats in size). Containing a revered and ornamental alcove called a *tokonoma*—a sort of private-home sanctuary—and bordered by a broad veranda that leads to a lovingly cultivated garden, this room is the spiritual core of the house.

Among the admired aspects of Japanese architecture are the outdoor-indoor relationships (fig. 4-33) and the concept of continuous or "flowing" space. A small garden, even under the limited conditions of city living, is considered a minimum requirement, one linked visually and psychologically to the inte-

4-33   Old Samurai's House, Miyagiken, Japan.

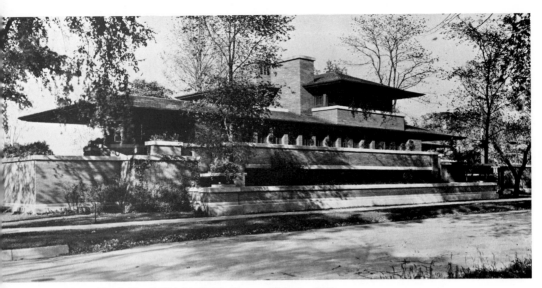

4-34   Frank Lloyd Wright, Robie House, Chicago, 1909.

rior by a veranda. In addition to the continuity between exterior and interior, movable partitions and the modular coordination of rooms lend to the Japanese house a sense of uninterrupted flow between interior spaces.

Yet wholesale application of Japanese principles of architecture to Western architecture would be superficial. The differences in life-style related to the custom of entering the home have already been mentioned; basic occidental attitudes toward physical comfort and hygiene require an assortment of furnishings that would suffocate a Japanese interior. Even more fundamental are the traditional differences in personal philosophy that always operate as underlying premises in domestic architecture. A Japanese interior, with its small scale and thin walls, is not conducive to the expression of individual personality.

Frank Lloyd Wright successfully assimilated into his early homes some elements of architecture that could be attributed to Japanese inspiration (fig. 4-34). Ground-hugging horizontal lines accentuated by deep overhangs, indoor-outdoor relationships occasioned by floor-to-ceiling glass, and the opening up of interior spaces are hallmarks of the Prairie Style he began to develop in the first decade of this century. But the elegant, romantic sensation of luxury is strictly American in spirit. Way beyond the pocketbook of the average American, the prairie house has nevertheless left its indelible mark (and thus a Japanese touch) on every suburban ranch house with its familiar overhanging eaves, picture window, and "scientific" floor plan.

CONCENTRATED-FAMILY DWELLING The single-family dwelling is too expensive for most Americans, let alone peoples of other parts of the world. And if the $125,000 ranch house on an 80-by-150-foot lot were multiplied to keep up with a population that increases by two percent every year, the whole country would soon be suburbanized. Clearly there is a need for forms of concentrated living that will permit large numbers of people to occupy relatively small surface areas.

High-rise projects like Chicago's Marina City (fig. 4-35) have been the most popular approach to the problem. These tall, ferroconcrete structures, located along the marina and within walking distance of shopping and work, are comfortable and convenient for the upper-middle-class people living there. Even the parking problem has been solved by turning over 18 floors to the residents' automobiles. But for average families, high-rise projects are not always as comfortable and convenient. The dream of a vertical garden city can become the nightmare of a vertical slum. One of the most notorious examples is the Pruitt-Igo project in St. Louis, which eventually became a ghost city. Among the reasons for its troubles was the fact that outdoor play areas were inordinately small, unsupervised, and relatively inaccessible to the children. Hallways and elevators soon became the play areas—eventually the targets of vandalism— leading to the complete disruption of family living.

The high-rise apartment is not the only type of high-density housing available. An alternative consists of individual units linked together, each unit having a patio—if not its own ground space. Called "urban low-rise group housing," this scheme is a solution that is attracting architects and urban planners today. Yet this type of housing is not new. It existed in the Western Hemisphere before the time of European settlers and long before land started to become scarce. The Anasazi Indians of the Southwest, for example, began living in concentrated settlements as early as the first century A.D. The Cliff Palace in Mesa Verde National Park (fig. 4-36) was a multistoried, masonry-walled community containing over 200 dwelling rooms. In Africa, the Dogon style of living resembles that of low-rise group housing (fig. 4-22). Although each house is separate, the complete unit of house, plot of ground, and granary bins is connected with those surrounding it.

4-35   Bertrand Goldberg, Marina City, Chicago, 1964.

The experimental apartment complex, Habitat, which suc-
ceeds in looking like a hillside town without the benefit of a real
hill, is a contemporary example of high-density group housing
(fig. 4-21). The nearly identical modular units were ingeniously
designed so they could be attached to each other in enough
different ways to lend a degree of individuality to each unit and
prevent the entire complex from looking monotonous. (The lack
of central hallways and elevator shafts, however, makes garbage
disposal and access to the apartments difficult.) In Europe,
where lack of space is more a problem than in America, there are
already many interesting but less radical examples of new apartment complexes. Terraced, staggered, linked, and patioed—

4-36   Cliff Palace, Mesa Verde National Park, Colorado, *c.* A.D. 1100.

they retain many of the advantages of detached single-family dwellings and the attractive qualities of garden-house life (fig. 4-37). Surprisingly, low-rise urban housing was found to be almost as economical as high-rise housing, both with regard to site requirements and to cost of construction. Further, it was found that concentrated living, if effectively designed, can contribute to the quality of life rather than detract from it.

Summary   The first part of this chapter surveys certain basic principles of architectural construction while providing one or two examples for each. Post and lintel was the method used for much of the world's architecture for centuries, and with that method people were able to make buildings as different as an Egyptian temple and a frontier house. A few new methods, developed within the last 150 years, provide architects considerably more freedom. Using ferroconcrete, they have been able to make structures as unique as Habitat and Sydney Opera House. Yet, although today's architecture takes a variety of forms, it is not as free as today's fine art. To erect a roof over people's heads, architects—no matter how experimental they may be—cannot afford to ignore certain laws of nature and the practical matters of function, materials, and technological expertise.

The second part of the chapter reviews various levels of architectural environments that affect the ways people live and function. Some of the examples, such as the Athenian Acropolis, qualify as distinguished architectural monuments; others, like the pocket park, are unpretentious pieces of people's daily surroundings. All of them exist as examples of humankind's constant and unceasing alteration of the physical environment. It is an enterprise that satisfies practical needs and also, sometimes, gives pleasure and inspiration.

4-37   **Low-rise housing units, Bern, Switzerland.**

II Human Context

Artists who work with images use them as writers use words—to interpret the human experience of the time and place in which they live. In primitive societies, where groups of people share a common history and set of beliefs, their conceptions of the world are interpreted in their art, their ceremonies, their ritual objects, and in the ways they build and decorate their houses. In a society such as contemporary America, where religious, educational, regional, class, and ethnic differences distinguish the population, such a degree of unity is impossible; the pluralism of beliefs and values is reflected in the pluralism of artistic expressions.

Nevertheless, certain themes seem to exist in the artistic expressions of all periods and cultures—primitive or modern, simple or complex. These themes usually relate to such basic questions as: What is the nature of the world? Who are we? What is our place in the world? Part II presents some of the ways that artists in other times and other places have responded to certain of these themes and how they have dealt with them in their art.

5
Images of Nature

"Almost every Englishman," Kenneth Clark once said, "if asked what he meant by 'beauty,' would begin to describe a landscape. . . . " The same might be said of a Japanese, or an American, or, in fact, almost any citizen of a modern society. To the average person, the art of painting is often identified with the landscape—despite the fact that today relatively few serious artists make landscape paintings.

This popular conception of art is reinforced by the endless number of inexpensive and tawdry reproductions of landscape paintings sold in stores for the decoration of American living rooms. Perhaps the proliferation of these images in our culture has led to their self-cheapening and has reduced them to little more than household clutter. If this is so, it obscures the fact that landscape painting is a sophisticated product of art and human consciousness. It is the result of a long artistic evolution linked to a history of changing human attitudes toward the natural environment. The varieties of attitudes toward nature and how these have been expressed in art (not only in terms of landscape) are the subject of this chapter.

Ice-Age Painting   Animals appear to have been the very first subject matter of art. So far as we know, the earliest image makers were Ice-Age hunters that lived more than 12,000 years ago in western Europe not far from the melting ice of the last major glaciation. Members of a Paleolithic (Old Stone Age) culture, they did not farm but eked out an existence by gathering food from wild plants and hunting wild animals that furnished food, furs, hides, bones, and ivory. On the walls of subterranean caves they left an amazing artistic record of these animals. Ever since the discovery of this art about a century ago, observers have been impressed by the evidence it provides of an extraordinary level of artistic observation and image-forming ability.

Although some of the species painted in caves near Lascaux in southern France may no longer exist, the artists made their images so vivid that we have no trouble recognizing them as various types of grazing animals—bison, mammoths, horses, bears, and reindeer (fig. 5-1). The outlines and proportions seem to have been based on fairly accurate observations of the profiles of real beasts.

5-1   *Hall of Bulls*, **Lascaux**, *c.* **15,000–10,000** B.C. **Dordogne, France.**

We can only guess at what the artists used for paints and brushes. They may have mixed pigments of red ocher and manganese with animal fat, and then used reeds or animal tails for transferring this mixture to the caves. There is also reason to believe that hunter-artists painting at other sites used blowpipes to spread the mixture. The images in the caves of Font-de-Gaume and Altamira (fig. 5-2) are more lifelike than those of Lascaux, primarily because of a chiaroscuro effect—not unlike that in a modern picture made with an airbrush—that brings out the bulky qualities of the animals.

Not all subjects were treated with as much sophistication as the animals. Representations of people are mostly stick figures; the rare references to landscape features such as rocks, plants, and streams are more like schematic symbols than images. Likewise, the arrangements of the animals (with or without other images) reveal none of the sophisticated methods—overlapping, vertical placement, variations in size, and linear perspective—now employed by artists to suggest spatial depth. Indeed, few

5-2   Bellowing bison and fragments of another galloping bison, Altamira, *c.* 15,000–10,000 B.C. Altamira, Spain.

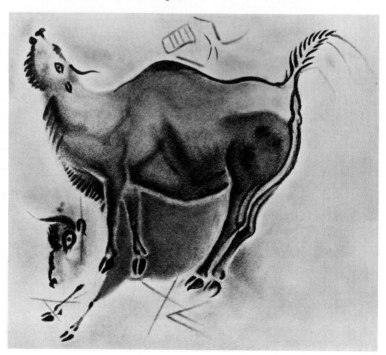

of the arrangements seem determined by any identifiable logic. Randomly placed—sometimes overlapping but usually unrelated to one another in size or narrative—the images are, in this respect, reminiscent of modern graffiti. The impressive realism of Ice-Age art is confined almost entirely to the portrayal of individual animals.

But if we speculate on the kind of lighting (or lack or it) that was available in these caves, we can speculate that prehistoric people probably could not have viewed more than one painting at a time anyway. Imagine what it must have been like to see one of these beasts leap into view as a torch was waved in front of it. This intriguing mental image leads us to wonder what an animal picture meant to these hunters. It requires both research and imagination to piece together the few bits of evidence and consider the purpose and meaning of prehistoric art. The awkward locations of many of the murals and the poor ventilation of the various chambers make it seem unlikely that these caves were used as art galleries or dwellings. This, plus the fact that many of the images of beasts show the marks—real or painted— of weapons, suggests that they did not serve purely aesthetic purposes.

The best guess may be that the awkward locations served as privileged sanctuaries for religious rites and that the images of beasts contained within served magical purposes. Animals, which the Ice-Age hunters depended on for survival, must have been at the center of their religion.

Image-making similar to that of the Ice-Age peoples have been found in some modern African societies (fig. 5-3). And totemism, a belief that animals are ancestrally or spiritually related to human beings, has continued to thrive in many places in the world. The mythologies of preliterate peoples are filled with stories of humans turning into animals and vice versa. Accordingly, it seems likely that Ice-Age societies probably also believed in some form of totemism.

In such societies, distinctions were not made between the natural world and the spiritual world. Since Ice-Age life was totally bound to animals, art depicting animals must have had awesome significance. Its magic was not only important for ensuring success in the hunt but was part of the very structure of belief and social continuity. In a sense these paintings were not images but real spirits, occupying the same magical stage as the hunter-dancers.

5-3 Bushmen defending their herds from a band of Zulus, rock painting.

Egyptian Tomb Art

Human beings—and the dead rather than the living—were represented in most Egyptian art, for one of the principal uses of paintings was the decoration of tombs. Here, too, art had a magic function. The image served to provide a home for the spirit of the deceased, especially if the mummified remains should deteriorate. The tomb of Ti, located at Saqqara, provides an excellent example of this custom. Ti, who lived around 2400 B.C., was an important bureaucrat, the overseer of the pyramids and the Sahura temple. Consequently, his remains were privileged to reside in a *mastaba* (a type of tomb) in a special burial ground for deceased officials.

One of Ti's earthly privileges was that of fishing and hunting in the marshes of the Nile. Because Egypt was an agricultural society, fishing and hunting were a sport—not a principal means of survival. In order to continue this sport in the hereafter, Ti commissioned a relief mural depicting it (fig. 5-4). Along with his own image, magical images for servants, boats, animals, and plants were also necessary. Other painted reliefs in his mastaba illustrate the many needs of his rich estate in eter-

5-4 *Hippopotamus Hunt,* tomb of Ti, Saqqara, *c.* 2500 B.C.
Painted limestone relief, approx. 48″ high.

nity: workers polish his statues, cooks and bakers prepare his food, craftsmen build boats for his favorite sport, and peasants harvest his grain and care for his cattle.

In order to guarantee that an image would be an adequate home for a soul, the Egyptian artist was compelled to follow certain rules. Ti's body, for example—which seems pinned in an upright position to the corrugated thicket of reeds—has its head, legs, and feet shown in profile while one eye and the trunk of the body are shown frontally. This formula (sometimes called *fractional representation*) was applied to almost all human figures, whatever their activity. Had the artist shown the back rather than the front of the nobleman's head, or one of his arms hidden behind his body, or his feet hidden inside the boat, then according to the rules of magic—he would have tragically omitted some of Ti's anatomy, leaving him literally without a face, two arms, or two feet. The artistic solution was to provide the most adequate and characteristic full view, not only of Ti but of the people and creatures that were to serve him forever.

The same type of thinking that considered anatomy a sum of the parts was applied to the organization of the picture. Although various elements of nature, people, and animals are logically connected (to an extent never achieved in Ice-Age art), they are not at all integrated in the realistic sense that we customarily associate with landscape art. Divided into tidy zones, the relief clearly spells out the proper neighborhood of each figure. The aquatic animals are relegated to their own environment, symbolized by neat rows of vertical ripples. The scarcely broken line on top of the water is the baseline for the boats. Overhead is another clear zone of fowl and smaller animals among the papyrus tops. Little if any overlapping is permitted, even where there are swarms of animals.

In the rigid structuring of this mural we can also perceive the symptoms of a highly organized civilization that was physically and emotionally dependent on the Nile. Although the river and its banks provided much of what they needed to live—fish and game, papyrus to write on, clay for pottery—the vital and abiding resource was the annual overflowing of the Nile that irrigated and enriched the fertile valley with silt. All Egyptian agriculture, hence Egyptian survival, depended on this event. So regular was the flooding—between July 19 and 21 at Heliopolis (now Cairo)—that the river imposed its rhythms on the life and thinking of the people. Thus the dependable fluctuations of the Nile, sanctified in Egypt's mythology as well as its law, helped produce what was perhaps the most rigid and stable society ever seen on this planet. This conservatism was exemplified by Egypt's art—an art that changed very little over a period of three thousand years.

Roman Wall Painting

It is believed that Greek landscape painting grew out of Greek theater sets, the word "scenery" coming from the Greek word for "stage." Yet we can only guess about the origin and development of Greek landscape art from pottery painting or from written sources, because almost no Greek painting still exists. We can, however, obtain a secondhand reflection of the later forms of this art from Roman frescoes and mosaics, which frequently were imitations of Greek works. Indeed, Greek artists were sometimes imported to Italy to decorate the walls of wealthy Romans' homes.

In a painting on a wall of a Pompeii villa (fig. 5-5), we see a few trees and buildings on a gentle hillside, a quietly romantic setting for strollers and a modest herd of goats. This view of nature, as well as the feeling it inspires, represents an enormous leap from Egyptian art. The separate figures and objects are lighted by the sun; some even cast shadows. The temples and the bases of monuments, unlike the Egyptian boats in figure 5-4, expose two of their sides instead of one (although their oblique angles do not always create a consistent perspective). The people and animals are not restricted to their profile views but are free to stand or relax in any natural position. Everything—trees, architecture, creatures, and the ground on which they rest—is integrated into a single visual event. A pervasive light blends the elements by de-emphasizing edges and boundaries. But this integration is also achieved by some of the logic and controls of optical space. We interpret an Egyptian picture vertically or horizontally, like a floor plan, but we can view the Roman picture—because of overlapping, relative sizes, and other visual cues—in much the same way as we see real objects in space.

The Romans, fascinated by the illusionistic potential of a more realistic form of painting, decorated their walls with numerous false architectural features such as columns, lintels, arches, and gables perhaps to tease their guests into seeing nonexistent courtyards and temples (fig. 5-6). Landscapes were often framed by false window mouldings to give the impression of seeing beyond the wall.

Paradoxically, the mental attitude that allows one to view an illusion as a surrogate of a real scene is the product of a more

5-5 Wall painting transferred to panel, from the Villa of Agrippa Postumus, late first century B.C. Portion shown approx. 26″ high. Museo Nazionale, Naples.

scientific approach to reality. The awakening of the intellect that began with the Greeks—to which the Romans were heirs—introduced scientific explanations not shared by other ancient cultures. Eventually this more objective attitude drove totemism out of nature. Image-making, liberated from taboos and its primitive magical function, was free to be used to represent natural appearances. But hand in hand with science and the art of appearances came an attitude of detachment from nature, signifying that the Greeks and Romans were no longer *participants* in but *witnesses* to the drama. The primitive hunters and the Egyptians were so much a part of nature that they were incapable of detachment—of standing apart to view the world scientifically and artistically.

5-6   Architectural wall painting from the bedroom of the Villa Boscoreale, first century B.C. Metropolitan Museum of Art, New York (Rogers Fund, 1903).

On holidays the traffic of our freeways, jammed with cars and campers, is headed mostly away from the city. The view of nature as being not only beautiful but a place to escape to is, in our day, taken for granted. Roman citizens, especially those who could afford wall paintings, seemed to have held a similar view. They, too, were urban dwellers, enjoying public services— water, sewage, paved roads, markets, courthouses, theaters, and public baths—that were remarkable for a preindustrial society. But despite the amenities, city dwelling then, as now, must have inflicted some psychological pressure. The idea of "opening up the wall" to imaginary porticoes and parks was probably intended to satisfy a need to be in closer contact with nature—even if it was a fictitious nature.

Chinese Landscape Painting

To the Chinese of the Sung Dynasty (960–1279), landscape art was much more than a stage prop. Nature itself was the protagonist of a drama in which humans were merely minor actors. By the tenth century, Chinese artists had translated their feeling for nature into a pictorial language that produced glowing images of landscape.

With just ink and paper, Tung Yuan created *Clear Day in the Valley*, a radiant landscape that evokes sensations of boundless space (colorplate 8). Indications of human life—fishermen, strollers, and buildings—are barely discernable in the vastness. This effect is due not to a system of one-point perspective but to the artist's skillful use of ink washes with which he suggested mountains, forests, and shrouds of mist. In places he used areas of empty paper to hint at the deepest layers of mist and the plane of the lake. This kind of landscape and the feelings it evokes can be related to the traditional Oriental attitude of respect for and cooperation with nature rather than the subjugation of it. Even the making of the picture required respect and cooperation; an ink wash cannot be forced.

However, *Clear Day in the Valley* is more than just a collection of nebulous vapors. Its ink washes are endowed with structure by a system of lines and details. The feeling of distance and altitude indicated by the washes is enhanced by the device of placing small trees and pavilions at the bottom of the picture. (The sensation of potentially falling into the scene is due perhaps to this "plunging" perspective.) Lines also complement the tonal areas in defining the craggy land formations and the textures of leaves and rocks.

5-7 Kuo Hsi, *Clearing Autumn Skies over Mountains and Valleys* (detail),
eleventh century. Ink and light color, 81⅜″ × 10¼″. Freer Collection,
Washington, D.C.

In addition to aiding the realism of the picture, the lines are
also responsible for rhythmic, abstract patterns. Artistic use of
line was a tradition in ancient China where handwriting (*calligraphy*), like painting, was looked on as a fine art. Chinese artists
received extensive training in calligraphy. And Chinese painting
was nurtured by the freedom and fluency of Chinese script and
by the cults that refined the art of calligraphy over the centuries.

Rather than directly copying a section of nature, Chinese
artists gathered impressions while walking. They absorbed the
subject matter from many angles, in the process savoring it and
mentally translating it into forms for trees, water, and mountains learned earlier from their masters. Everything was stored
in the memory, to be released later during an act of creativity.
Like a stage performer, the artist felt the need for mental preparation before the act. According to documents of the time, some
Chinese artists depended on wine for this creative release. But
the artist Kuo Hsi (fig. 5-7), who lived in the eleventh century,
relied on a private ritual that was described by his son.

> Whenever he began to paint he opened all the windows, cleared his desk, burned incense on the right and left, washed his hands, and cleansed his ink-stone; and by doing so his spirit was calmed and his thought composed. Not until then did he begin to paint.

The absorption and filtering of reality before transferring it to paper was an artistic habit founded on a philosophy of life. The goal of the Chinese artist was to reveal the essentials of nature rather than to record its outward appearance. The twelfth-century Confucian philosopher Chu Hsi compared the ultimate knowing of anything to the act of peeling an orange: An artist who merely imitated outer appearances was one who stopped at the peel. Educated artists, like the philosophers who meditated on religion and philosophical subjects until these became engraved on their inner consciousness, studied nature from all angles until they could internalize its universal character. Central to this philosophy of art was the concept of *Ch'i*— life force, or energy. *Ch'i*, to which artists had to attune themselves, became not only the source of their creativity but the measure of the value of their work.

Ideas connecting nature and human beings run deep in Chinese thought. By the time of the Sung painters, a cult of nature had arisen from elements of all three of China's religions (Buddhism, Confucianism, and Taoism). Both Taoism and Ch'an Buddhism—the sect to which most painters and intellectuals belonged—involved the search for an escape from reality, an escape that took the form of a withdrawal to nature. This was motivated by more than purely religious insights and metaphysical speculation, since at that time China was being divided by internal upheavals and barbarian attacks on its borders. Artists, however, received salaries from the government or rich patrons and were insulated from the mainstream of Chinese living, free to fulfill their need for withdrawal. Their art was not shared with the average Chinese but was circulated among a cultural and economic elite. Love of nature, it seems, was a privilege of the wealthy.

Christian Manuscripts

At the time Tung Yuan and other Sung painters were glorifying nature, Christian artists in Europe were glorifying the gospels. *Christ's Entry into Jerusalem* from the *Gospel Book of Otto III* (fig. 5-8) is a fair example of medieval landscape at the time—which

5-8 *Christ's Entry into Jerusalem* from the *Gospel Book of Otto III,*
c. 1000. Bayerische Staatsbibliothek, Munich.

serves to show how far European art had retreated from Greco-
Roman realism by the year A.D. 1000. Christian artists, totally
committed to the spiritual world, communicated their message
of salvation with an art of symbols. Theologians held that na-

ture, like the human body, was ultimately sinful, and were therefore essentially hostile toward artistic imitations of nature as well. Not that nature was entirely excluded. For example, illustrations of animals were often used to decorate gospel texts. But they were turned into emblems for beings or ideas other than themselves: The ox, the lion, and the eagle, among others, were symbols of the Evangelists Luke, Mark, and John. Nature, downgraded in medieval Christian life, was used in art largely for symbolic or ornamental purposes.

An anecdote about mountains illustrates the great difference between the Chinese and Christian attitudes toward nature. The Alps, so attractive to tourists today, were not considered a fit subject for human attention in the Middle Ages. Petrarch, a famous fourteenth-century scholar, talked his brother into accompanying him on a climb of Mt. Ventoux. In those days, climbing a mountain for aesthetic reasons was almost unheard of. But when they reached the top, Petrarch read a passage from Saint Augustine that made him feel guilty about enjoying himself and forgetting the needs of his immortal soul. "I turned my inward eye upon myself," he says, "and from that time not a syllable fell from my lips until we reached the bottom again."

Leonardo Five hundred years after Tung Yuan's *Clear Day in the Valley* and the *Gospel Book of Otto III*, a Florentine artist named Leonardo da Vinci painted the portrait of the young wife of Francesco del Giocondo (fig. 5-9). Since then, she has become the most famous woman in the Western world; her famous smile has fascinated every generation. The fact that it was possible to make such a portrait in 1503 shows the vast distance that European art and intellectual life had come. The intellectual interest of Europeans was shifting—as suggested by the expression on Mona Lisa's face—away from the mysteries of the Church and beginning to focus on the mysteries in themselves. Humanism, a system of thought based on the interests and concerns of people, had become pervasive in Renaissance Italy. Even before Leonardo, artists had experimented with the problems of expressing the human spirit in more secular terms. The people's interest had turned from the heavens to the earth—in keeping with a Renaissance marked by a revival of scholarly and scientific investigation. For example, it was during this time that the principles of linear perspective were developed by the mathematically minded Florentines (including Leonardo himself). It is the form of the landscape behind Mona Lisa, as well as its newly discovered human meanings, to which we must now turn our attention.

As might be expected from Petrarch's experience, the Europeans' historical lack of rapport with the land appears to have made it difficult at first for their artists to incorporate land features into their pictures. Early attempts, especially with mountains (fig. 5-10), were naive or fantastic (not unlike the papier mâché concepts of moon scenery that appeared in movies before the days of space travel). Even the tool of one-point perspective, which worked well for representing the shape of a building or room interior, was relatively useless for forests and streams. Renaissance artists before Leonardo also seemed to have a diffi-

5-9
Leonardo da Vinci, *Mona Lisa,* **1503–05. Oil on panel, 30″ × 21″. Louvre, Paris.**

5-10   Giovanni di Paolo, *Saint John in the Wilderness* (detail), *c.* 1450.
Tempera on wood, 27″ × 14¼″. The Art Institute of Chicago (Collection of
Mr. and Mrs. Martin A. Ryerson).

cult time fitting their people into continuous landscapes. Either
the people were the wrong size or the foreground was discon-
tinuous with the background—or both.

Leonardo, a scientist as well as an artist, was more observ-
ant and less committed to abstract formulas in his approach to
landscape than were his contemporaries. He solved the problem
of harmonizing the subject with the background by placing the
young woman on a high ledge overlooking a landscape (fig.
5-11). The networks of cliffsides and valleys, roads and river-
beds, jagged mountains and sky, join to forge a single environment—one held together by a pervasive atmosphere. (Leonardo
perfected the technique of *sfumato*—blurred outlines and smoky
ambiences that tend to fuse figures and objects.) But his landscape images were a product of strong emotions as well as scientific observation. It is no accident that the geological forms behind Mona Lisa seem to throb like a living organism. Leonardo
believed that a life force, not unlike that of the Sung concept of
Ch'i, flows through all things of the earth. Yet lurking in Leon-

ardo's mountains and valleys there is a forbidding quality not found in Chinese art. Nature, as he once observed in his notebooks, "often sends forth pestilential vapours and plagues upon the great multiplications and congregations of animals, and especially upon mankind." Some of the chill of medieval art survived the Renaissance thaw and lingered in Leonardo's landscapes.

5-11   Leonardo da Vinci, detail of the upper-right background of the *Mona Lisa.*

Constable   The landscape of cool trees and distant meadows in the nineteenth-century English painting *The Hay Wain* by John Constable (colorplate 9) radiates serenity and optimism. Long before Constable, European artists had mastered virtually all the principles—linear and aerial perspective, gradient of textures, cast shadows, and so forth—associated with creating an optical illusion of nature. Indeed, his countrysides are indebted to seventeenth-century art, in particular Dutch paintings of low horizons, scudding clouds, moving shadows; and French paintings of tree-lined, classical stillness (5-12). But even though he was a thorough student of the techniques of other artists, he was also a keen observer of nature itself. Constable's dedication resulted in his extending the vocabulary of outdoor art to perhaps its finest manifestation in the Western world. His particular contri-

5-12   Nicholas Poussin, *Landscape with the Burial of Phocion*, 1648. Oil on canvas, 47″ × 70½″. Louvre, Paris.

bution was that of capturing the transient phenomena of nature's "dews, breezes, bloom and freshness" by means of broken color—touches of bright color and flecks of pure white, often applied with a palette knife (fig. 5-13). Such effects are not simply a matter of facile painting technique. Constable's fresh vision was a result of both his closeness to nature and continual experimentation with the oil medium. His belief that painting should be pursued as an inquiry into the laws of nature is reminiscent of Leonardo da Vinci's attitude. And as was the case with Leonardo, Constable's reliance on careful observation was enhanced by a reverent passion for his subject.

Nature worship swept Europe in the early nineteenth century. On the Continent, the writings of Jean-Jacques Rousseau had challenged the hearts and minds of Europeans by upholding the virtues of primitive simplicity over the vices of civilization. In England, the Romantic poetry of Wordsworth (read by Constable) extolled the spiritual revelations of nature in even its most humble aspects. Literature and art reflected an intellectual revolution that seemed to be steering Europe toward an outlook like that of eleventh-century China—the common ground being a mystical feeling for nature. (One symptom of this shared state of mind was the mutual affinity in China and nineteenth-century England, for large informal gardens.) Constable's temperament and personal religious views coincided perfectly with this cultural movement. The natural universe, in which the philosophers of the time believed the highest moral feelings were revealed, was considered to be the handiwork of God. And this handiwork extended to every last thing—mill dams, willows, old rotten planks, shiny posts—that Constable revered in the English countryside. His finest landscapes, like *The Hay Wain*, were painted in the East Anglian countryside around the river Stour where he grew up.

Ironically, the works of Constable—the artist who most successfully expressed the moral, philosophical, and visual ideals of the people of England at that time—were more popular in France than in his own land. English artistic tastes, which favored a more finished-looking and idealized product, had not as yet caught up with English spiritual values. But in France *The Hay Wain* received a prize in the Salon of 1824, and was to profoundly influence many French artists—including the Impressionists, who based an entire style on the technique of breaking up color. But Constable had his greatest effect on the artists of the movement known as *Romanticism.* The extremes of Romantic painting either sank into sentimental depictions of rustic life or soared into extravagant visions of idealized nature. However, Constable's complete respect for nature seems to have enforced an artistic honesty that helped him to resist the seductions that so tempted other artists of his generation.

5-13 John Constable, *Willy Lott's House near Flatford Mill, Suffolk, c.* 1816. Oil on paper, 9¼" × 7". Crown copyright, Victoria & Albert Museum.

After Constable

Landscape art and nature worship have declined since Constable's time. The French Impressionists of the latter half of the nineteenth century helped set in motion the separation of art from many of the social and spiritual values essential to a landscape tradition. Nature, no longer felt to have any religious significance, became a source of color sensations and patterns and a stage for portraying the newly developing middle class. After the Impressionists a preoccupation with color and the formal elements of art became a more central concern, and nature became less and less important—even as a point of departure.

The general public, however, still likes to visit the countryside, enjoys breathtaking scenes of nature in the movies, and hangs landscape pictures in the living room. Paradoxically, real nature has not always received its due from the public. Its relevance has been diminished by architecture and highways—and its very existence threatened by pollution.

Meanwhile, there is great opportunity in our time—in terms of both motives and means—for artists to deal with nature. The possibilities of ecological disaster may be reason enough for many to begin dramatizing an awareness of the prospect. For others, the possibilities of new images of nature may be the main inspiration. Before now our view of the world was limited not only by our eyes but by our position on earth. One extreme is represented by Leonardo's portrait of Mona Lisa, the other by Tung Yuan's distant view of mountains. Now the limits have been considerably extended, permitting us—with the help of such tools as the electron microscope—to look at the inner world of matter and—with the help of space travel and television—to see our own planet from a distant vantage point.

Some artists are already dealing with nature in ways quite different from the oil-on-canvas methods of people like Constable. _Earth Art_ calls for these artists to expand the scale of their work to that of their subject, using the land itself as material. With such tools as picks, shovels, trench-hole diggers, and earth-moving equipment, Michael Heizer transformed large areas of the landscape into works of art (fig. 3-31). By creating interesting shapes and spaces on a large scale, he brings our imagination into a contact with nature that may cause us to experience new aspects and beauty where they might be least expected. Thus his function as an artist is not very different from that of such older landscape artists as Constable, Leonardo, and Tung Yuan.

6
Men and Women

The nude has been a pervasive subject in Western art for centuries. It has remained popular even when—as in the nineteenth century—public display of the disrobed body in real life was taboo.

The primary reason for the popularity of nude images is not surprising. After all, what is more interesting to us than ourselves? However, the human beings in many paintings and sculptures do not always resemble ordinary mortals like us. Human figures in art are usually idealized to represent gods and goddesses, angels, heroes and heroines, and so forth. Yet regardless of their special status, these images ordinarily resemble us in at least one respect: They are either male or female. Sexual distinction in art is important—especially if the figure is that of an idealized naked adult—because it is an essential and fascinating dimension of our lives.

In the first part of this chapter we consider images of men and in the second part, images of women—concentrating on works that particularly reflect the sexual ideals of different cultural periods. We will see how the aesthetic object has played a major role in creating a set of standards for the sexual object. But we will also view the development of the nude tradition in Western art and examine some of the ways in which it has been used for the expression of ideas. Finally, we will consider images of men and women together using an example that is not from the Western tradition.

Men   In contemporary American culture, physical beauty is usually associated more with the female body than with the male body. To the ancient Greeks, male beauty was just as compelling as female beauty—if not more so. From the eighth century to the fifth century B.C.—known as the *Archaic* period—sculptors created nude images of men, not women.

The Greeks   Statues of males were often associated with the cult of Apollo, god of youthful manly beauty and reason—but they were also associated with athletic sports, particularly the Olympic games. As early as the Archaic period young noblemen competed in those events in the nude. Whereas to us nakedness, the "natural" state of humans, is often thought to be a trait of primitive peoples, to the Greeks—who by this time were emerging as an important Mediterranean civilization—it was a sign of their superiority, a trait setting them apart from the surrounding "barbarians." The nude became an expression of the essentially human concern in Greek philosophy and religion.

Early sculptures of males, which may be statues either of Apollo or portraits of young athletes (Kouroi), display an alertness and self-confidence typical both of young athletes and a young culture (fig. 6-1). But they also have a marked stiffness—a result of the influence of Egyptian sculpture—that tempers their vitality and naturalism. In Egyptian statuary (fig. 6-2), this stiffness seems appropriate, emphasizing its monumentality and royalty; in Archaic Greek statuary, it is worn somewhat awkwardly.

The early part of the fifth century saw the beginning of the period known as *Classical* (*c.* 480–323 B.C.), an era of extraordinary progress in art and philosophy that was to set the Greeks apart from all other ancient civilizations. The aesthetic instinct that had given Archaic Kouroi statues their human alertness gave Classical statues a hitherto unknown realism and beauty, exemplified by the 480 B.C. Kritios Boy (fig. 6-3). Kenneth Clark, who has made an important contribution to the subject with his book *The Nude: A Study of Ideal Form*, says of this statue:

> Here for the first time we feel passionate pleasure in the human body . . . for the delicate eagerness with which the sculptor's eye has followed every muscle or watched the skin stretch and relax as it passes over a bone could not have been achieved without a heightened sensuality.

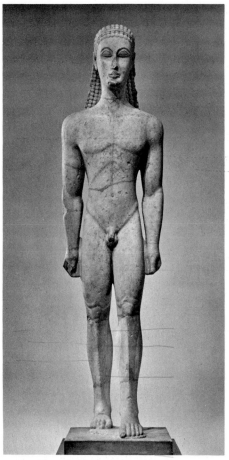

6-1
Kouros, c. 615–600 B.C.
Marble, 7′2″ high.
Metropolitan Museum of
Art, New York (Fletcher
Fund, 1932).

6-2
Mycerinus and Queen, from
Giza, *c.* 2500 B.C. Slate, 4′8″
high. Museum of Fine Arts,
Boston (Harvard-M.F.A.
Expedition).

Greek art was progressing rapidly during this period in developing models of male beauty, in bronze and stone, that gave tangible form to Greek concepts of humanism and idealism. Humanism was fundamental to Greek science and philosophy which, in Classical times, began to seek answers to questions about the workings of the world and human nature through rational thought rather than through appeal to divine authority. It was reflected in art by the increased realism of the human body. Idealism was evidenced in the writings of Plato, a prominent fifth-century philosopher, who theorized an ideal world outside of time and space in which there were not only the eternal "verities" of Truth, Beauty, and Goodness but the ideal forms for everything—including the bodies of people. To Plato, this ideal world was more "real" than the world on earth, the latter being a mere imitation of the former. Idealism was reflected in art by the beauty and supposedly perfect proportions of the statues, qualities which were also built into Classical architecture such as the Parthenon (fig. 4-3).

By mid-century the famous sculptor, Polykleitos, had created the *Spear Carrier*, known to us today only through marble copies by Roman artists (fig. 6-4). Because our perceptions have been conditioned by photography, movies, television, and even

6-3
Kritios Boy, c. 480 B.C.
Marble, approx. 34" high.
Acropolis Museum, Athens.

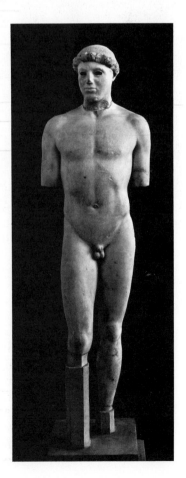

6-4
Polykleitos, *Doryphoros
(Spear Carrier),* original
c. 450 B.C. Roman copy,
marble, 6'6" high. Museo
Nazionale, Naples.

realistic statuary in public parks, we may not be overly impressed by its realism or the significance of its contribution to the art of representing the human body. But if we compare it with the Archaic example, we quickly see how far Greek artists had progressed in articulating the structure, proportions, and movement of the body. Unlike the seventh-century Kouros— whose individual parts seemed to have been pieced together— the fifth-century *Spear Carrier* is an organic, indivisable unit. Perhaps the single most significant aspect is the manner in which he is standing. His slight step, placing the majority of his weight on one foot, was as important to Western art as the first step taken by the first astronaut on the moon's surface was to space science. The position of the feet and the effect it has on the posture and the character of the body is a moon's distance away from the rigidly symmetrical stance of earlier works. The slant of the shoulders (downward slightly to the figure's right), countered by an opposite slant to the hips, is achieved by the figure's weight being centered over the right foot. This is known as *weight shift,* a convention for representing the human body that is still found in every life-drawing class. In real life it is a natural way to stand or walk.

Polykleitos, as if anticipating Plato's writings (which came later), developed a code of proportions and movements for the ideal male body that is manifested in the copy of his statue. Naturalism is actually modified by the artist's concept of perfection, in this case starkly revealed by the incisive clarity of individual parts such as the chest, thorax, pelvis, and even the kneecaps.

In late, *Post-Classical,* art, the idealism exemplified in *Spear Carrier* often gave way to a sense of elegance as reflected by the late fourth-century *Apollo Belvedere,* also a Roman copy (fig. 6-5). The latter work does not exhibit the same rigor—the effect of a controlling, committed intellect—that the Classical work does. In other Post-Classical statues, extreme realism or dramatic displays of human expression took the place of idealism. This lack of commitment to a doctrinaire idealism in art was a symptom of a corresponding sophistication and lack of philosophical unity in late Greek society.

The Romans, the inheritors and the assimilators of Greek culture, added little to the male nude—apparently content with reiterations and variations of the themes already perfected by the Greeks. Believing that it enhanced their divinity, Roman rulers had their portrait heads placed on top of ideal nude bodies. Despite this decline in its earlier significance, the practice of sculpting male nudes continued until medieval times.

After the Roman world was overturned by the new order of Christianity, images of nudes fell into disfavor for approximately a thousand years. Except for the story of Adam and Eve, Christian theology of the Middle Ages had little interest in nudity, and then only as a way to exemplify the sins of the body rather than its virtues. Many, but not all, pagan statues were destroyed during this period.

The Italian Renaissance	In the fifteenth and sixteenth centuries, the artists of the Renaissance rediscovered Greek and Roman sculpture, and once again the naked body appeared in art. But when applied to the heroic figures of the Old and New Testaments instead of the gods of Mt. Olympus, the male image underwent a transformation.

6-5
Apollo Belvedere, **original
c. 330 B.C. Roman copy,
marble, 7'4" high. Vatican
Museum, Rome.**

Michelangelo, perhaps the greatest artist of the time, frequently included male nudes in his sculptures and murals, and probably contributed more to the development of the male image than any artist since Polykleitos. Considering the human body divine, he made images of it that added a new and vital dimension to masculine beauty in art. But beauty alone is only a part of the total content of his sculpture. He carved his monumental *David* (fig. 6-6) for the city of Florence in the early years of the sixteenth century—about the same time that Leonardo, another Florentine, was painting *Mona Lisa* (fig. 5-9). It shows the young hero in the moments before battle, his head turned toward the approaching Goliath. We can certainly see something of the *Spear Carrier* in the stance and proportions of the *David,* for Michelangelo was an enthusiastic student of the an-

6-6
Michelangelo, *David*,
1501–04. Marble,
approximately 18′ high,
including base. Galleria
dell'Accademia, Florence.

tique statues that could be found everywhere in Italy. But after looking at the defiant head held in place by a column of muscle, our eyes move down across a torso that barely conceals a storm of tensions underneath, tensions that are vividly revealed even in the right hand of the statue. We see that although Michelangelo's treatment of the *David* may have been influenced by the *Spear Carrier*, its intensity belongs to a world very different from the Classical calm of the older sculpture.

Artists of the Renaissance, including Michelangelo, often dealt with subjects from Greek and Roman mythology as well as from Christianity. But even when creating images of gods and heroes, they did not attempt to idealize physical beauty so much as to emphasize the strength and energy of these muscular and active figures. To Renaissance artists, the naked male was a powerful and novel subject—one which let them breathe new life into religious and mythological themes while showing new masculine ideals.

Neoclassicism

After the Renaissance, interest in the male nude declined, although the female nude—as we shall see in the following section—became very popular. Not that the male nude was discontinued; it remained an established but not vital artistic tradition. And for specific subjects—battle scenes, crucifixions, and episodes from Classical myths—it was still appropriate (though not essential). As an end in itself—whether exemplifying beauty, power, or energy—male nudity no longer captured many artists' imaginations. As a symbol, it usually alluded to the glory of the Classical past—glory that was becoming more of an empty memory, if not a fantasy, in an increasingly modern age. Still, the late 1700s and early 1800s witnessed the rise of *Neoclassicism* in the arts, a renewed interest in the simplicity and grandeur that some artists associated with the high point of Classical Greek civilization. The influence of the Neoclassical movement can be seen in a work by the American sculptor Horatio Greenough, who chose to represent George Washington naked from the waist up (fig. 6-7). Washington's wigged head rests upon an idealized body, one with broad shoulders and well-defined planes of chest and abdomen that hark back to Polykleitos. But Greenough's attempt to ennoble his subject through the symbolism of the nude did not succeed with the public. Apparently Americans were uncomfortable with the idea of a former president looking like a Roman emperor or a Greek god.

The Late Nineteenth Century

The nude male images by the French sculptor Auguste Rodin are among the most successful ones made since the Renaissance. Perhaps this is because Rodin's images rarely referred to the Classical past. His *Age of Bronze* (fig. 6-8) brings to mind Michelangelo's *David;* both seem to have a reserve of energy waiting to be released. But while the *David*'s firm, aggressive posture announces the violence the young man is about to commit, the tentative posture of the Rodin youth does not clearly indicate what action is contemplated. The youth seems to be taking a step, clutching his head with one hand and gesturing

Plate 9 John Constable, *The Hay Wain*, 1821. Oil on canvas, 51¼″ x 73″.
Reproduced by courtesy of the Trustees, The National Gallery, London.

Plate 10 Sandro Botticelli, *The Birth of Venus*, c. 1480. Tempera on canvas, 5′ 8″ x 9′ 1″. Galleria degli Uffizi, Florence.

Plate 11 Marc Chagall, *Double Portrait with Wineglass*, 1917–18.
Oil on canvas, 7′ 7¾″ x 4′ 5½″.
Musée National d'Art Moderne, Paris, ⓒ by A.D.A.G.P., Paris 1986.

Plate 12 Michelangelo, *Creation of the Sun and the Moon*, detail from the Sistine Chapel ceiling, 1508–12. Fresco, approx. 9' 2'' x 18' 8''.

Plate 13 Rembrandt van Rijn, *The Night Watch (The Company of Captain Frans Banning Cocq)*, 1642. Oil on canvas, 12' 2'' x 14' 7''. Rijksmuseum, Amsterdam.

Plate 14   Vincent van Gogh, *The Night Cafe*, 1888. Oil on canvas, 27½″ x 35″.
Yale University Art Gallery: Bequest of Stephen Carlton Clark, B.A. 1903.

Plate 15 Jackson Pollock, *One (Number 31),* 1950. Oil and Duco enamel on canvas, 8' 10'' x 17' 5⅝''. The Museum of Modern Art, New York (gift of Sidney Janis).

Plate 16   Edward Hopper, *House by the Railroad*, 1925. Oil on canvas, 24'' x 29''.
Collection, The Museum of Modern Art, New York.

6-7
Horatio Greenough, *George Washington*, 1832–41. Marble, approx. 11′4″ high. Courtesy National Collection of Fine Arts, Smithsonian Institution.

vaguely with the other. Apparently Rodin himself was unsure of the theme, for he originally called the work *The Vanquished*. However, despite this lack of clear intention, the sculpture's rising, striving movement is clearly suggestive. Physically, it expresses the restless energy that seethes beneath the surface of every living thing; psychologically, it expresses the restless emotions of human beings' spiritual longing.

Art Today Although in Rodin's time the idealized figure was still able to convey abstract ideas, it was soon to fall from favor altogether. The modern art movement was already underway, and by the early 1900s interest in the nude male—along with other traditional subject matter—was replaced by a preoccupation with abstract forms and color. Only very recently has the male nude begun to reappear as a subject of any importance. And the reasons for this do not seem related entirely to aesthetics, for the artists who paint nude males today are mostly women, many of them identified with the growing feminist movement.

Sylvia Sleigh's paintings of naked men are provocative even

6-8
Auguste Rodin, *The Age of
Bronze,* **c. 1876–77. Bronze,
5'11" high. Minneapolis
Institute of Arts (John R.
Van Derlip Fund).**

in an age that thinks of itself as sexually liberated. Not only are her subjects nude, but the view is usually frontal and the pose casual—reflecting a candor about the male body that has been almost nonexistent in art outside of life-drawing classes. Because most people are not accustomed to this, a painting like *Walter Finley Seated Nude* (fig. 6-9) seems brash, if not a little shocking. But Sleigh's purpose—like that of the Greek artist who made the *Kritios Boy* (fig. 6-3)—was probably to emphasize the beauty of the male subject, which is supplemented by the ornately flowered wallpaper of the background as well as reflected in his relaxed, self-confident pose. Most of Sleigh's models are young men with an abundance of health, good looks, and body hair, which she has called "natural embroidery."

Women   Living in a culture in which images of the naked female body constantly appear on the newsstands and in the movies while images of male nudity are still somewhat rare, we may have difficulty understanding attitudes in Greece before the fourth century B.C.—where sculptures of young women were usually clothed while those of Apollos and young athletes were likely to be nude.

The Greeks   By the fifth century B.C., after the long tradition of nude Kouroi and when Greek artists like Polykleitos were refining their Classical masterpieces of nude athletes, statues of women were normally clothed in a loose-fitting—often revealing—garment called a chiton. Women, of course, were considered sexually attractive. Apparently, however, the idea of expressing female attractiveness through nude images was not yet of interest to Greek artists. By the fourth century, though, statues of nude women were beginning to be made for the sake of experiencing their ideal nudity. Appropriately, this ideal developed around the cult of Aphrodite, the love goddess, and her Roman equivalent, Venus. Statues of these and other nude figures of women became increasingly popular in the Greek (and Roman) world.

The first significant Aphrodite statue was created by the fourth-century Greek Master Praxiteles for the people on the island of Cnidos (fig. 6-10). By this time the challenges of repre-

6-9
Sylvia Sleigh, *Walter Finley Seated Nude,* 1976. Oil on canvas, 56" × 52". Collection Dennis Adrian, Chicago.

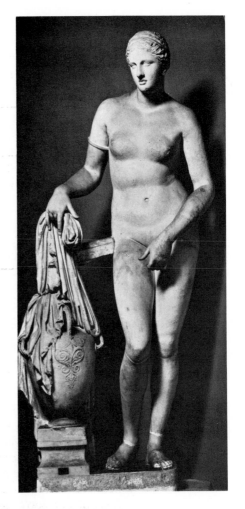

6-10
After Praxiteles, *Cnidian Aphrodite*, original *c*. 330 B.C. Roman copy, marble. Vatican Museum, Rome.

senting the human body had been overcome by sculpting male nudes. But the posture of weight-shift, Polykleitos's legacy, takes on a voluptuous character when applied to the female body. The curve of her left hip, as well as the smaller curve below her armpit, is much fuller and more pronounced—its smooth line less broken by bone and muscle. The S shape of the female body, often called sinuous, becomes a familiar symbol of desire. Praxiteles was well suited to sculpt Aphrodite; even his statues of men have a sinuous quality, together with a delicate modeling of the surface that almost gives the appearance of flesh. Unfortunately, Praxiteles' Aphrodite is known to us only through Roman copies.

**The
Middle Ages**

The basic formula established by Praxiteles was scarcely varied in any major way through the rest of the Greek and Roman periods. And just as was the case with nude images of men, the Christian world prior to the Renaissance professed little interest in naked women except in instances where there was a need to symbolize fleshly lusts. In one culture the body had been a focus of religious veneration; in the other it was, at times, considered antireligious. However, in the twelfth and thirteenth centuries, at the height of medieval civilization, women began to play a more important role in courtly life and were celebrated in the arts and letters. The age of chivalry flowered and the cult of the Virgin Mary appeared in the Church. The worship of the Virgin helped to offset the notion of Eve the Temptress that had dominated thinking during the earlier years of the Middle Ages. And Mary had her earthly counterpart in the medieval lady of the court, who achieved a position of honor and even of power in the masculine world of knighthood and the Crusades. Images of women, whether those of the royal courts or the Virgin Mary, were of course depicted fully clothed. Yet their femininity was not completely hidden; witness the seductive S-curve posture present in *the Virgin of Paris* as she holds the baby Jesus (fig. 6-11). Furthermore, her clothes and general appearance were probably based on those of the chic ladies of the court. But aside from her indubitable femininity and the apparently accidental similarity between her pose and that of the *Aphrodite,* the two women are quite different. *Aphrodite* is a goddess of beauty whose nudity implies an acceptance of the human body. *The Virgin of Paris* is a spiritual figure whose beauty exemplifies a beatitude transcending the earthly body. This beatitude is reflected by the tranquility of her face and the impression of lightness of her body (despite the fact that she is made of stone). Even the way she holds the baby seems to defy gravity.

**The Italian
Renaissance**

As the feudal system of the Middle Ages gave way to another form of society based on city-states, the influence of the Church was weakened and artists began to work instead for the wealthy noblemen who held political power. Men like Lorenzo de' Medici of Florence cultivated the study of the past, inspiring a new interest in the myths, poetry, and sculpture of the Greeks. And with this, inevitably there came an admiration for the Greek and Roman portrayals of the nude. But it was not an easy matter for the artists of the fifteenth century to bridge the gap between the goddess of love and the Christian Virgin. A medieval attitude

6-11
The Virgin of Paris, **early
fourteenth century.
Cathedral of Notre Dame,
Paris.**

toward the image of the naked female persisted even when images of naked men had come to be sanctioned as symbols or as
representations of biblical heroes—like Michelangelo's *David.*

Thus, most artists concentrated on images of men—clothed
or nude—to represent or symbolize the burgeoning middle-
class society of traders. Femininity, once again, was out of style;
a surprising amount of the art of the period, whether dealing
with religious subjects or the nobility, seems to have stressed
the attributes of powerful masculinity. With little to go on,
therefore, in terms of precedent for painting the female nude
within a Classical theme, Sandro Botticelli created one of the
most enduring versions of Venus Aphrodite in art history

(colorplate 10). Initially inspired by an Italian poet, Botticelli's version of the love goddess's birth harks back over 20 centuries to the original hymn to Aphrodite by the early Greek poet Homer:

> . . . where the moist breath of Zephyros blowing
> Out of the west bore her over the surge of the loud-roaring
>   deep
> In soft foam. The gold-filleted Hours
> Welcomed her gladly and clothed her in ambrosial gar-
>   ments . . .
> And around her delicate throat and silvery breasts
> Hung necklaces inlaid with gold, . . .*

Venus's pose was probably based on that of the Venus de Medici, a Classical marble statue. Botticelli created an image of a nubile woman who is both desirable and dignified. To this extent his achievement is true to the spirit of Greek female nudity but is not especially Greek in other respects. None of the figures, including Venus, is standing solidly on the ground (or the shell). Even allowing for allegorical license and the need to illustrate the fantasy of someone being born out of the sea, Botticelli's Venus is more like the lightweight figures of angels and virgins that populate medieval Christian art than the solidly physical types of the Classical marbles. The delicately ornate details of waves, leaves, and strands of hair are repeated in the decorative treatment of the billowing drapery. But for the nudity, the picture could almost be a medieval tapestry.

There is nothing medieval about the nudes of the Venetian artist, Tiziano Vecelli (known as Titian). Painted nearly 60 years after Botticelli's *Birth of Venus*, Titian's *Venus of Urbino* (fig. 6-12) is, without reservation, a goddess of love. She reclines languidly in full display on a couch shared by a small dog while servants work in another room of what appears to be an opulent Venetian villa. Her facial expression together with her passive posture signifies she is available for pleasure—an aspect echoed in the luxury of her surroundings. By this work Titian established a convention of female nudity that was to endure for centuries. Versions of this pose and ambience were to be repeated in

*Reprinted from *The Homeric Hymns, A Verse Translation* by Thelma Sargent. By permission of W. W. Norton & Company, Inc. Copyright © 1973 by W. W. Norton & Company Inc.

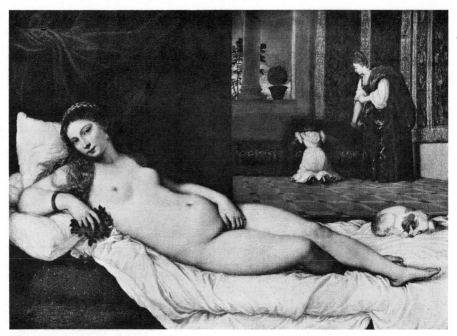

6-12   Titian, *Venus of Urbino, c.* **1538. Oil on canvas, 47¼″ × 65″.**
Galleria degli Uffizi, Florence.

countless works, both good and bad. Titian also became the leader of a school of painting centered in Venice known for its practice of using the paint medium more directly. He and his colleagues omitted the step of first outlining a picture in tempera, preferring to use oil paint from the start—a pursuit that resulted in paintings rich in color and surface textures. (See chapter 3.) Compared to the *Venus of Urbino,* Botticelli's *Birth of Venus* appears rather "lean," not only in the shape of the central figure but in all the shapes, the colors, and even its atmosphere.

The Seventeenth Century   The paintings of Peter Paul Rubens of Flanders (now Belgium) owe much to the pioneering work of Titian and his school. Like Venetian paintings, they are imbued with sensuous colors and textures, and soft forms that blend with their surroundings. Further, Rubens' nude women, like Titian's goddess, seem uninhibited about their nakedness—lacking the medieval reserve that still lingers in Botticelli's Venus. By the seventeenth century—the *Baroque* period of art—painters had become skillful in rendering pictorial effects, and Rubens was first among equals. In his *The Judgement of Paris* (fig. 6-13)—a Greek story of a beauty contest between Athena, Aphrodite, and Hera—the spatial organization is more complex than that in either a Titian or Botticelli painting. And the nudes are more energetic and vital—this despite the fact that they appear to be heavier.

The generous dimensions of Rubens' women raise interesting questions about the effects of historical versus local influences on what artists depict. Are Rubens's nudes a reflection of the tastes of a period or an expression of some northern European preference for hearty and healthy women? Or, indeed, are these wondrous women an expression of the artist's personal tastes? (The central nude, Aphrodite, is a portrait of his wife.) Such questions have often been asked but never satisfactorily answered. So many factors affect the work of any artist that we can only offer a partial answer—that art is always created through a filter of experiences both personal and cultural. In this particular case it would certainly be inaccurate to claim that the

6-13   Peter Paul Rubens, *The Judgment of Paris, c.* 1636. Oil on canvas, 57" × 75". National Gallery, London.

artist's perferences were determined by where he lived—for Rubens, an aristocrat, was also a successful statesman who held ambassadorial posts and painted in many of the courts of Europe. And there is no doubt that his trio of naked women were intended to be just as desirable as Botticelli's slim and (by more contemporary standards) appealing goddess.

Neoclassicism   Painted about a century and a half after *The Judgment of Paris,* Marie Guillemine Benoist's *Portrait of a Negress* (fig. 6-14) presents a view of womanhood radically different from Rubens's. Although Benoist stressed simplicity in composition and clarity of line and texture in her treatments of figures and clothing, her portrait is more graceful and warmer than most Neoclassical art.

According to some observers, paintings of nude females reflect a male point of view. English critic John Berger went so far as to say, "Women are depicted in a quite different way from men—not because the feminine is different from the masculine—but because the 'ideal' spectator is always assumed to be male and the image of the woman is designed to flatter him." If this is

6-14
Marie Guillemine Benoist,
Portrait of a Negress, 1800.
Oil on canvas, 31¾" × 25¾".
Louvre, Paris.

true, Benoist's portrait seems to be an exception. In addition to presenting her sitter's sensitive face, long neck, full breasts, and elegant hands, she has emphasized the subject's tenderness and quiet dignity. Benoist captured something of the woman's personality that transcends the anonymity of a sex object.

Victorian Images   Nude images continued to appear in art, managing to survive even the nineteenth-century Victorian period when public antipathy toward the body was at a peak—when the sight of an ankle was considered provocative and the use of the word "leg" was held to be indecent. Oddly enough, the art of the time was full of sexually titillating displays of Turkish harems, Roman slave markets, and decadent orgies. So long as the nudes in a work were sufficiently classical and the subject matter could be interpreted as intended to teach historical or moral lessons, the most voyeuristic scene was guaranteed public approval. The works of French artist Adolphe William Bouguereau, one of the most popular painters of the late nineteenth century, vividly illustrate this paradox. Though an "official" painter who enjoyed the benefits of public patronage, his treatments of classical themes—like *The Birth of Venus* (fig. 6-15)—amount to little more than lavish exhibitions of female flesh. In this respect he was the equal of Rubens. However, unlike the seventeenth-century master, Bouguereau suppressed all evidence of painted surface to achieve a slick realism to rival that of the camera. It was as if the artist had photographed a group of actors in a *tableau vivant*. The illusion of optical reality and the provocative posturing of the figures, especially that of Venus, simply magnify the aspect of exhibitionism. To grasp how far Western painting and the Venus theme had come over a period of 400 years, compare Bouguereau's version of The *Birth of Venus* with Botticelli's.

The Twentieth Century   As a vital theme in art, female nudity virtually came to an end in the twentieth century. As the modern movement gained momentum, paintings like Bouguereau's symbolized all that was bad about established art—not only because of their hypocrisy but also because of their commitment to pictorial realism. The traditional practice of vividly illustrating a subject, nude or otherwise, was considerably downgraded and classical themes lost whatever credibility they continued to have during the nineteenth century in an increasingly scientific and materialistic world.

Yet the Venus theme persisted in a somewhat contrary way during the early years of the twentieth century as artists sought solutions to what they perceived to be the limitations of realism. Picasso's solution was one of willful violence that shattered the rules of composition—and with them the conventions of the nude (fig. 6-16). Matisse's response was to "dry up" the nude by turning it into just another compositional element (fig. 6-17). Later in their lives, both these artists occasionally returned to slightly more traditional methods of representation—often portraying the female nude in ways that demonstrated they had nothing against the physical appearance of women.

After the initial battles with form were fought, many artists began to apply the new techniques to traditional subject matter. The sculptures of the British artist Henry Moore were among the more successful efforts at interpreting the female figure in new ways. While he certainly could not be said to be celebrating the

6-15
Guillaume-Adolphe Bouguereau, *The Birth of Venus, c.* **1879. Present location unknown.**

6-16
Pablo Picasso, *Dancer*, 1907.
Oil on canvas, 4'11" × 3'3¼".
Collection
Walter P. Chrysler, Jr.,
New York.

6-17
Henri Matisse, *Le Luxe, II*,
1907–08. Distemper
on canvas, 82½" × 54¾.
Statens Museum for Kunst,
Copenhagen
(Rumps Collection).

body beautiful, Moore's work was often very sexual in nature because he used semiabstract shapes that suggested rather than represented parts of the body (fig. 6-18). Moore combined this fascination with the figure with experiments in open sculpture, a direction that had been initiated a few years earlier in France by Julio González (fig. 3-20) and other artists. Frequently, as in the early reclining figure shown here, Moore began with "natural" open spaces—such as that formed by the elbow the woman is leaning on or that which exists below her raised knee—and distorted them, making a space larger or smaller than viewers would expect, sometimes even eliminating parts of the body. Here he seems to have left out part of the torso, perhaps to emphasize the breasts and the physical strength of the arms.

6-18 Henry Moore, *Recumbent Figure,* 1938. Stone. 4'4" long. The Tate Gallery, London.

Many associations are likely to occur to viewers as they move around the massive form. Some may stem from the body shapes and sexual allusions. Others from the landscape-like forms and the surface qualities of the stone, which call to mind mountains and caverns and suggest a reassuring permanence. More than just the body of a woman, this work is an affirmation of life itself.

By the 1960s, the quest for new images had gone so far that it had brought many artists all the way back to more realistic representations of the human figure. Using the "overlooked" vocabulary of comic strips and advertising, artists such as Andy Warhol and Tom Wesselmann created satirical versions of the modern Venus. With cold indifference—and equally cold insight—Warhol took the ideal woman off her pedestal and put her on the supermarket shelf, as interchangeable as a line of soup cans or any other marketable commodity (colorplate 28). The judgment implied in this act—not only about the status of women but about the dehumanization that occurs in a mass-media, mass-production world—is far more devastating than the violence in Picasso's forms. Wesselmann's long series of Great American Nudes—set in collage environments of sexual symbols and products that advertising has made "essential" to life—comments on this from another viewpoint, emphasizing the blandness of a Venus whose only features are sexual (fig. 6-19).

Yet it is largely among the cliché images of popular culture that the traditional concept of Venus survives. Born Aphrodite and arriving naked from the sea, she quickly usurped the stage-center of artistic nudity from Apollo. And when her role in art was compromised—if not obliterated—by the abstract emphasis of twentieth-century painting, she was reborn from the sea of mass media and arrived naked in the centerfold of *Playboy* magazine, enacting the fantasies of the American male. Although realistic painting and sculpture have lately returned to prominence in the galleries, sexuality is no longer as marked or as myopic as it once was. Artists, reflecting a new attitude toward women, have abandoned the sex object in favor of the art object; nudity, when it is portrayed, is often dealt with in a matter-of-

6-19   Tom Wesselmann, *Great American Nude No. 99*, 1968. Oil on canvas, 60″ × 81″. Courtesy Sidney Janis Gallery, New York.

fact way—as in the case of John de Andrea's sculptures of women (fig. 3-19) or Sylvia Sleigh's portraits of naked men.

Man and Woman

To merely show how artists have represented men and women separately would be literally incomplete. The union of a man and woman is, after all, the fulfillment of the promise implied by their separateness. The balance of this chapter will complete the theme by surveying a few examples that deal with the relationship between men and women.

Indian Temple Art

One of the most noteworthy—and unusual—depictions of the male-female relationship is found in the Khajuraho temples of northwest India, which were constructed in the tenth century A.D. by a people called the Chandels. The major temple of the group is so covered with relief sculptures and other carvings that it resembles coral deposit more than a building (fig. 6-20). The visual energy of the busy carvings suggests that the builders intended the temple's exterior to reflect the primal energy of life. Sculptures of gods and goddesses, saints and mortals, decorate the niches and bands around the turrets, some carved in high relief, others fully round—and nearly all engaged in one form or another of sexual activity. The majority of the figures are *apsaras,* heavenly courtesan-nymphs, who occur either singly or in conjunction with a male figure, and who may in fact be representations of the *devadasis*—women who served as attendants to the temple's deity and as public dancers and musicians. Many of the figures represented actual princes and their wives and courtesans, a fact that calls to mind a parallel with Europe of the same period: the Royal Portals of Chartres Cathedral in France, so called because the Old Testament figures carved alongside the doors represented the kings and queens of France (fig. 6-21). But the comparison only serves to demonstrate the vivid difference in outlook between the two faiths. The stiff, formal figures on the cathedral were clearly intended to de-emphasize the body; the sensuous creatures that populate the temple were sculpted with greatly exaggerated sexual attributes. Their postures and gestures create a sensation of movement, and the jewelry and flimsy scarves that cling to the curves of their bodies accentuate the eroticism of their acts (fig. 6-22).

Unlike most of the artists of the Western tradition, these Indian sculptors did not use live models. Instead, they based

6-20   Walls of the Kandarya Mahadeva Temple.

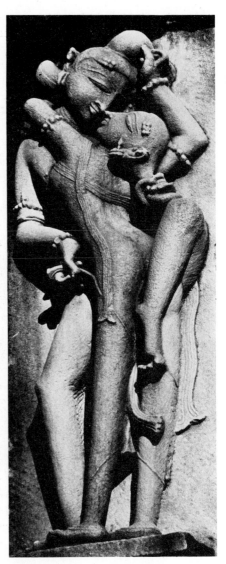

6-21
Detail of the Royal Portals,
Chartres Cathedral, twelfth
century.

6-22
Detail of the Kandarya
Mahadeva Temple, tenth–
eleventh centuries.

their work on earlier sculptures and evolved their conventions for representing the human body by relying more on their religious and sexual views than on their observations of anatomy. Much of the imagery was inspired by literary sources—such as the myth of the creation of woman in which Twashtri, the Divine Artificer, took the roundness of the moon, the clinging of tendrils, the trembling of grass, the glances of deer, and many other qualities and compounded them to make woman. Accordingly, the young maidens tend to be adorned with breasts that resemble wine-palm fruit. Both men and women seem to have smoothly flowing body envelopes that ignore the relationship of muscle to bone structure. They have volume without seeming to have weight, and their movements deny the sterner mechanics of the real body. Theirs is a liberated anatomy of supple rhythms that effectively expresses the feelings of erotic love.

In the Western world, habits of thinking and conduct in both philosophy and religion have long been guided by the concept of a division between mind and body. Most of the time the body comes out second best, treated as something to be ashamed of—a tradition that reaches back as far as the story of Adam and Eve (fig. 6-23). Only in recent times has the Western world come to accept the depiction of sexual activity as a possible, if not a proper, subject matter for art. Yet the forthright celebration of human sexuality was completely in keeping with the beliefs of Hinduism, a major theme of which is the life-giving energies: the male-female principle. At times the female aspect, often personified by Shakti, is emphasized; at other times it is the male aspect, Siva, that is stressed. But the principle of wholeness always prevails, necessitating the union of male and female. In certain rites, sexual intercourse itself is considered a divine act whereby the participants become like Siva and Shakti, or god and goddess. Physical sensation and idea are fused, obliterating the divisions between mind and body, heaven and earth.

Chagall   The expression of love between the sexes is as strong in the work of the twentieth-century painter Marc Chagall as it is in the Kandarya sculptures, but it is expressed in a strictly monogamous context. Chagall and his wife Bella first met in their small home town in Russia when he was about 22. At the time she was studying in Moscow he was studying art, without much success, in St. Petersburg. They fell in love immediately; she

6-23
Jacopo della Quercia, *The Expulsion from the Garden of Eden, c.* 1430. Istrian stone, 34" × 27". Main portal, San Petronio, Bologna.

even posed in the nude for him. But marriage between the two was delayed when Marc left in 1910 to continue his studies in Paris, then the art capital of the world. In a short time he became a successful artist. The natural naiveté of his style appealed to the progressive critics and dealers of Paris who, at the time, were interested in nontraditional approaches.

Despite his phenomenal success he had not forgotten Bella, and in 1914 returned to Russia to marry her. Although both families objected, especially hers, the two were married in 1915. Chagall painted several works on the subject of love shortly before and after his marriage. In *Double Portrait with Wineglass* (colorplate 11), the fantasy come true is revealed by Marc, intoxicated with happiness, sitting on the shoulders of his wife—with their newborn child hovering angel-like over both. Below them lies a quaint Russian village, perhaps Vitebsk, near their hometown. Logic and the forces of gravity are overcome by their private happiness. Floating figures are common in Chagall's works; here they symbolize the flight of lovers—the buoyancy of the human spirit in marital bliss.

Chagall's art is an extension of his private world, a world that freely unites the real with the unreal and the present with

6-24   Oskar Kokoschka, *The Tempest*, 1914. Oil on canvas, 71¼" × 87".
Kunstmuseum, Basel.

the past. In many ways it is similar, both in form and content, to the sculptures of Kandarya Mahadeva. But the passion of Chagall's visual poetry reflects his dedication to the love of a single person, and to the physical and spiritual celebration found in a genuine monogamous union.

Kokoschka   A contemporary of Chagall, Oskar Kokoschka, painted *The Tempest* (fig. 6-24) in 1914, at almost the same time as *Double Portrait with Wineglass*. Like Chagall's painting, it is a young man's artistic response to a personal experience with love. When we look at the painting, several other parallels suggest themselves: for example, the pair of lovers in *The Tempest* also seems to be floating. In fact, the German title is *Die Windsbraut*—literally "the bride of the wind"—which would be an apt name for Bella, whose figure floats in so many of Chagall's works. And like the earlier Chagall painting, *The Tempest* is a double portrait of the artist and a particular woman.

Kokoschka's three-year love affair with Alma Mahler—daughter of an artist, widow of a celebrated composer, and one of the most beautiful women in Vienna—nearly destroyed him. The dual trauma of passionate romance and high society was too much for Kokoschka; love, hate, ecstasy, fear—above all, disillusionment—were combined in the relationship timely ended by World War I. Kokoschka's poetry during the period refers to the turmoil—like the color and forms in his painting—that threatened to devour his identity and creativity.

We could speak of both Chagall's *Wineglass* and Kokoschka's *Tempest* as being emotional paintings: The Chagall is intoxicated with joy and the Kokoschka is agitated. But the two are quite different in spirit. *The Tempest* is heavy and turbid like a gathering storm yet to release its fury; Kokoschka's couple is neither airborne nor firmly on the ground. On the other hand, Chagall's lovers seem as free of gravity as a kite in an April breeze. The man's face in the Kokoschka, rather than expressing joy, projects the glazed expression of one who is deep in thought. In *Wineglass* the love of a man for a woman is without reservation. In *The Tempest* the love is, at best, ambivalent—more desperate than happy, more restless than satisfied.

Summary

Of all the subject matter available to the artist, perhaps none has proved more universally and consistently appealing than the human body. Whether as an ideal form or as the portrait of a particular person, it has been viewed and treated differently by the artists of every age. Simply looking at the way in which a naked body was represented can tell us as much about an age as all the objects, clothing, and other things recorded in the work. Style and content tell us whether the people of a given time believed that a man should be athletic or elegant, or whether a woman was considered a piece of decorative property or an object of worship. The relationship between the sexes is often expressed indirectly in these works, but it has less frequently been the subject matter of art. To be sure, a hidden trove of sexually explicit works produced by artists great and small does exist, yet these works are rarely meant to be more than stimulating or amusing. Only in rare cases—such as the Indian temple carvings—has the sexual relationship been treated in a religious way. Western art, needless to say, has had little of this. In the twentieth century, however, it has become more possible for artists like Chagall and Kokoschka to come to terms with the sexual as well as the emotional ties between men and women—and to express their infinite variety in a variety of ways.

7 Four Artists

The lives of the four artists discussed in this chapter span nearly five centuries of Western history and represent very different artistic, social, and religious points of view. Yet these artists also shared a number of things.

For one thing, their names are four of the best known in the history of art, their works continuing to maintain prominence in the public mind long after their deaths. For another, their artistic careers were marked by a drive to seek new expressive possibilities within the art of their time or, sometimes, a new artistic language altogether. The search was often fueled by a need to express new ideas or meanings that their contemporaries were only dimly aware of. In some cases it led to a significant modification of the artistic traditions they had started with.

All four succeeded in evolving unique artistic statements that stood out sharply from those of their fellow artists. And, in different ways, all four suffered for their rebellion and uniqueness. In every case, the problems related to their artistic careers were compounded by serious personal problems.

These similarities help to make meaningful the vast differences between them. These differences relate not only to their art but to their relationships with the public, the various intellectual, religious and political issues that involved them, and the challenges they faced when rebelling against established ways of thinking.

Michelangelo (1475–1564)

Michelangelo Buonarroti's early life was spent in Florence, Italy, at a time when that city was at the peak of its glory as the principal artistic and intellectual center of Renaissance Europe. It was there that the famous circle of gifted writers and artists gathered around Lorenzo "The Magnificent," the greatest patron of all the Medicis and the ruler of Florence at the time.

Michelangelo discovered at a young age that he preferred sculpture. His earliest training in the medium was under a sculptor named Bertoldo, who conducted his classes in the splendid Medici Gardens. There the 15-year-old Michelangelo not only learned something about his craft and explored the many classical sculptures of the Gardens but also had the opportunity to talk with some of the humanist scholars and poets of Lorenzo's circle. It was because of their influence that he himself became a scholar of classical and early Renaissance writings. He also became an enthusiastic follower of *Neoplatonism*, a synthesis of Greek and Christian beliefs and a major intellectual movement in Renaissance Italy. Indeed, Michelangelo's artistic development was in many ways more influenced by the ideas he gained from his contact with Lorenzo's scholars than by the training he received from Bertoldo.

The Early Pietà

When he was about 25 years old, Michelangelo was commissioned to sculpt a Pietà—an image of the Virgin Mary holding the dead Jesus—for a chapel in St. Peter's Basilica (fig. 7-1). In spite of its sorrowful subject matter, the Pietà's beauty and technical mastery are stronger than its suggestion of pathos. The limp body of Christ, slumped in the heavy folds of the Virgin's skirt, has the graceful proportions of a slender Apollo. The heroic figure of Mary is too large—perhaps larger than the figure of Christ—and too youthful to be the mother of a 33-year-old man. The artist's goal, however, was not objective realism but the harmonious relationship of the two figures—which meant that Mary had to be larger than usual—and the expression of an ideal, a Neoplatonic Mother of God who is as beautiful as she is tender.

The qualities of idealization, monumentality, and harmony found in the *Pietà* were beginning to be reflected in the works of other leading Italian artists of the time, particularly Leonardo da Vinci, a generation older than Michelangelo. In the famous *Mona Lisa* (fig. 5-9), Leonardo's aim was to make an idealized portrait in which the foreground figure harmonized with its landscape background. But a sketch of a group of figures, *The Virgin and Child with Saint Anne and the Infant Saint John* (fig. 7-2),

7-1
Michelangelo, *Pietà,* 1498–
1500. Marble, 5′9″ high.
Saint Peter's, Rome.

is a better example to compare with the *Pietà*. Da Vinci endowed each of the women and children with the handsome proportions and noble bearing of Greek statues, and by giving careful attention to the position and movement of each figure, ensured they all related to one another as a group—united by a single flow of rhythmic movement.

But the magnificent *Pietà*, which established Michelangelo as the leading sculptor in Italy, is not typical of his later work. For although the later pieces often consist of idealized figures, they also contain elements that tend to contradict the sense of harmony characteristic of the *Pietà* and other art of the period. These elements were already present in his statue of David (fig. 6-6), which was commissioned by the city fathers of Florence in 1501, the same year the *Pietà* was finished. This work's intensity and defiance symbolize the civic virtues and the force and anger needed to arouse the courage of the citizens in their struggle for liberty. But these qualities are also signs of the artist's own ferocity of spirit (his contemporaries referred to it as *terribilitá*), which was to show up more and more in his art as time went on.

There has been a great deal of speculation about the links
between the events of Michelangelo's life, his personality, and
his work. He was certainly a man of paradoxes: a servant of the
Medicis and a follower of Savonarola, the fiery monk who denounced the Medicis and their culture; a passionate admirer of
physical beauty who was ashamed of his own body; a devout
Catholic who was enthusiastic about pagan art and ideas; and a
celebrated artist who was withdrawn and alienated from those
around him. Some scholars allude to events of his early childhood to explain these paradoxes; others believe that he suffered
from repressed homosexuality. But all agree that his life was
torn with neurotic conflict that generated enormous creative
energy as well as being the source of some of the restless and
disturbing qualities that make his work so fascinating.

**The Sistine
Ceiling**

In 1505, Michelangelo was summoned to Rome by the ambitious
and powerful Pope Julius II to build a grandiose tomb. But soon
after the artist started work on the project, the Pope lost interest
in it and began instead to pressure him to paint a fresco on the

immense ceiling of the <u>Sistine Chapel</u> (fig. 7-3). Michelangelo, after protesting that he was a sculptor and not a painter, reluctantly accepted the commission in 1508 and began what was to be his greatest enterprise.

The work required <u>four years</u>. Lying on his back atop a scaffold some 65 feet above the floor, Michelangelo painted a fresco of more than <u>700 square yards</u> (fig. 7-4). Just the painting itself was an awesome technical feat, but the concept and the scope of the ideas are equally awesome. Using the <u>story of Genesis</u> as his basic source and the human figure as his principal means of expression, he constructed a complex interpretation of the Judeo-Christian Creation liberally infused with Greek ideas.

The episodes of Genesis are chronicled in a series of nine

7-3   Interior of the Sistine Chapel, Vatican, Rome.

rectangular panels running down the center—the crown of the ceiling—beginning with scenes of the Creation and ending with the drama of the Flood. God, who appears in each of the Creation panels, is represented by two figures (the one on the right shown with some of His heavenly assistants) in the *Creation of the Sun and Moon* (colorplate 12). Both figures are clothed in loose-fitting, billowing gowns that reveal God's muscular, athletic body—like that of a pagan Titan or perhaps of Zeus, regent of Mount Olympus. But the face of the figure on the right does not have the distant stare of a Greek statue, the classical calm that we expect of a Greek god. Instead it has the fierce look—full of holiness and wrath—that we often associate with the Old Testament God. In the four corners of the panel, as well as in the corners of all of the central panels, are naked youths, each restlessly perched on a pedestal. Although Greek in their nudity, the roles they play in this work are similar to those of Christian angels; in a more traditional work they would probably have wings and wear long gowns.

7-4   Michelangelo, ceiling of the Sistine Chapel, 1508–12.

Flanking the panels on all four sides of the ceiling is a series of large figures—the biblical prophets and pagan sibyls who predicted the coming of Christ—each seated within a shallow niche. Between the prophets and sibyls are lunettes (triangular spaces directly above the chapel's arched windows) containing the kings and queens of Judah, the ancestors of Christ. The larger lunettes at the corners contain events from the Old Testament that are believed to have foreshadowed Christ's crucifixion.

Perhaps the most impressive aspect of the Sistine Chapel ceiling is the sense of order that Michelangelo managed to impose on it. No work in the history of art can compare with its scope, conception, or sheer expressive power. Over 300 figures populate the space and are drawn to several different scales. Worlds are being created and destroyed. Christian, Jewish, and Neoplatonic themes intermingle. Yet the artist has managed to contain it all by using every bit of the inconveniently parceled space to further his ends—dividing it up into an architectonic

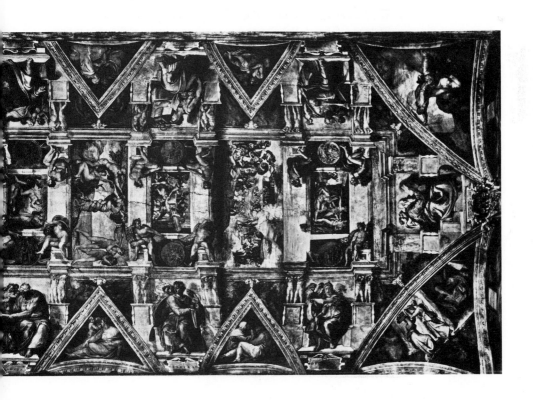

arrangement of rectangular and triangular spaces that bring order to the complex narrative and symbolic components as well.

The Last Judgment

Twenty years later Michelangelo was prevailed upon by one of Julius's successors, Paul III, to paint an interpretation of the Last Judgment on the altar wall of the same chapel. By now the artist was nearly 60 and, in addition to the trials of aging, he was depressed by the deterioration of the world around him. The foundations of the Catholic Church were being threatened by the Protestant Reformation; Rome, the seat of the Church, had been sacked and laid waste seven years earlier by Spanish and German soldiers; and the Medicis had been forced to leave Florence, only to return as tyrants who eradicated its freedoms. Meanwhile, Michelangelo had involved himself in far too many projects. He was harassed from all sides by those who had commissioned him—including the executors for Pope Julius, who were still trying to get him to finish the tomb. It would appear that Michelangelo's mounting frustrations were released in all their fury in his painting of *The Last Judgment* (fig. 7-5).

Rather than Christ the Redeemer, Michelangelo's *Last Judgment* portrays Christ the Avenger—whose image discourages any interpretation other than one of fear and despair. And rather than a vision of human beings as a divine creation, there is a dark and pessimistic view of them as being virtually incapable of achieving grace. The saved are not easily distinguished from the damned, for neither group looks happy or possesses the physical beauty that characterizes the creatures on the ceiling. Once again the human body is naked—and even larger and more muscular than before—but this time it is brutish rather than heroic, base rather than glorious. The scene is a thunderous vision of doom, an unleashed *terribilitá*. Clumps of twisting flesh whirl around the angry Christ as souls are wrenched from the earth (lower left) to be lofted before Christ, who decides which are to remain with him and which are to be dragged struggling into hell (lower right) where devils and figures from Greek mythology await them. Finally, there is a sign of Michelangelo's own sense of guilt—as well as of his perverse sense of humor—in his self-portrait, the flayed skin held by the martyred St. Bartholomew (fig. 7-6).

The structure of *The Last Judgment*, like its content, is a turmoil of unevenly distributed clusters of figures arching around the central figure of Christ. When we compare this with the

7-5 Michelangelo, *The Last Judgment*, altar wall of the Sistine Chapel, 1534–41. Fresco, approx. 43' high.

ceiling—with its balance of figures and spaces and its rectangular, ordered composition—we become aware not only of the vast difference between the two works but of the lengths to which Michelangelo had gone in breaking with the values of his earlier art.

The achievements of Michelangelo were legendary throughout Europe even during his lifetime—which lasted another 25 years after the completion of *The Last Judgment*. Yet rather than bask in his celebrity, he continued his prodigious work (including, in addition to murals and sculptures, several significant architectural projects, such as the Capitoline Hill (fig. 2-22).

The Last Pietà Michelangelo's last sculpture was, once again, a Pietà (fig. 7-7). These two sculptures present interesting contrasts as landmarks at either end of a difficult artistic and spiritual journey. Whereas the first was a celebration of beauty, the last is an expression of death—a requiem in stone made by an artist who was personally close to death. Its unpolished surfaces and unfinished figures are, of course, partly the result of a faltering hand and an aging spirit, but they are also the result of a religious beatitude at the end of a long and troubled life. Michelangelo's struggle was finally relieved.

Between the two Pietàs, Michelangelo's enormous reputation had come about more because of his painting than because of his sculpture—although sculpture was his preferred medium. The Sistine ceiling enlarged the concept of the heroic in art and revealed how the human figure could convey energy and drama. *The Last Judgment* demonstrated that great art did not have to be pleasant and that the figure could convey terror. Michelangelo dealt with the most august themes of Western culture, and gave them visual forms that left lasting impressions.

Rembrandt (1606–1669) The Dutch Republic of the early seventeenth century—a union of cities in the northern Netherlands—had recently achieved independence from Spain. Among other things, self-determination had meant economic opportunity and religious freedom for the mainly Protestant population of the tiny nation. Taking advantage of the Netherlands' ports and seafaring history, the hard-working Calvinist traders proceeded to dominate the oceans and establish commercial relations in all parts of the world—including the Far East and America. Amsterdam, which was an insignificant fishing village in the fifteenth century, be-

7-6
Michelangelo, detail of fig.
7-5 with "self-portrait."

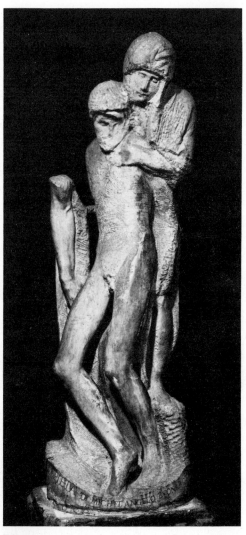

7-7
Michelangelo, *Pietà
Rondanini, c.* 1555–64.
Marble, 77½" high. Castello
Sforzesco, Milan.

came in many ways the Florence of the seventeenth century. By the time Rembrandt van Rijn was born (in Leiden, the second city of the Netherlands at the time), Amsterdam was the richest and most powerful city in the Dutch Republic and the commercial metropolis of the world.

Dutch art at the time that Rembrandt came of age was almost completely outside the seventeenth-century mainstream. There were, basically, two schools of art in Holland at the time. One, called the Italian school because the artists studied in Italy, was partial to historical or religious subjects filled with posturing, idealized bodies, and impressive settings. Its roots went back to the High Renaissance (and the works of Michelangelo) and its principal counterpart internationally was the Baroque art of the Catholic countries, a style magnificently exemplified by the Flemish painter Rubens (fig. 7-8). The other was the emerging Dutch school, which favored the portrayal of everyday life

7-8
Peter Paul Rubens, *St. Ignatius Exorcising Demons from the Church,* 1619. Oil on canvas, 17′6½″ × 12′11½″. Kunsthistorisches Museum, Vienna.

in the form of household objects, down-to-earth people, and landscapes—subject matter that is commonly referred to as *genre*.

The patrons of Protestant Holland were not the Dutch Reformed Church—which refused to harbor art in its buildings—but individual people, particularly well-to-do burghers who found comfort in the images of genre painting and therefore created a demand for it. Yet there were also many patrons and artists in Holland who still admired the Italian school, among them Rembrandt's teacher Pieter Lastman. Rembrandt, of course, was influenced by elements of both schools, but his own work lacked the exaggeration and idealization of the Baroque style and the trivial content of genre. He was, in a sense, out of step with both of the principal alternatives of the art of his day. Unlike most genre painters, he persisted in making religious pictures; unlike Baroque painters, he endowed his religious pictures with a simplicity and realism characteristic of genre art.

Some believe Rembrandt's interest in the Bible was inspired by his mother. If so, it was strengthened and given some artistic direction by Lastman, who liked to do biblical subjects. Whatever the reasons, Rembrandt created a great many paintings, prints, and drawings that could be thought of as biblical illustrations, such as *Christ Healing the Sick* (fig. 3-9). Unlike Michelangelo's religious interpretations, Rembrandt's did not depict larger-than-life beings inhabiting an abstract world but ordinary-looking people living in a concrete, personal world familiar to all of us—a Protestant conception that emphasizes the personal relationship between God and the lives of human beings.

The Blinding of Samson

In some of his early biblical paintings, Rembrandt displayed an affinity for heightened effects that was reminiscent of Baroque art. But the theatrical elements of Rembrandt's religious dramas were derived from realism, lighting, and a vivid imagination rather than from superhuman figures and grandiose gesturing. The ten-foot-long *Blinding of Samson* (fig. 7-9) may have been made to please one of Rembrandt's patrons, Dutch poet and statesman, Constantyn Huygens, who allegedly had a taste for violence and horror. Huygens was probably not disappointed, because Rembrandt portrayed the savagery of the attack with a forcefulness and terror that few of his contemporaries would have dared to match. The scene is in the tent of Delilah, who is fleeing with Samson's hair as soldiers wrestle him to the ground and commit the atrocity. The terrible agony of the stabbing is

7-9 Rembrandt van Rijn, *The Blinding of Samson*, 1636. Oil on canvas, 93″ × 119″. Staedelisches Kunstinstitut, Frankfurt.

seen not only in Samson's face but his entire body, arching and kicking—even the toes are clenched with pain.

Violence, moreover, is expressed by the picture's strong diagonals: the figure of the soldier on the left, his spear, the flaps of the tent, the figure of Delilah, Samson's right leg, and the alignment of the metal-clad soldiers, almost all of which point to Samson's face. The major means of creating dramatic effect and focusing attention is the contrast of light and dark. The greatest area of this contrast is around Samson's body and face, as if the ugly act were starkly exposed by the glare of a spotlight shining through the tent opening. In addition to highlighting the victim, the glare silhouettes the soldier with the spear. The fleeing Delilah, on the edge of the light, appears somewhat spectral while the soldiers, defined chiefly by the highlights on their armor, are partially concealed in the murky shadows.

Rembrandt's greatest period of personal happiness and professional success was the decade of the 1630s. After moving his studio from Leiden to Amsterdam he obtained several important commissions, enjoyed the esteem of the social world of the city, and married Saskia van Ulenburgh, the daughter of a wealthy burgomaster. By the end of the decade he was the most celebrated painter in Holland, and was wealthy enough to make a down payment on a spacious house in Amsterdam. But the year 1642 proved to be a turning point in his career and for his family.

In that year, Rembrandt completed a major work, a group portrait of the civic guard under Captain Cocq that came to be known as *The Night Watch* (colorplate 13). Not content merely to use the traditional solution of portraying the company of men sitting in rows around a banquet table, Rembrandt decided to show them at the moment of being called to parade formation. Caught in the act of hasty preparation, each figure is doing something different—cleaning a musket, hoisting a banner, grabbing a halberd, or scurrying to position. Each also seems to be wearing something different; their "uniforms" are a conglomeration of colors, lace collars, embroidery, chain mail, sashes, plumed hats, and metal helmets. To add to the tumult, Rembrandt included a few strays: a boy dashing off to the left, a girl bathed in an eerie light (and carrying a chicken and a dagger on her belt) in the middle left, and a barking dog on the right. Yet in spite of the confusion, each man's face is at least partly visible—and, supposedly, a faithful likeness.

The Night Watch surpassed its simple portrait function and came to be regarded as the most exciting work of Rembrandt's middle period and one of the greatest paintings in the history of art. It is a truly heroic piece—not in the sense associated with Michelangelo of superhuman theme and scale but in a swashbuckling sense—full of pomp, fanfare, and martial splendor. One can almost hear the shuffle of boots and the clang of metal. It is also full of movement, demonstrating the artist's remarkable inventiveness and his ability to record a variety of gestures. At the same time, it is full of enough contradiction—the chaos of actions, the oddities of dress, the presence of the girl—to endow it with a certain amount of mystery and poetry and to make it something more than a picture of a military company.

Augmenting the drama, movement, and even the sense of mystery is Rembrandt's employment of light and dark, which serves here, as in the Samson painting, to structure the whole composition. The hour of the scene is probably late afternoon rather than night (the nocturnal appearance is due to the darkening of the layers of varnish), but the lighting does not conform to the rays of the sun. It conforms instead to the pictorial needs of emphasis and balance and the expressive needs of mood and excitement. The eye, guided by the distribution of light and dark, focuses on the two officers in the foreground and scans the fascinating throng of men behind them.

The painting, for all its virtues, was not well received by everyone. Apparently some of the men in the company, who had paid a hundred guilders apiece for it, were dissatisfied with their lack of visibility. Others were critical of the painting's unconventional characteristics. While Rembrandt's reputation did not plummet because of *The Night Watch*, it was undoubtedly hurt by the public reaction.

A Self-Portrait   Still, Rembrandt never compromised his frank realism and his self-proclaimed right to paint a subject with the full freedom of his considerable imagination—no matter how idiosyncratic that imagination might be at times. This obstinacy—especially his refusal to flatter his portrait subjects—contributed to his continuing decline in popularity. The fact that he also refused to flatter himself was probably of little comfort to his public. A 1652 self-portrait (fig. 7-10), in which the artist appears at once defiant and vulnerable, is unsparing in its disclosure of the effects of aging and stress. It also reflects changes that had taken place in Rembrandt's art. The composition is simpler, the details and textures of the things represented are less emphatic, and the texture of the paint itself—because of looser and broader brushwork—is more in evidence. Light is still the chief means of emphasizing objects and of focusing attention, but Rembrandt has used it differently. Instead of a spotlight for creating excitement, it is a tool for probing the subtler aspects of the subject's inner life and emotions revealed by the face and body.

Commitment to his own artistic values, together with changes in taste on the part of the public, eventually led to Rembrandt's financial ruin. Seventeenth-century Holland was the first society to develop a system of patronage based on the middle class rather than the church or the courts. Arnold Hauser, a social historian of art, has explained that such a system helped Rembrandt's powers to grow because it gave him freedom to experiment. On the other hand, it did not provide the security

of the former system, thereby causing him to lose everything when his popularity dropped.

Rembrandt's professional problems were further aggravated by the death of Saskia and then by the public disapproval of his living with Hendrickje Stoffels, a young servant girl with whom he fell in love about seven years after Saskia's death (and whom he could not marry because he would have lost his deceased wife's estate). Surprisingly, none of his many problems affected the quantity of his production; he continued to paint in spite of deaths, lawsuits, and bankruptcy proceedings. His troubles, however, seemed to have had the effect of making his work even more subdued and profound.

The Return of the Prodigal Son

Hendrickje died in 1662. Rembrandt himself was to live for only seven more years, during which time the prices of his works were absurdly low and he became financially destitute. In one of his last paintings, *The Return of the Prodigal Son* (fig. 7-11), there is a softness and an apparent tendency to dematerialize reality that is reminiscent of Michelangelo's later Pietà (fig. 7-7). The simplicity of the scene, without any distracting movement in the sacred stillness and halflight, allows the miracle of reunion to take place. Although leaving much unsaid, this painting effectively suggests the meaning of the parable and the significance of family bonds in general. The son surrendering himself to the tender embrace of his father summarizes the healing message of Christian pardon. The depth of feeling can be related to Rem-

7-11
Rembrandt van Rijn, *The Return of the Prodigal Son*, c. 1665. Oil on canvas, 8'8" × 6'8¾". Hermitage Museum, Leningrad.

brandt's own life, which saw the old artist outlive almost his entire family.

Rembrandt did not leave behind a family of artists, either. None of his students produced a significant body of work in his style and other artists of his time ignored it. By contrast, Rubens's grand style was extended and modified in the next century by a host of artistic heirs. Indeed, Rembrandt's work went relatively unnoticed until the nineteenth century, when its distinctive qualities were finally recognized and appreciated by the Romantics. And although Rubens's art is still respected today, it is not nearly as honored as Rembrandt's, which has grown steadily in stature—and which now is appreciated more for its insights into human character than for its romantic qualities.

The artists of seventeenth-century Holland, discouraged by their Calvinist religion from glorifying God or the church through art, turned to representing the world around them. So did Rembrandt, but unlike his countrymen he also applied his remarkable gifts to the task of making gospel stories real and vivid. In his earlier work—both religious and secular—he strove for dramatic effects that often required elaborate compositions. In his later work, he stressed the psychological aspects of his subjects in simpler, more restrained compositions. Perhaps because of the problems he faced in his own life, his later art was extremely penetrating in its portrayal of human feelings. When using a story from the Bible, Rembrandt was able to express its religious content in very human terms. His later work constitutes a rare—perhaps the greatest—collection of artistic interpretations of the Scriptures from the Protestant perspective.

Van Gogh (1853–1890)

In the eighteenth century, Holland's influence among the nations of Europe began to decline sharply. By the middle of the nineteenth century, after a series of disastrous struggles with England on the seas and France on land—including French occupation from 1795 to 1813—Holland's importance as an international power and Amsterdam's influence as a major city were severely reduced. In art, especially, Holland was a provincial country.

Vincent van Gogh, the son of a Protestant minister from the North Brabant province of Holland, decided to become an artist at the relatively late age of 27. He had already failed as an art dealer (in a business owned by his relatives), a theological student, and an evangelist. His failures were not due to incompetence but to a chronic inability to relate to people and to periodic outbursts of emotion followed by self-recrimination. Theories about his mental disorders vary from epilepsy to cerebral tumor and from schizophrenia to turpentine poisoning. Yet regardless of the explanation, his life consisted of alternating, almost unbearable, extremes of feeling that were barely concealed by his outer behavior and relationships with others. Immersing himself in something—first religion, then art—was a way of overcoming his loneliness and avoiding complete mental chaos.

As both artist and former evangelist, Vincent often looked to the works of Rembrandt for inspiration, feeling "there is something of Rembrandt in the Gospel, or something of the Gospel in Rembrandt." To Van Gogh, the seventeenth-century master—more than anyone else—had blended art and religion, making them virtually synonomous; like Rembrandt, he sought to express his feelings of compassion and tenderness through depictions of common people.

The Potato Eaters

Van Gogh's first important work, *The Potato Eaters* (fig. 7-12), painted in 1885 when he was 32, summarizes his thinking and artistic direction at the time. There is a significant difference in approach between Van Gogh and Rembrandt—indeed between Van Gogh and almost all other artists to that time. Rembrandt conveyed emotion through realistic depictions that were based on his profound understanding of human nature. Van Gogh expressed emotion primarily through line, color, texture of the paint, and distortions of some of the shapes. In *The Potato Eaters*, the emotional focus is not just on the humble peasants and their existence as it is depicted but also on the earthy, lumpy qualities of their forms. The painting itself, as Van Gogh explained, is "like the color of a very dusty potato."

Even after finding his vocation in art, Van Gogh's behavior did not change enough to keep him from experiencing periodic emotional crises or having trouble with the people around him. He moved often, living with this relative or visiting that one, and spending some time studying art in both Holland and Belgium. Through it all he received financial support from his brother Theo, who had become an art dealer in Paris. In 1886, deciding that the environment of the Netherlands was physically, intellectually, and emotionally stifling, he went to Paris to join Theo and to gain what he could from what was then the world's most progressive center of art.

7-12 Vincent van Gogh, *The Potato Eaters,* 1885. Oil on canvas, 32¼″ × 44⅞″. Vincent van Gogh Collection, Stedelijk Museum, Amsterdam.

At first that city was a tonic for Van Gogh's spirits. In the gallery where Theo worked and in Fernand Cormon's studio where Vincent studied, he met many of the younger and more advanced artists. His style was influenced by the lighter, brighter colors favored by Impressionists like Monet (colorplate 19) and the flat and precise designs of Japanese prints (fig. 7-13), with which nearly everyone in the Paris art world was fascinated. For a while his temperament improved, perhaps because his feelings of being an outcast were overcome by his being a part of the lively crowd of artistic rebels (including such people as Gauguin and Toulouse-Lautrec). But he soon wearied of Paris as tensions grew between him and Theo and his bouts of melancholy returned. In February of 1888–perhaps at the suggestion of Toulouse-Lautrec, who wanted to get rid of him—Van Gogh left for Arles, a small city in the south of France.

View of Arles   The two-year period that Van Gogh spent in southern France was the most brilliant in his short life as an artist. Like the Paris

7-13 Hokusai, *The Great Wave,* from *Thirty-Six Views of Mt. Fuji,*
Tokugawa period. Woodcut, 10″ × 14¾″. Museum of Fine Arts, Boston.

episode, that of Arles started out happily—even more so. The
fresh air and warmth of that first spring had a good effect on his
art and, at least for a time, his feelings about life. Each painting
of orchards, fields, drawbridges, and the like tended to suggest
optimism rather than pessimism. *View of Arles with Irises in the
Foreground* (fig. 7-14), painted in May, is a celebration of spring
and an affirmation of life in general. The strong colors and bold
shapes woven together by thick, lively brushstrokes not only
convey the radiance of spring but reveal the artistic self-confidence Vincent had acquired in only eight years. Every form—
iris, buttercup, tree, building—is brilliantly delineated from inside to outside, with each brushstroke doing the job of drawing
as well as painting. *View of Arles,* like so many paintings he
made in his first months there, demonstrates that Van Gogh—in
spite of his tendency to become depressed—could make very
positive paintings. Southern France in the spring had brought
out his enthusiasm for life; according to one art historian, "the
painting of Arles was a return to Eden."

The Night Cafe   *The Night Cafe* (colorplate 14), painted in September of the same
year, characterizes another side of this region as well as Van
Gogh's changing feelings about it. The city of Arles, according
to many witnesses of the time, was a miserable working-class

town full of taverns, brothels, and people who were prone to violence. Van Gogh's painting is of the inside of one of the taverns that stayed open all night as a refuge for night-prowlers, the Cafe de l'Alcazar. It is a taut, unreal environment, a night-time scene flooded with an unearthly light that suggests frustrations and tensions. The acrid colors—citron yellow in the lamps and floor, chartreuse in the pool table, bar, and ceiling, and blood red in the walls—clash with one another; their violence, along with the exaggerated perspective, contradicts the sullen, eerie stillness. Van Gogh wrote, "I have tried to express the idea that the cafe is a place where one can ruin oneself, go mad, commit a crime."

In that same month, Vincent also made a self-portrait (fig.

7-14 Vincent van Gogh, *View of Arles with Irises,* 1888. Oil on canvas, 21¼″ × 25½″. Vincent van Gogh Collection, Stedelijk, Museum, Amsterdam.

7-15
Vincent van Gogh, *Self-Portrait*, 1888. Oil on Canvas, 24½″ × 20½″. The Fogg Art Museum, Harvard University (bequest—collection Maurice Wertheim, Class of 1906).

7-15). Like the *View of Arles*, it has tapestry-like brushstrokes that define the structure of head, face, neck, and clothing. The same lively paint texture animates the background by forming a whorl around the subject's head. At the same time, this consistent textural treatment tends to reinforce the face's staring expression as well as the severity of the facial features and closely shaved head. Like *The Night Cafe*, Van Gogh's self-portrait has a tautness that suggests the barely controlled tensions of a man who could "ruin himself, go mad, commit a crime."

That fall Paul Gauguin had arrived in Arles at the invitation of Van Gogh, who hoped that the two would form the nucleus of a brotherhood of artists—a dream Van Gogh had had since Paris. He admired, almost worshiped, Gauguin—a mystic, adventurer, notorious debauchee, and a potentially important painter of the modern movement. Unfortunately, Gauguin either could not or would not return Van Gogh's admiration, and his instinct for sarcasm and provocation found an easy target in the sensitive younger artist. The circumstances of their association led to a series of nervous breakdowns for Van Gogh, including the now-legendary story of his cutting off an earlobe and

7-16   Vincent van Gogh, *The Starry Night,* 1889. Oil on canvas,
29″ × 36¼″. The Museum of Modern Art, New York (acquired through
the Lillie P. Bliss Bequest).

presenting it to a prostitute on Christmas Eve of 1888. From this
time on, he was in and out of hospitals until he commited suicide in the summer of 1890.

The Starry
Night

During this time, however, he never ceased to paint and draw.
Much of his work from this period, not surprisingly, is even
more subjective and charged with even greater energy than his
earlier pieces. *The Starry Night* (fig. 7-16), painted from the window of his room in the hospital at St. Rémy-de-Provence, is
overflowing with excited forms. At the lower right is a village
sheltered by the mountains and dominated by a church spire
reminiscent of those in Holland. Commanding the left side is
the flamelike shape of a huge cypress tree—an ancient symbol
of death—which extends from bottom to top and overlaps the

dramatic sky, the main feature of the picture. The town is painted with short, measured strokes, and is relatively quiet; the tree is painted with long, thick, serpentine strokes and is quite restless; the sky, a phantasmagoria of celestial activity depicted with sweeps and spirals of thickly applied paint, represents the ultimate stage of frenzy.

Like the late works of Michelangelo and Rembrandt, *The Starry Night* seems to reflect the thoughts and feelings of a man anticipating his own death. But here, reality has yielded to the artist's inner vision far more than it has in the late Pietà or *The Prodigal Son.* The painting stands on the edge of a period in which emotional content would be generated less through subject matter and symbols and more through the visual qualities of spontaneously created abstract forms.

Except for one favorable article appearing in a French magazine six months before his death, Vincent received very little recognition during his lifetime. Yet not many years after his death he became a hero among the artists of the modern movement, many of whom were greatly inspired by his work. Although Van Gogh's style and approach influenced much of the art of the twentieth century, the spirit of his art is clearly a part of the same religious-humanistic tradition of Michelangelo and Rembrandt. His intense concern for life can be equated with the theological doctrine of immanence—God's love and presence in all things—which he expressed in a subjective style that transformed every person and object included in his pictures.

Pollock (1912–1956)

During the early years of the Great Depression, Jackson Pollock studied art at the Art Students League in New York. Each summer he hitchhiked, rode freight trains, or drove an old jalopy across the country to his family's home in California. On the way he would do some sketching, but mostly he would observe the life of America—especially that of people whose lives had been broken by the Depression. His travels provided the opportunity to see the impressive murals then being painted by Mexican artists like José Clemente Orozco and Diego Rivera (fig. 3-6) and to discover Indian sand painting—two things that undoubtedly influenced his later art.

Seascape

In 1934, Pollock painted *Seascape* (fig. 7-17), in which a tiny sailboat is nearly engulfed by a stormy sea that symbolizes the overwhelming forces of nature. Its content, together with its curvilinear forms and dark brooding colors, is reminiscent of *Starry*

7-17   Jackson Pollock, *Seascape*, 1934. Oil on canvas, 12″ × 16″.
Collection of Lee Krasner Pollock, New York.

Night—except that the Van Gogh work, for all its halucinatory energy, is more disciplined. *Seascape* reflects some influence of the teachers at the Art Students League, especially that of Thomas Hart Benton (fig. 7-18), but it also displays the robust brushwork and rhythms that were to characterize Pollock's mature paintings. His early works, like those of Van Gogh, did not attract much attention outside of the artist's immediate circle of friends and relatives.

In 1935, Pollock signed on with the newly created Federal Arts Project—part of a relief program set up by the government for the purpose of creating jobs—as a member of a division that was supposed to create art for schools, post offices, and other public buildings. He remained with the project, with few interruptions, until 1943.

One of those interruptions related to a four-month hospital stay for treatment of acute alcoholism in 1938. No one is sure just when Pollock's drinking problem started, but by his mid-twenties he was an alcoholic. Moreover, he tended to become violent when drunk and was often involved in barroom fights, reckless driving, arrests, and generally aggressive behavior. Like Van Gogh, he seemed to be on an emotional roller coaster with good times followed by crashing lows—and when he was

7-18 Thomas Hart Benton, *Arts of the West,* 1932. Tempera, 8′ × 13′.
New Britain Museum of American Art, New Britain, Connecticut
(Harriet Russell Stanley Fund).

low, he drank. Otherwise, his personality was not like Van
Gogh's; he did not have that artist's chronic inability to relate to
people. When he was not drunk he was warm and likeable,
even charming, and maintained several enduring friendships
with both men and women—among them the painter Lee Krasner, who later married him.

The late thirties and early forties were difficult and challenging times for young American artists. The social crises of the
Depression and World War II were, of course, bad enough, but
the real problem for artists was a kind of identity crisis. The
relationships between American art and the nation and between
American art and the international art world were inconsistent if
not contradictory. *Regionalism*—exemplified by the paintings of
Benton—was the leading American movement of the time. But
its old-fashioned realism, rural subject matter, and homespun
values were inappropriate for a nation that was becoming increasingly involved in international affairs. European art, particularly that of Paris, seemed equally inappropriate. It was looked

7-19   Joan Miró, *The Harlequin's Carnival*, 1924–25. Oil on canvas, 26″ × 36⅝″. Albright-Knox Art Gallery, Buffalo, New York (Room of Contemporary Art Fund, 1940).

upon by some as effete, and American efforts to emulate it did not sell well or receive much critical attention. However, several important European artists had fled to America at the onset of World War II and had settled in New York. Pollock, among others, was stimulated by their presence and their ideas. But the direction of American art—not only its form and content but its potential role in American and world culture—was essentially an enigma at that time.

By 1940, Pollock had dropped what Regionalist tendencies he ever had, retaining at most the taste for vigorous curvilinear forms and interlocking compositions he had inherited from Benton. He was becoming increasingly interested in the ideas and methods of European modernism—especially the work of such artists as Joan Miró (fig. 7-19)—and was being influenced by those European artists in New York who emphasized the function of the subconscious in making art. Another important influence was a series of sessions with a Jungian psychiatrist who stimulated Pollock's interest in archetypes—basic images and ideas that are supposedly present in everyone's subconscious—and how these might be used and expressed in art.

Pasiphae   *Pasiphae* (fig. 7-20) was painted when Pollock was 31, about the same age Van Gogh was when he painted *The Potato Eaters.* Pollock's painting represents his attempts to this point to bring together the many themes of his life and artistic influences into a new artistic expression. The figurative images of earlier work had by this time been replaced by abstract signs and symbols that can be related to ancient myths—as the title *Pasiphae* implies—or to the Jungian subconscious. In addition, the opulence of its rhythms and colors contains an echo of the Mexican murals Pollock had seen in his earlier travels, while the calligraphic character of the lines reflects American Indian art. But this painting's most unique quality, a curious and compelling mixture of awkwardness and force—sort of an American *terribilitá*—was what caught the attention of the New York art world.

The abstract signs and symbols of *Pasiphae* and other works of that period began to disappear in some of the paintings Pollock made in 1946. Consisting of freely painted, primarily circular brushstrokes, they implied an approach to painting that could be thought of as "automatic writing." In other words, the

7-20   Jackson Pollock, *Pasiphae,* 1943. Oil on canvas, 56⅛″ × 96″.
The Metropolitan Museum of Art, New York.

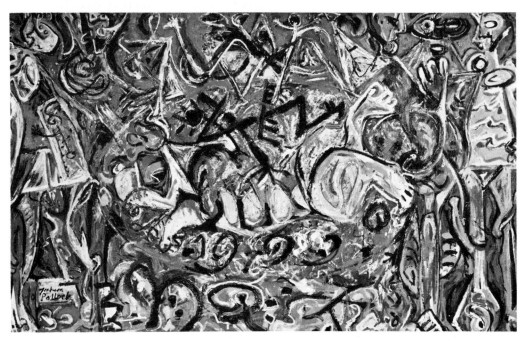

forms were produced spontaneously, rather than by conscious use of images or symbols.

Cathedral   The following year, Pollock developed a new way of working that made the 1946 paintings appear restrained and inhibited by comparison. No one knows for sure how it came about—whether it was a suggestion of the Surrealist painter Roberto Matta, an accident, the result of a fit of frustration, or just one of those revelations that surface quietly and unexpectedly. Pollock's revolutionary method? Not brushing the paint onto the canvas.

Cathedral (fig. 7-21), made with liquid Duco and aluminum paint, was one of the first made this way. The canvas was not fixed to a wooden frame and hung on an easel, but spread on the floor so that Pollock could walk around and across it and apply paint by dripping, spilling, splashing, and scraping. Not only had he dispensed with signs and symbols—indeed with form itself as it had been known to this point—but also with the traditional techniques of painting. What remained was the art of pure freedom that he had been looking for. Beginning a painting with very little premeditation, he would develop it intuitively as he went along (fig. 7-22). According to Pollock:

> When I am *in* my painting, I'm not aware of what I'm doing. It is only after a sort of "get acquainted" period that I see what I have been about. I have no fears about making changes, destroying the image, etc., because the painting has a life of its own. I try to let it come through. It is only when I lose contact with the painting that the result is a mess. Otherwise there is pure harmony, an easy give and take, and the painting comes out well.

His new work was met with both praise and antagonism, but there was no question that Pollock was the artist that everyone was talking about—and "everyone" this time was more than just the tiny New York art world. In the fall of 1948, *Life* magazine devoted 24 pages to a "Round Table on Modern Art" in which, among other works, Pollock's *Cathedral* was discussed (and roundly defended by critic Clement Greenberg). A year later, *Life* devoted an article just to him—"Jackson Pollock: Is He the Greatest Living Painter in the United States?"—with photos of him working in his barn-studio. In the days before the omnipresence of television, an article in *Life* was the ultimate in mass-media coverage. How did Americans respond to Jackson Pol-

7-21
Jackson Pollock,
Cathedral, 1947.
Oil, 75″ × 35″.
Dallas Museum of Fine Arts
(gift of Mr. and Mrs.
Bernard J. Reis).

lock? Having little knowledge of modern art, they were startled by his radical paintings and working methods and also—as Pollock's biographer, B.H. Friedman, points out—impressed with his image as "a new, nonarty American-style painter."

One   Some people denounced paintings like the enormous *One* (colorplate 15) as chaotic and unintelligible, but many others recognized what Pollock called "pure harmony." They were also moved by the scale of such works, which filled the viewers' visual space and made them feel a part of the work—as Pollock himself did when he made *One.* At the same time, the colors and tones reminded viewers of the natural environment, although without reference to a specific landscape. Because Pollock's work was unfamiliar, it allowed people from different backgrounds to read into it almost anything they wished. Marxists saw the gestural lines as radical signs of social protest; Existentialists related them to Pollock's search for a personal form of expression; others connected them with the artist's western origins and the mythology of cowboys. But they all recognized in the painting's dancing lines and rhythms a radical new art of total spontaneity.

In spite of his fame, Pollock did not prosper financially or emotionally. The work of the "shining new phenomenon in American art," as *Life* referred to him, did not sell very well. The actual market for abstract art—especially in his day—has always been small in America—and after expenses and dealers' commissions the Pollocks had very little left. In addition to a serious lack of money, Pollock experienced a certain amount of critical backlash along with the inevitable pressures of being in the spotlight. *Time,* for example, referred to him as "Jack the Dripper," and even Greenberg, who had been a strong supporter, cooled toward his later work. In the last two years of Pollock's life, his drinking problem became more acute than ever and his artistic production almost stopped entirely. He died at the age of 44 when the car he was driving crashed into some trees not far from his home.

Pollock was an important force in bringing American art out of its cultural isolation and into a position of world leadership, where it has been ever since. Regarding this achievement, a fellow painter once said that Pollock had "broken the ice" for other American abstract artists. Indeed, some believe that Pollock's success inspired and influenced other aspects of the pro-

7-22   Jackson Pollock painting, 1950.

gressive culture of the 1950s—the Beat Generation's poetry, cool jazz, and other forms of fine and popular art—whose emphasis on the artist's personal freedom and improvisation was similar to that of Abstract Expressionism. Pollock's work reflects the modern obsession with one's own inner life. By a leap of insight, he developed the idea of painting as a pure psychological event—supposedly eliminating the gap between the subjective world of the artist's thinking and feeling and the objective world of paint and canvas.

Summary   From Michelangelo to Pollock, we have seen a trend away from religious content or, at least, a progressive modification of that content. Almost all of Michelangelo's subjects were religious; Rembrandt's were both secular and religious; Van Gogh's were nearly all secular—although most had some religious significance. Pollock's art was not religious at all, at least not in the traditional sense.

We have also seen a progressively stronger emphasis on the individual personality. Although Michelangelo's art was intensely emotional—to that extent reflective of his personality—its content had to do with major theological issues, and its emotional qualities were intended to relate to those issues and not to the artist's or anyone else's personality. By the time of Pollock, however, the emotional qualities of the work were not simply reflective of the artist's personality but supposedly a direct result of his subjective state at the time the painting was made.

Considered within their own time periods, the four artists have some things in common. Like all other artists, they started their careers within the available art styles and themes of their time, but unlike most others, they challenged tradition. In each case they were successful, but the measure of their success was not always immediately apparent. Both Michelangelo and Pollock lived to see the impact of their ideas on the art of others. Rembrandt experienced success early in his career only to see his work actually decline in value—its rebirth in popularity coming long after his death. Van Gogh never received recognition from more than a small group during his lifetime.

Finally, all four experienced various crises in their artistic careers and personal lives. Was this an important factor in their art? According to scholar of mythology Joseph Campbell, suffering is revered in nearly all the world's myths and religions as a positive experience leading to significant revelation. He quotes, as an example, this statement by an Eskimo shaman: "Privation and suffering alone can open the mind to all that is hidden in others." In many ways the creative artists are the shamans of our own culture: Witness how the sentiment expressed in the line above echoes those of a poem by Michelangelo:

> Not without fire can any workman mold
> The iron to his preconceived design,
> Nor can the artist without fire refine
> And purify from all its dross the gold.

8

Images of America

It has often been said that art is a reflection of the society that produces it, affected by a particular geography, climate, historical background, set of attitudes, and other factors. In essence, art reflects a place and a people. This chapter concerns a relatively young art that expresses an acute awareness of place and people. Perhaps because most Americans—at one time or another in their family histories—came from someplace else, they seem to be uniquely conscious about where they are and who they are in America. And much of their art has focused on the American continent as a specific place on this planet and the American people as a particular species in the history of human civilization.

Like the American people, American art was an immigrant. And its ambivalent relationship to the art traditions of Europe continued to be a dominant theme in its history. The search for a specific artistic identity, both in form and content, has been a major preoccupation. Images of America, therefore, relate to discovering not only what America is but what American art is. The following examples, spread over approximately a century, reflect a many-sided interpretation of the American experience.

Before the Civil War: Painters of the Land

Throughout the greater part of its history, the growth of American civilization was virtually synonymous with the settlement of its land. The American countryside, therefore, played a central role in establishing the American mentality. Its vastness was seen not only as a physical challenge to the ambitions of the settlers but also as a symbol of the scale of American dreams. Both the land and the state of mind conducive to a tradition of landscape art were present almost from the first days of independence. But in the late 1700s and early 1800s—when Constable was painting the English midlands—no significant landscape painting had yet appeared in America.

Cole Thomas Cole was the first artist to demonstrate the epic qualities of the American landscape. When he started painting, fashionable art consisted of portraits and historical subjects. But Cole preferred to depict landscapes and satisfied this desire by hiking through the Catskill Mountains in New York with a sketchbook. His work soon began to attract the attention of artists and patrons, and by the time he was 28 he had achieved sufficient popularity to secure financial backing for his first of two trips abroad to study European art.

In *The Oxbow* (fig. 8-1), a gnarled tree on a wedge of hill in the left foreground sets off a spacious view on the right, where we see a great bend in the Connecticut River. The leading edge of the storm coming in from the left tends to continue the line of the hillside in an arc that goes off the canvas, further dividing the picture between the left and right—and between dark and light. It is a dramatic re-creation of the lighting that accompanies a summer storm, when some parts of the land are darkened while others remain bathed in light—an alternation that Cole repeated in the highlights on the tree and the cloud shadows of the distant hills. The drama unfolding in the atmosphere adds to the quality of wildness that Cole admired, and that he further emphasized by the unruly underbrush on the hill and the sense of unencumbered distance beyond. European landscape paintings of the time were more "civilized," depicting more serene vegetation and including more familiar reference points to counteract the impression of openness.

This kind of landscape, appropriate to the American sensibility, captured the people's imagination and fostered the American version of Romanticism. Cole expressed in paint what certain writers of New England expressed in words. Among these, philosopher Ralph Waldo Emerson believed that a profound encounter with nature was also a profound religious experience: "Standing on the bare ground—my head bathed by the blithe air . . . the currents of the Universal Being circulate through me; I am part and parcel of God."

Cole enjoyed a major following of east-coast artists who came to be known as the *Hudson River School*. Like Cole, they

8-1   Thomas Cole, *The Oxbow*, 1846. Oil on canvas, 51½″ × 76″.
Metropolitan Museum of Art, New York (Gift of Mrs. Russell Sage, 1908).

were European trained and applied their skills mostly to making heroic images of the wooded hills of New York. But not all good landscape painting was by the Hudson River artists, nor was that part of the country the only area being painted.

Duncanson   Robert S. Duncanson, a black artist who spent most of his life in Ohio, was largely self-taught, but his work reflected the influence of the Hudson River School and expressed a deep reverence for nature. His *Blue Hole, Flood Waters, Little Miami River* (fig. 8-2) is a quiet paradise that emphasizes nature's peace and equilibrium rather than its power and drama. The painting is evidence of Duncanson's interest in the minute details of rocks, foliage, and clouds, and of his ability to re-create them. Yet because of his careful organization of the shapes and the lights and darks, the variety of texture and detail does not overwhelm the

8-2   Robert S. Duncanson, *Blue Hole, Flood Waters, Little Miami River,* 1851. Oil on canvas, 29¼" × 42¼". The Cincinnati Art Museum (Gift of Norbert Heermann).

picture's unity. The basic compositional scheme is that of four triangular shapes—the sky, the lagoon, and the right and left tree masses—all pointing toward the center, located at the far side of the lagoon. On the near side are a few shaded figures who establish the scale of the scene and contrast with the brightly illuminated water—the major focus of the painting.

Bingham   George Caleb Bingham grew up in the frontier state of Missouri where, as a boy, he decided to take up art after meeting a frontier portrait painter. He studied briefly in the East, where he learned how to make monumental figures. But rather than remain there to learn more about painting in the grand manner, he returned to Missouri and adapted the concept of heroically proportioned figures to the representation of the scruffy trappers and raftsmen who became his favorite subjects. The Mississippi River, the setting for many of those subjects, was the dividing line between the East and West and has become a significant part of the myth and legend of America. And Bingham's interpretation of river life played a part in creating the legend.

Watching the Cargo (fig. 8-3) shows three rivermen relaxing on a mudbank of the Mississippi while their barge is stranded on a sandbar in the shadows behind them; a sunlit piece of driftwood, to the right of the men, returns our attention to the foreground and provides some visual balance. The lazy late-afternoon atmosphere, accented by long shadows, expresses a peacefulness more like Duncanson's painting than Cole's. But because of the emphasis on the earthy people, together with

8-3   George Caleb Bingham, *Watching the Cargo,* 1849. Oil on canvas, 26″ × 36″. State Historical Society of Missouri, Columbia, Missouri.

their work-a-day belongings and a faint suggestion of humor, this painting is not nearly as lofty in sentiment as either Duncanson's or Cole's.

Watching the Cargo is a good example of American genre art. In Bingham's era, genre artists were well known for recording America's village and country life in terms of the anecdote—some event considered amusing or sentimental—and Bingham showed a definite preference for the anecdotal. However, some of his paintings, like *Watching the Cargo,* transcend mere recording and remind Americans of the majestic and timeless qualities of their land.

The Hudson River School and genre art flourished in the decades preceding the Civil War, a time of robust optimism when the adventures of industrialization and westward expansion were just getting underway. America was moving away from being the simple, nonmanufacturing utopia of small farmers that Thomas Jefferson had dreamed of. In many ways the spirit of that change is reflected in the works of Cole, Duncanson, and Bingham which, for all their emphasis on the outdoors, do not celebrate American agriculture but the American wilderness—the symbol of freedom and of the potential for economic and social growth.

After the Civil War

In the period after the Civil War, the industrial and territorial expansion set in motion earlier became more pronounced than ever. And in the process, immense fortunes were made as tycoons fought for control of the railroads and the new industries like petroleum and meat-packing. Although the late nineteenth century in America was an age of rampant materialism, the new wealth also demanded culture—or at least the display of it. And culture to the new-rich Americans meant Europe. It was axiomatic that quality would be sought overseas rather than at home, and American millionaires vied with one another to acquire European art and associate themselves with the art of the old world. Needless to say, it was a depressing period for America's artists—many of whom gave up on their own country and settled in Europe.

Sargent

One American artist, John Singer Sargent, enjoyed the best of both the Old and the New Worlds. Like so many nineteenth-century American artists, he had studied in Europe. He had acquired a broad, fluid-line painting style in a Parisian studio at the age of 18, and a few years later traveled to Spain to learn about shadows and luminosity from the works of *Velázquez*. Equally at home in Europe and America, his reputation was international and "European" enough to make him popular in his own land. A good eye, a deft brush, and a taste for elegance were the ideal requirements for a portrait painter of the time, and he was in demand by fashionable people during the period Mark Twain called the Gilded Age.

One of Sargent's best paintings, *The Daughters of Edward D. Boit* (fig. 8-4), is of four girls who appear to have momentarily stopped playing. The signs of nineteenth-century gentility are seen everywhere: in their scrubbed faces, their crisp clothes, the spacious interior, and the furnishings of the room—especially the pair of large oriental vases. Sargent made the scene seem quite casual, not only by his facile painting style and unerring sense of draftsmanship but also by boldly placing one girl off on the left. Yet if we look closely, we see that he offset her weight in the composition by the pull of several things on the right, including the edge of the vase and the light coming from the deep space of the room behind the girls. The shadowy atmosphere that flows around every figure softens their forms and makes the light seem all the more luminous. It is a scene of refinement and grace that skillfully uses some of the stylistic advances of European art without taking the risks; it is also a domesticated art that reflects the values of a particular class of Americans.

Homer

Winslow Homer's art reflects the life-style of a different class of citizens. Homer began his artistic career as a free-lance illustrator for picture magazines, an experience that probably developed his ability to observe contemporary subjects and re-create their moods as well as their appearances. Although he had spent some months in Paris and may have seen the work of the young Impressionists—whose directness of approach and emotional detachment were compatible with his own tendencies—Homer was largely self-taught.

Compare the plain, well-lighted interior of the *The Country School* (fig. 8-5) with the softly-shadowed interior of the Boit mansion. The walls display little more than the patina of wear, their plainness accentuated by the expanse of unvarnished floorboards in the foreground. About the only similarity between Homer's schoolchildren and the Boit children is the naturalness of their appearance and actions. Otherwise the people and setting of *The Country School* are as ordinary and humble as a school lunch.

Plate 17   Fritz Scholder, *Super Indian #2 (with ice cream cone)*, 1971.
Oil on canvas, 7' 6'' x 5'.
Collection Solomon Schechter Day School of Nassau County, New York.

Plate 18   Edouard Manet, *Luncheon on the Grass*, 1863. Oil on canvas, 7' x 8' 10''. Galerie du Jeu de Paume, Paris.

Plate 19 Claude Monet, *La Grenouillère*, 1869. Oil on canvas. 29½″ x 39¼″. The Metropolitan Museum of Art. The H.O. Havermeyer Collection. Bequest of Mrs. H.O. Havermeyer, 1929.

Plate 20 Paul Cézanne, *Still Life with Basket of Apples,* **1890–94. Oil on canvas, 25¾″ x 32″. The Art Institute of Chicago (Helen Birch Bartlett Memorial Collection).**

Plate 21 Paul Gauguin, *The Vision After the Sermon (Jacob Wrestling with the Angel)*, 1888. Oil on canvas, 28¾″ x 36¼″. National Gallery of Scotland, Edinburgh.

Plate 22   Henri Matisse, *Window at Collioure*, 1905. Oil on canvas, 21¾'' x 18⅛''. Private collection.

Plate 23 Max Beckmann, *Departure*, 1932–33. Triptych, oil on canvas, center panel 84¾″ x 45⅜″, side panels each 84¾″ x 39¼″. Collection, The Museum of Modern Art, New York. Given anonymously.

Plate 24   Piet Mondrian, *Composition*, 1929. Oil on canvas, 17¾'' x 17¾''.
Collection, The Solomon R. Guggenheim Museum, New York.
Gift of Katherine S. Dreier Estate.

8-4 John Singer Sargent, *The Daughters of Edward D. Boit*, 1882. Oil on canvas, 87⅝" × 87⅝". Museum of Fine Arts, Boston.

If we sense any nostalgia in Homer's work, it is not because of the artist's treatment of the subject—which lacks any trace of sentimentality—but because of our own conceptions (or misconceptions) about an America that existed a century ago. In its day, the apparent lack of charm in this and others of Homer's paintings troubled his critics. Henry James, who was familiar with European art, once commented that Homer "cares not a jot for such fantastic hair-splitting as the distinction between beauty and ugliness" and complained about "his barren plank fences . . . freckled, straight-haired Yankee urchins . . . flat-

8-5   Winslow Homer, *The Country School,* 1871. Oil on canvas, 21⅜" ×
38⅜". The St. Louis Art Museum.

breasted maidens. . . . " Yet to the general public, it was the
simple factualism and the lack of high-flown subjects that made
Homer's pictures appealing. Apparently the American people
sensed that he portrayed them honestly from *their* point of view.

**The Ash Can
Artists**

The story of the great westward movement tends to dominate
people's thinking about America in the late 1800s, crowding out
another story that is even more important—the growth of
American cities and the steady migration of people from rural to
urban areas. By 1890, five urban areas had populations of one
million or more, and 30 percent of all Americans were city-
dwellers. The modern city, furthermore, was responsible for a
new social phenomenon—the inner-city slum. In a preindustrial
city, the elite lived in the center while the poor lived on the
unprotected fringes; in a postindustrial city, the elite fled to the
relative cleanliness of the edges, leaving the center to the poor.

Sloan

It was not until the first decades of the twentieth century that
artists like John Sloan began to observe and depict the life of the

8-6   John Sloan, *McSorley's Bar*, 1912. Oil on canvas, 26″ × 32″.
Detroit Institute of the Arts (gift of The Founders Society).

inner city. The shadowy atmosphere of *McSorley's Bar* (fig. 8-6) is something like that of Sargent's picture, but here the interior is a smoke-filled tavern—a murky refuge from the noisy street rather than a spacious Victorian parlor. Sloan was a member of a group that specialized in the portrayal of the heretofore ignored urban lower classes. And this group's work was so offensive to gallery goers that it came to be known as the *Ash Can School*.

In terms of style, however, the Ash Can School's rebellion was mild—for these artists painted in ways that the more advanced painters in Europe had already rejected. Sloan's broad brushwork, although earthier and blunter, is not essentially different from Sargent's. His simplified but accurate observation of human anatomy was influenced by his earlier career of illustrating for a newspaper—a fact that may also have accounted for his interest in working-class themes. When he settled in New York in 1904, he was impressed by the throbbing street life of the city.

His portrayals of beach scenes, grubby buildings, broken fences, and clotheslines were extremely provocative in the years before World War I, but the city and its slums have become such a commonplace experience that these subjects no longer shock.

Bellows   George Bellows, although not a member of the original group, was closely associated with the Ash Can School. Also a former newspaper illustrator, Bellows's style was even more exaggerated than Sloan's. In *Stag at Sharkey's* (fig. 8-7), he used long, fluid strokes to render the bodies and forceful movements of the boxers. And, somewhat in the manner of both Sargent and Sloan, he emphasized the central figures by highlighting them against a shadowy background. The overstated postures of the fighters approach caricature, and the ugly audience of cigar-chomping fans surrounding the ring would probably make the spectators at a contest of Roman gladiators seem genial by comparison.

8-7   George Bellows, *Stag at Sharkey's,* 1907. Oil on canvas, 36¼″ × 48¼″. Cleveland Museum of Art (Hinman B. Hurlbut Collection).

The people in Sloan's and Bellows's paintings are in many ways the same working-class Americans celebrated by Bingham and Homer a few decades earlier—the principal difference being that they live in the city instead of the country.

Early Modernists

After World War I, some American painters moved in the direction of abstraction. This was partly due to the influence of styles that had begun to develop in Europe, for a large colony of expatriate American painters and writers had sprung up in Paris—and there was a great deal of communication between the artists of that city and New York. Other forms of abstraction developed independently, in large part inspired, it appears, by a strong desire to find a fresh way to approach American subject matter.

O'Keeffe

The work of Georgia O'Keeffe is one example of the new approaches. The highly personal form of abstraction she developed was derived more from an interpretation of nature than from any particular twentieth-century school of abstract art. Her work aimed at simplification, a tendency that can also be seen in the paintings of Sloan and Bellows. But O'Keeffe's brushwork is much more refined and her forms are far less detailed. These factors made it possible for her to create powerful and evocative paintings out of subjects as banal as flowers. By taking a single blossom and enlarging it until the shapes filled an entire canvas, she turned the sensual curves and colors into an almost erotic display. O'Keeffe liked living and working in the American Southwest because the clean, austere forms of the landscape lent themselves to her style. In *Black Cross, New Mexico* (fig. 8-8), we see the cool, clear, economical approach that characterizes all her work. Combining abstraction with realism, she reduced the sand dunes in the background to almost geometric forms, yet modeled them to appear three-dimensional. The portion of black cross in the foreground is so smooth that it looks like it might be carved from a hard stone. Much of the excitement of O'Keeffe's work lies in these tensions between the real and the abstract, nature and the spirit. The abstract element is due not so much to distortion as to a stark revelation of the latent harmony in nature—an art that strongly implies a form of nature worship. In this sense, artists like O'Keeffe belong to the American tradition that began with Cole.

8-8   Georgia O'Keeffe, *Black Cross, New Mexico,* 1929. Oil on canvas, 36″ × 30″. The Art Institute of Chicago (Special Picture Fund). Copyright Georgia O'Keeffe.

Stella   Joseph Stella found lyricism in the city rather than in nature. He had come under the influence of the Italian Futurists, whose principal stylistic device was to break up their subjects and rebuild them into an overall harmony of planes and surfaces. Their objective was to express the dynamism of the modern world. Stella found their approach well-suited to his enthusiasm for the subject matter of New York. Unlike the Ash Can artists, Stella was interested in portraying the city's technological aspects rather than its sociological aspects—the new architecture, engineering, and methods of travel and communication that were becoming part of modern urban living.

In *Skyscrapers* (fig. 8-9), the planes of city forms have a geo-

8-9
Joseph Stella, *Skyscrapers*, 1920–22. Oil on canvas, 54″ × 99¾″. Collection of the Newark Museum (Purchase 1937, Felix Fuld Bequest).

metric precision similar to that of the shaded volumes of O'Keeffe's natural forms. Despite the abstraction, we can still make out familiar features of the city—skyscraper towers, bridges, cables, and smokestacks. Though less specific, other features are suggestive of the city, such as the radiating lines that could be searchlight beams and the numerous hollows that might represent the city's many cavernous alleyways and subway tunnels. We can almost hear the noise of buses and cabs and the wails of sirens. To many people these things spell confusion and chaos; the very thought of the city inspires indigestion and frayed nerves. But to Stella it was all poetry—a kaleidoscopic harmony of exciting impressions. His extravagant statements reflected the vision of his paintings: "The steel had leaped to hyperbolic altitudes and expanded to vast latitudes . . . " His faith in the man-made world was comparable to the Romantic's faith in the natural world; he intended his art to "affirm and exalt the joyful daring endeavor of the American civilization."

Critical Views

Not all the artists who worked in the period between the two world wars shared the Modernists' enthusiasm for abstraction. During the twenties and thirties many artists began to stress American subject matter in more traditional styles. Regionalists, like Thomas Hart Benton, turned to an idealized version of rural America that praised the virtues of the simple life. Others focused instead on the problems of urban life, such as unemployment, the decay of neighborhoods, and the growing demoralization of the average citizen.

Hopper

Edward Hopper had more than a casual knowledge of the work of the Ash Can School, having studied with Robert Henri—a leading teacher of the time—who was to become one of the more important members of that group. Because he had spent some time in Europe at the beginning of the century, Hopper also had some knowledge of the newer trends. But he remained an original artist who rejected both the excesses of the Parisian avant-garde and the New Yorkers' tendency to sentimentalize their subjects. Hopper's America, epitomized in *House by the Railroad* (colorplate 16), is immobile and remote rather than vital and lusty.

Hopper was a skillful pictorial composer, not because he mastered fixed principles of design but because he precisely arranged a limited selection of details to evoke a great amount of content. In *House by the Railroad*, just enough detail is used to depict an old house in a forlorn environment. The reflected light and its complementary shadows reveal the houses's volumes but also help to emphasize its starkness. The railroad track and its roadbed brutally cut off the bottom of the house, while the empty sky completes the feeling of isolation and loneliness. Hopper seems to suggest that the alienation of neighborhoods (and the people in them) is brought about by railroads, empty lots, thoroughfares, or any number of things to which declining areas of the city are susceptible. In this forbidding context, human occupation is suggested only by the randomness of the window shades. As Hopper's biographer Lloyd Goodrich pointed out, "Seldom has an inanimate object expressed such penetrating melancholy as *House by the Railroad*."

The general content of *Nighthawks* (fig. 8-10) is more immediately apparent: a few people in a lonely cafe on a street isolated by the night. But because of Hopper's economy of means and studied arrangement, every detail—a triangle of reflected light in an upstairs window, a cash register in the window below, a snap-brim hat, a row of bar stools, a door to the

8-10   Edward Hopper, *Nighthawks,* 1942. Oil on canvas, 33⅛" × 60⅛". The Art Institute of Chicago (Friends of American Art Collection).

kitchen—seems to have its own mysterious private meaning, just as these lonely people seem to be separated by their private worlds.

Lawrence   *Tombstones* by Jacob Lawrence, painted in the same year as Hopper's *Nighthawks,* makes a much more explicit criticism of America (fig. 8-11). If we were to regard Hopper as a painter of the dream that failed, Lawrence would have to be the painter of the dream that never began. His social comments were made all the sharper by his hard-edged, caricature-like images and brightly colored shapes. *Tombstones* records a group of people in front of an apartment building that houses a tombstone shop on its

8-11
Jacob Lawrence,
Tombstones, 1942. Gouache on paper, 28¾″ × 20½″.
Collection of the Whitney Museum of American Art, New York.

ground floor. The people are of all ages, from an infant in a mother's arms to an old man slowly climbing the steps. The collection of tombstones, like a small cemetery, not only suggests the end of a life cycle (implied in this range of ages) but also the eventual death of the neighborhood.

The simplified, schematic character of Lawrence's forms led art historian David Driskell to identify his work as "neo-primitive." But this does not mean that Lawrence, who studied art in New York and worked in the Federal Arts Project, was not a sophisticated artist. On the contrary, he intentionally adopted some of the characteristics of folk art and comic strips in order to endow his own art with a greater power and directness. Other critics have related Lawrence's bold patterns and intense, flat colors to similar tendencies in African art and modern European art. But Lawrence's images and compositions are individual, and his work has a definite message: It makes statements about the life of a particular group of people. It is realistic art, not in the optical sense of being true to outward appearances but in the sense of seizing, by means of exaggeration and caricature, the essence of what life is like under dehumanizing circumstances. As Driskell said of Lawrence, "His work is tough, urbane, unsentimental."

Contemporary Viewpoints

By the 1950s, the avant-garde of New York had become deeply involved in abstract painting, but this was not the only important movement in America at the time. A number of artists in the San Francisco Bay Area had experimented with totally abstract styles and then returned to basing their paintings on the human figure.

Diebenkorn

Richard Diebenkorn was one of the members of this group, and perhaps the most successful in applying the dynamic brushwork and bold forms of the prevailing abstract style to the subject matter of everyday life. In *Man and Woman in a Large Room* (fig. 8-12), we can easily recognize the forms of two people and detect a crude perspective in the shape that appears to be a carpet and in the lines of the wall and door on the right. The static qualities of the scene are reminiscent of the world that Edward Hopper painted; indeed Diebenkorn's man and woman seem every bit as isolated and pathetic as the nighthawks. Yet the sense of tragedy is offset by the emotional qualities of the

8-12   Richard Diebenkorn, *Man and Woman in a Large Room*, 1957.
Oil on canvas, 71″ × 63″. The Hirshhorn Museum and Sculpture Garden,
Smithsonian Institution, Washington, D.C.

color and the broadly conceived composition—carryovers from his earlier abstract style. Beyond the open door, a mere crack in the right-hand wall, we see a few daubs of warm, glowing color— like a glimpse of the California countryside. Ironically, the sliver of the California dream only serves to emphasize the element of disenchantment that dominates the room.

Goings   A generation later the art of northern California had changed radically. Not only was the rebellion against abstraction complete, it had been carried a step beyond: The Bay Area school of the seventies was one of photographically precise realism. The

8-13   Ralph Goings, *Kentucky Fried Chicken*, 1973. Oil on canvas, 48″ × 68″. Private collection.

emotional subjectivity of works like Diebenkorn's had been replaced with the scrupulous objectivity of artists like Ralph Goings.

Kentucky Fried Chicken (fig. 8-13) shares certain elements with the Diebenkorn painting and, for that matter, with those of Hopper—but it does not share the spirit of any of them. Goings was concerned entirely with painting problems—the reflections of light on surfaces, the varying degrees of color on a wall seen through one, three, or five windows—and made no judgments on his subject matter. No meaning was attributed to the Colonel's roost or the snack bar other than that which is visible to the eye. They are not presented to us as friendly gathering places or tragic refuges but as simple facts of the California landscape. But it is easy to read things into those simple facts. Even though Goings was concerned with painting problems, his consistent choice of such subject matter implied an interpretation. Just as Cole and the Hudson River painters recorded the epic qualities of the American landscape, Goings and other realists like him recorded the spirit-numbing banality that had spread across the continent.

Conclusions   One of the most intriguing things about American art is that it has so often been torn between polar alternatives. In the nineteenth and early twentieth centuries, there was constant disagreement about whether the emphasis in our native art should be on the word *native* or the word *art*. Nearly everyone tried to reconcile the two, but the Europeans were so much more advanced that it was impossible for Americans to be innovative in anything other than subject matter. Only after World War II did they catch up with the masters of European art—and, a short time later, surpass them. By the early 1960s their position was so secure that the next important movement, Pop Art, carried an unmistakably American stamp in style as well as subject matter.

Scholder   But America's art has also been subject to other divisions, those that are typical of all art—the lyrical versus the dramatic, a love of nature set against a preference for the diversions of the city, the subjectivity of the emotions contrasting with the belief that art should be an objective record—and a few others all its own. The paintings of Fritz Scholder often capture some of this distinctly American mood, for he is both a successful contemporary American artist and an Indian. Though he was originally determined not to become known as an ethnic painter, he eventually began to incorporate Indian elements into his work. He now uses Indian themes and content almost exclusively, believing that a marriage of traditional subject matter with the contemporary idiom will provide a truer statement of the Indian (fig. 8-14). The figure in Scholder's *Super Indian #2 (with ice-cream cone)* is assertively large, set in the middle of the canvas, painted in a dark brooding brown, and surrounded by rich colors (colorplate 17). He stares out at us from deep inside this image of himself. Like the people in the Diebenkorn, the Hopper, and even the Lawrence pictures, he too is a tragic figure—but for different reasons. He is dressed in a ceremonial costume that identifies him with the folkways of an all-but-obliterated culture; yet he holds an ice-cream cone, a folk object of the culture that overwhelmed his. Like the often-contradictory art and history of America, the painting mingles the past and present, pathos and humor, and radically different ways of life.

8-14   Fritz Scholder, *Indian #16*, 1967. Oil on canvas, 71″ × 71″. Collection
Mr. and Mrs. Robert E. Herzstein, Washington, D.C.

III HISTORICAL CONTEXT

The first two parts of this book consider art's relationship to perception and to the expression of important themes; Part III examines art as a phenomenon in itself, concentrating on the ways it exists in history. By looking at some of the major artworks of the past in their order of appearance, we can begin to discern a definite pattern—almost as if we were watching a time-lapse movie of a blossoming flower. This overall pattern is sometimes more revealing than the individual works themselves. Yet because art is a product of human behavior, the process of change and the directions it takes are neither foreordained nor inevitable. Art is subject to the will and actions of individual artists as well as to the circumstances of history. In this section we first see how art-historical change relates to major styles and to individual artists. Then we examine a specific period of art history in detail.

The period examined is the modern one—that is to say, the long sequence of images and ideas that has developed during the past hundred years or so. Modern art did not begin with a sudden change; it had complex roots that extended back centuries. Underlying it were not only the attitudes and technical discoveries of many artists but also such things as the invention of photography, scientific discoveries about the nature of light, and the great social upheavals that grew out of the rise of democratic forms of government. Conditions have changed greatly since then; so, of course, has art. It is by studying these changes in their historical context that we are able to understand something of the how and why of contemporary art.

9
Art and Change

A painting or sculpture can be described as existing in time as well as space—not the "real" time of music or poetry but the "abstract" time of history. That is to say, each object of art can be thought of as an event that marks a specific point in time and offers some clue to understanding the character of that time. As you recall from Chapter 7, Michelangelo's *Last Judgment* (fig. 7-5) communicates something of the agony of the Reformation and Counter-Reformation struggles without making any direct reference to the politics of the period. And Edward Hopper's *House by the Railroad* (colorplate 16) expresses something of the melancholy and social isolation of twentieth-century life without containing a single human being.

Another effect of time on an object, art or otherwise, is that of physical wear and aging. In this sense every object is a continual event, undergoing constant but not necessarily visible change. And finally, in a dynamic society like ours, the art object also undergoes a change in people's perceptions. What seemed to be stylish a few years ago now seems old-fashioned; what seemed outlandish now seems pleasing. New designs are created that surpass others and new ideas emerge to replace the old—a new context evolves that is sometimes alien to an old object or sometimes helps to make it more acceptable. Every new and different object forces us to see other things in a slightly different way; we might say it changes the appearance of those objects that came before.

Prime Objects

In 1934, a revolutionary car called the Chrysler Airflow (fig. 9-1) was exhibited for the first time. A critic wrote that it looked strange at first but that after a while " . . . you are quite likely to come around to the viewpoint that these cars look right and that conventional cars look wrong."

The Chrysler Airflow

As it turned out, the Airflow sold badly; after three years of production, it was discontinued. The Airflow was not a bad car in the engineering sense; it had demonstrated remarkable capabilities in road tests. But apparently the buying public rejected it on the basis of its looks.

Before we discount the critic's prediction, we should look at the history of automotive design during and just following the appearance of the Airflow. A Chrysler product, the Plymouth (fig. 9-2), was typical of the year 1934. The rear seat was directly over the rear wheels and the engine was situated behind the front axle. Although showing some evidence of modern "sculptured" styling, its basic contours were still square—and the fenders, body panels, headlamps, and spare tires were separately attached. On the other hand, in the Airflow the rear seat had been moved ahead and the engine was placed over the front

9-1   The 1934 Chrysler Airflow.

9-2
The 1934 Plymouth.

9-3
(above) The 1939 Plymouth.
(left) The 1936 Plymouth.

axle. An "aerodynamic" frame gave the car a unique shape, while the continuous body sheath gave it the appearance of a single organic unit. When we look at the automotive industry *after* 1934, we find that the Airflow's radical styling was gradually incorporated into the design of other cars throughout the rest of the decade. Again, the Plymouth is typical (fig. 9-3). In the 1936 version, the rear seat and engine were moved forward; the slanted windshield and the more aerodynamic body line resemble the 1934 Airflow more than they do the 1934 Plymouth. In the 1939 model, the headlamps and grill were finally blended into the body shape. Plymouth, along with other American cars, did maintain the long, straight hood and vertical front end—an accent that probably symbolized power to the American buyer. Despite this and a few other minor modifications, the entire automobile industry turned out products that were essentially descendants of the 1934 Airflow. One direct descendant is still around today: the German Volkswagen. Its basic lines are almost identical to those of the two-door Airflow—even the sloped front end and round fenders (fig. 9-4).

9-4
The 1963 Volkswagen and the 1934 Chrysler Airflow.

The Shape of Time

Relative time and formal change are the subject of art historian George Kubler's book *The Shape of Time*, which provides a useful scheme for considering artworks and artifacts in their historical context. His system not only gives us some insight into why some works are accorded more recognition than others but also explains the mechanisms of stylistic evolution.

The basic ingredient of Kubler's theory of change is a concept of relative time as opposed to absolute (calendar) time. In other words, saying that the Airflow came out in A.D. 1934 tells us very little by itself. What we need to know is when this car made its appearance in relation to other models of passenger cars. This leads us to his concept of *formal sequences:* "Every important work of art can be regarded both as a historical event and as a hard-won solution to some problem." A radical change in the shape of a significant art object (or an artifact such as a car) is usually a purposeful solution within a sequence of designs. The solution is related to those that came before and, if it is successful, will be connected with solutions that follow. Within a sequence of linked solutions there are *prime objects* and *replications.* Prime objects are successful major inventions; they affect certain traits of all the objects that follow them in such a way that these traits cannot be traced directly to any of the objects that came before them. Replications, on the other hand, are merely simple variations on the theme created by the previous prime objects. (In the case of mass-produced objects, a model may have thousands of identical "editions," but this is not what is meant by replications in this usage.) In Kubler's scheme, the Airflow deserves the label *prime object*; the Plymouths of the late 1930s were its replications. If we were to look at a large enough span of automobile history to discover the next prime object (or the one just prior to the Airflow), we might see an example of a formal sequence or series of design solutions that significantly modified the shape of the car.

The series of Greek sculptures of nude youths in Chapter 6 gives us a fair idea of the steps taken by the Greeks over nearly 200 years in modifying the sculptural treatment of the human figure. Their architecture paralleled this process during the same period with the steady refinement of the Doric order, a system of architectural proportions that governed the building of temples. Compare the Temple of Hera (fig. 9-5) built by Greek colonists at Paestum, Italy with the famous Parthenon at Athens (fig. 4-3). They differ—even though both have basically the

9-5   Temple of Hera, Paestum, Italy, *c.* 460 B.C.

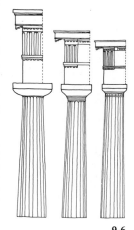

9-6
Changes in Doric-order proportions.

same kinds of columns, decorative motifs, and overall shape. The Paestum temple represents an earlier stage of development. Though smaller than the Parthenon, it looks much heavier. This is because of its proportions: The columns are stockier; there is less space between the columns; and the entablature—the part of the building supported by the columns—is larger. The diagram (fig. 9-6) shows the stages of evolution in the silhouette of the column and the entablature; it is a simple matter to perceive the changes that took place in the proportions of each part and between related parts. (The Parthenon, the final stage in the development of the Doric order, is represented by the columnar silhouette on the right.)

Unlike the development of the Airflow, the impulse to change the Doric order was not largely caused by the need for engineering improvements. Nor was it caused, as in Greek sculpture, by new discoveries about the subject. The motivation seems to have been almost entirely aesthetic. One thing should be noted: The 460 B.C. Temple of Hera is not really a prime object; the Archaic temple, the first to exhibit these traits, is no longer standing. Therefore, a replica has to represent this phase for our purposes.

In recent art history, the problem is not that of prime objects disappearing but of being able to recognize them at all in the profusion of artistic developments. The old adage of not being able to see the forest for the trees applies here; it is difficult for us to discern the broad outline of an artistic sequence in our own time simply because there are so many different objects and ideas.

The Modern Movement

Over a century ago a series of major changes began to take place in Western art. Many historians feel that the series began with a single work of art—one of those prime objects of which Kubler spoke—and that the revolution it started is still occurring in our own day.

The early stages of the revolution were directed against the art of the French Academy, of which Thomas Couture's *Romans of the Decadence* (fig. 9-7) is a good example. A jaded style of realistic painting that illustrated lofty moral themes in imaginary historical settings was surely out of touch with life and therefore ripe to be overthrown. But in the long run, the modern movement did much more than overturn the French Academy; it vir-

9-7 Thomas Couture, *Romans of the Decadence*, 1847. Oil on canvas,
15'1" × 25'4". Louvre, Paris.

tually annulled one of the most fundamental premises of Western art since the Renaissance—that a picture was supposed to imitate visual reality.

This was not the only issue of the modern movement. New possibilities for content and media were also investigated. But in the last part of the nineteenth century and the early part of the twentieth, the more advanced painters began to move away from the realistic treatment of subject matter toward an art in which the major focus was on structure—lines, shapes, and colors—and its capacity for conveying an aesthetic meaning independent of a recognizable scene.

Manet Thirty-one-year-old Édouard Manet, a Parisian painter (former student of Thomas Couture), submitted his *Luncheon on the Grass* (colorplate 18) for exhibition in the Paris Salon of 1863. Held annually, these Salons were the principal artistic events of nineteenth-century France; more than just a marketplace for artworks, they were the arena for establishing reputations and careers. (In this respect they resembled the American institution of the Academy Awards.) To show in one was a necessity; to

9-8   Giorgione, *Pastoral Concert,* 1510. Oil on canvas, 43" × 54". Louvre, Paris.

receive a prize or favorable public recognition was extremely advantageous.

Manet's painting was turned down. But the Salon turned down so many works that year that the government was prevailed upon to open another section for a parallel exhibition of rejected works—called, appropriately, the *"Salon des Refusés."* There, Manet's work was in a position to be noticed by the public—and it was. It received more attention than the works of either show, most of it negative. *Luncheon on the Grass* scandalized both the critics and the public.

Today it is somewhat difficult to understand why *Luncheon on the Grass* caused such a fuss. After all, nudes in art were quite acceptable to Couture's public. Moreover, the painting is reminiscent of and directly based on a distinguished sixteenth-century painting in the Louvre, *Pastoral Concert* by Giorgione, which also shows two naked women in the company of two clothed men in an outdoor setting (fig. 9-8). However, Manet's painting is neither a sermon on Roman decadence nor a classical fable. The figures in his painting are not Greek goddesses romping about a pictorial, fairytale scene with Venetian troubadours, but two young women—one clothed and wading in a pond, the other completely naked—in a contemporary picnic setting, accompanied by two young men dressed in contemporary clothing. Such behavior was considered extremely indecent; therefore the painting itself was looked upon as indecent. But perhaps what shocked the public most was that the naked woman shamelessly stared (or worse, smiled) directly at the viewer.

Manet's painting also upset viewers because it ignored the basic rules of composition to which they were accustomed. Great art meant the kind of grouping seen in *Romans of the Decadence*, where the artist took care to pose each character, to set off the central group, and to arrange everything so a viewer would not miss the point. The scenery, the costumes, and the props are all in place (one vase has been tipped over to suggest rowdiness). MGM in the thirties could not have done any better. Manet, on the other hand, presented a casual scene without heroic gestures or a contrived composition.

But equally controversial—and ultimately more important to the future of art—were Manet's methods of painting. *Luncheon on the Grass* does not strike us today as unusually colorful, but for a painting of 1863 it was. Ordinarily, bright hues—such as we see in the clump of clothing and basket of fruit—were not placed side by side without gradations or intermediate hues. Manet also took liberties with the lighting and the time-honored method of chiaroscuro, flattening out the forms of things, especially the nude, that people were accustomed to seeing as soft and sculptural.

Olympia (fig. 9-9) demonstrates Manet's radicalism even more vividly. Although it was also based on an established theme used in many classic paintings—in this case Titian's *Venus of Urbino* (fig. 6-12)—Manet's variation was a clearly provocative one because of its modern setting that suggests the reclining woman is a prostitute and not a goddess of love. Here again Manet discarded the subtle gradations of light and dark that indicate the roundness of forms, and flattened out the figures. He also reduced the amount of detail, indicating the forms of bedsheets and flowers with a minimum of brushstrokes. Commenting on this reduction, another artist complained that Manet's paintings looked like playing cards; a critic compared the woman's body to a corpse. Again, the protest probably stemmed more from the picture's realism than from the purported lack of realism. The woman's pose and facial expression—

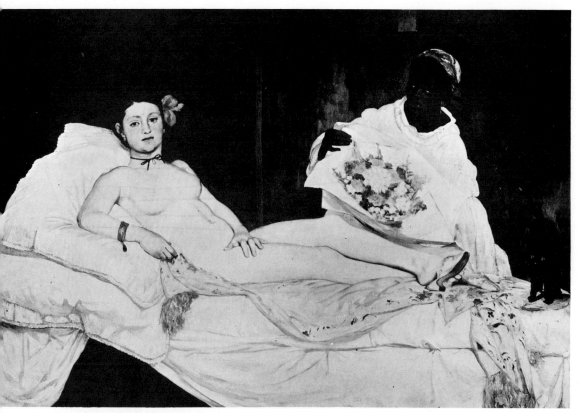

9-9 Édouard Manet, *Olympia*, 1863. Oil on canvas, 51¼″ × 74¾″. Louvre, Paris.

a subtle mixture of sex, detachment, and defiance—were, if anything, too lifelike for the time. Further, the lack of detail and traditional shading enhances the naturalism rather than detracting from it. Manet was well aware of the discrepancies between art and life, especially between the art establishment of his day and modern life as he perceived it.

Monet and the Impressionists   Another young Parisian artist, Claude Monet—almost the namesake of Manet—was for a time his close associate. Like Manet, Monet favored contemporary subjects, particularly the urban middle classes (though without the prostitutes). He also challenged established traditions of color, chiaroscuro, and composition. Indeed, Monet's early work was similar to Manet's, sharing the traits of flatness, simplification, and directness of approach. But Monet was to go far beyond Manet in developing an original style of art. _La Grenouillere_ (colorplate 19), a scene of city dwellers enjoying an afternoon on a lake, is a case in point. The appearance of rippling water is startlingly real; a closer look reveals that Monet constructed the picture out of nothing more than bright daubs of paint—not a single ripple or object has been "drawn" in the conventional sense.

In the 1870s Monet became the central figure of a small group of artists who eventually adopted the name _Impressionism_ for their style, a term invented by a journalist who wished to deride their work. Other members included Edgar Degas (fig. 3-5), Berthe Morisot, Camille Pissarro, Auguste Renoir, Alfred Sisley, and the American expatriate Mary Cassatt. Like Monet, they had been influenced by the colors and forms of Manet's paintings and shared a taste for contemporary subject matter— especially the life of upper-class Parisians who possessed the leisure and the means to enjoy horseraces, regattas, and week-end outings. All the signs of membership in this class are present in Mary Cassatt's _The Cup of Tea_, a painting of the artist's sister wearing a pink costume and sitting in a silk-covered armchair in front of white hyacinths (fig. 9-10). The affluence and tastefulness of the setting are reflected in the casual pose of the young woman and in the relaxed way in which she holds the saucer and cup in her gloved hands. These qualities are also reflected in the confident manner with which Cassatt painted the scene. The loose and spontaneous brushwork not only helps us admire the artist's facile style but flawlessly captures the appearance and mood of the subject.

The Impressionists preferred outdoor subjects in and around the city of Paris—painting scenes "on location" to capture their vitality and freshness. To the Impressionists, the whole world seemed to be a sunlit park. Yet their works are often impersonal—as detached as the expressions on the faces of Manet's and Cassatt's women—and notably lacking in romanticism (in that they do not emphasize the heroic and stately qualities of their subjects). If there is a romantic note at all, it is to be found in the daylight that was the glory of their paintings.

The Impressionists' methods of applying paint—often with short strokes and bits of color—were indirectly influenced by the broken color and flickering effects found in the landscapes of Constable (colorplate 9). Their preference for flat simplified planes, high points of view, and abrupt cropping of foreground objects is traceable directly to their fascination with Japanese prints—popular in the Paris art world of the late nineteenth

9-10
Mary Cassatt, *The Cup of Tea,*
1879. Oil on canvas,
36⅜″ × 25¾″.
The Metropolitan Museum
of Art (anonymous gift).

century (fig. 7-13). But their overriding obsession was with the phenomena of the world of vision—the raw materials of light and color—and the search for their equivalents in oil paint. Sometimes this led to an almost total neglect of the underlying physical structure of things. Monet, more systematically than any of the others, pursued a study of the effects of light by selecting a particular subject—it did not matter whether it was a haystack or a Gothic cathedral (fig. 9-11)—and painting it numerous times under differing light conditions. Carried to this extreme, color in his paintings became detached from the objects represented, came to have a life of its own, and suggested the possibility of an abstract art of colors, textures, and shapes that did not necessarily resemble those of the everyday world. Ironically, the Impressionists' contributions to realistic painting actually helped lead art away from realism.

9-11 Claude Monet, *Rouen Cathedral, Sunset*, 1894. Oil on canvas, 39½″ × 25¾″. Museum of Fine Arts, Boston (Juliana Cheney Edwards Collection. Bequest of Hannah Marcy Edwards in memory of her mother).

The Birth of the Avant-Garde

There was still another legacy that Manet passed on to later generations. The furor over *Luncheon on the Grass,* rather than repelling other artists, attracted many to Manet's way of thinking. The scandal itself helped bring about Manet's leadership among the more advanced young painters whose works were also attacked because of their unorthodox styles. If it did anything, ostracism served to encourage them; beginning in 1874, the Impressionists had the audacity to sponsor their own series of public exhibitions.

By the 1890s, the Impressionists had obtained the acceptance and acclaim of the official art world that had spurned their work earlier. But the lag in recognition and the temporary hostility between the artists and their public is a predicament that has continued to exist in the art world to the present day. Since the late nineteenth century, there has always been an *avant-garde*—a small number of artists whose understanding of art is more advanced than that of their contemporaries and who are for that reason perceived by the art establishment and general public to be nonconformist and experimental.

Rodin

One artist who especially exemplified the independent spirit of the times was Auguste Rodin, a sculptor the same age as Monet. While Rodin received enthusiastic support from the avant-garde painters, he also succeeded in gaining recognition from the general public. At the time academic sculpture was, if anything, in a lower state than academic painting, and the artistic and spiritual vacuum being filled by the bold works of young Rodin was appreciated even by some members of the regular art establishment.

However, Rodin's unusual ideas and style were not always greeted with wholehearted acceptance. His first major public monument—begun in 1884 for the city of Calais—engulfed him in a decade of controversy. The purpose of the monument was to honor the fourteenth-century heroes of Calais who offered to sacrifice their lives to the English army to save the entire city from destruction. Rodin elected to depict all six men at the moment each made the decision to sacrifice himself. However, the sponsors objected to his plans, preferring a more traditional monument with a statue of a single heroic figure to symbolize all six. But Rodin refused to compromise, and for a while the sponsors went along. However, when they saw the preparatory models for the six figures they objected once again, this time to the style. Rodin's roughly finished, extremely emotionalized figures bore none of the marks of conventional sculpture—which at that time were noble gestures, carefully planned proportions, and highly polished surfaces. Yet, despite the objections and other problems that arose, Rodin stuck to his original idea. *The Burghers of Calais* (fig. 9-12) was finally installed in the city in 1895.

The complex textures of Rodin's bronze are reminiscent of Monet's broken colors and reflect Rodin's interest in the Impressionists' methods. The rough surfaces affect the play of light, sometimes giving the figures the appearance of movement. Often when a Rodin sculpture—such as *The Age of Bronze* (fig. 6-8)—first received notice, critics accused him of casting from life, so suspicious were they of the vibrant modeling of the surfaces. The right kind of lighting can imbue a Rodin with an uncanny degree of life; on the other hand, the busy texture, like the many daubs in Monet's painting, can dissolve the form to such an extent that one becomes conscious only of its glittering abstract surface.

But the gravity of the subject matter and the heavy drama of Rodin's *Burghers* have little in common with the emotional de-

9-12 Auguste Rodin, *The Burghers of Calais*, 1884–86. Bronze, approx. 82″ × 94″ × 75″. Musée Rodin, Paris.

tachment of most Impressionist painting. The heroic sacrifice of these historical figures is a world away from the sun-filled, passive landscapes of Impressionism. It was to be the emotionalism of Rodin's works—not their Impressionistic tendencies—that would have the greatest influence on early twentieth-century sculpture.

Cézanne   By the late 1880s, when Impressionism was on the verge of its popular triumph, the avant-garde had already passed into the hands of new artists. Three of these—Cézanne, Van Gogh, and Gauguin—deserve special attention. While all three had been associated to a greater or lesser degree with the Impressionist movement, each broke away to pursue his own separate artistic goals. In different ways all three began to renounce pictorial reality. Collectively these three are often referred to as *Post-Impressionists* because their individual styles crystallized later than Impressionism's and their work was a more advanced phase of the modern movement. But these men and their work were so different from one another that Post-Impressionism, unlike Impressionism, never really amounted to a single movement.

Paul Cézanne—whose art was among the most influential in the modern movement—hardly resembled the self-assertive hero-artist of the avant-garde. Unlike Manet or Rodin, during his most productive years as an artist he was a conservative and serious provincial who attended early mass and spent the rest of the day at work on his paintings. But even though he was isolated from the activities of Paris, Cézanne almost rewrote the rules of painting.

The key to these rules had to do with a new translation of reality. Artists before Cézanne, including the Impressionists, generally attempted in one way or another to imitate the appearances of nature. Though Cézanne did not disregard appearances entirely, he substantially altered them in the process of painting—which to him was a difficult, methodical labor of penetrating the essence of a subject. Above all he wanted to capture the subject's inherent solidity. He did this for each apple in *Still Life with Basket of Apples* (colorplate 20) by juxtaposing distinct hues rather than shading with intermediate values. This de-emphasis of chiaroscuro was, of course, started by Manet and continued by the Impressionists, but they de-emphasized the solidity of objects in order to capture fleeting effects of reflected sunlight. This would not do for Cézanne, who methodically applied slablike strokes of red, orange, and yellow as he built each apple. This method of constructing forms is found throughout the painting. The white cloth, for example, has qualities of weight and tangibility that are never found in Impressionist works.

Cézanne's translation of reality also took liberties with the traditional rules of perspective and foreshortening. *Still Life with Basket of Apples* intermingles a number of contradictory viewpoints: The cookies stacked on the plate do not all lie on parallel planes, the bottle is tilted, and the surface of the table is distinctly higher on the right than on the left. These liberties are even more pronounced in his landscape painting *Mont Sainte-Victoire Seen from the Bibémus Quarry* (fig. 9-13). Rather than use a traditional one- or two-point perspective system, Cézanne combined the rock surfaces, trees, and bits of sky into a multiperspective system of several focal points. Such a system may in fact represent the conditions of normal vision more truthfully than traditional perspective. (Our field of vision is broad, but we can only focus on one small area at a time. Therefore when we scan a scene, we focus on several different points while not being conscious of all of them.) But the overall effect in a Cézanne painting is not that of visual reality but of visual energy. Although the competing viewpoints produce a certain amount of tension, they have been played off against one another to create a vital stability. Cézanne was a master at balancing opposing forces.

We can see from these works that another important element of Cézanne's approach to painting is his emphasis on composition. Every canvas was a problem to solve, not in transcribing nature but in translating the energy and order of nature into painted surface. Every color and every arrangement of objects had their purpose in the harmony of the whole. The many distortions and dislocations, far from being arbitrary, were absolutely necessary to this harmony.

Because of a substantial family inheritance, Cézanne did not paint for money. (Until the last decade of his life he scarcely sold a painting.) He did not paint for the public either. No works of his were ever accepted by the official Salon, and when they were shown in the Impressionist exhibits of the 1870s, they were the object of ridicule. He eventually left Paris and returned to his family's home in Provence, where he spent the rest of his years pursuing his demanding art to satisfy himself. He lived long enough, however, to see that art receive moderate recognition

9-13　Paul Cézanne, *Mont Sainte-Victoire Seen from Bibémus Quarry,*
c. 1898. Oil on canvas, 25½″ × 32″. Baltimore Museum of Art (The Cone Collection).

and come into vogue as a model for emulation by a new and
much younger avant-garde.

Van Gogh　Vincent van Gogh, whose story is told in Chapter 7, was, like
Cézanne, an outsider. Both were unknown to the public and
ignored by all but a small portion of the art world of their generation. Van Gogh was able to survive with his brother's help and
Cézanne inherited a fortune. Although both were most aware of
the work of the Impressionists, both came to reject the Impressionist philosophy and methods, sharing only Impressionism's
brighter palette and emphasis on color. But there was also a
fundamental difference between Van Gogh and Cézanne in
their approach to art. Cézanne's interest lay in discovering and

transforming the essential structure of material reality in art; Van Gogh's was that of possessing the most intense human meanings in everything around him.

Gauguin Paul Gauguin, the third major Post-Impressionist painter, aggressively pioneered the same basic principle as Cézanne and Van Gogh—that the elements of form have artistic power in their own right. A profound colorist, his paintings regularly display an exotic palette of purples, pinks, yellow greens, and bright oranges; yet their effect is usually ingratiating and never as provocative as Van Gogh's vivid colors. Instead of Cézanne's multiple planes and viewpoints, Gauguin's forms are generally flat and endowed with an ornamental vigor suggestive of tropical plants and reflective of Japanese prints. And instead of Van Gogh's thick texture of brushstrokes, Gauguin's painting surface is flat. In *Vision After the Sermon, Jacob Wrestling with the Angel* (colorplate 21), the artist simplified and stylized the bonnets of the peasant women to stress their abstract shapes and lines. The field where the struggle takes place tilts upward to provide a vertical backdrop for the foreground shapes, and is painted red orange to contrast with the white of the bonnets and the greens and blues in the rest of the picture. But despite his emphasis on abstract form, Gauguin did not disregard the importance of subject matter and religious content. His mysticism and love of myth are reflected in *Vision After the Sermon* as well as are his decorative tendencies. Indeed, the simplicity of the images lends the picture a naive flavor that heightens the sense of piety and mystery. Gauguin chose freely from primitive religions as well as Christianity for his themes. In fact, his enthusiasm for primitive culture, together with a distaste for "civilization," eventually led him to settle in Tahiti.

While still in France, Gauguin was a prominent figure in the avant-garde movement of the late 1880s. Gregarious and verbal, he was given to expounding on art—especially his theories about the "autonomy" of color, shape, and line. In this respect he differed markedly from his friend Van Gogh, who manifested these theories in his art but was too backward socially to circulate his ideas beyond writing letters to Theo. Gauguin had a striking personality, and young artists were naturally drawn to him. At informal gatherings in Pont-Aven, a small fishing village on the coast of Brittany, he kept them spellbound talking about his theories. His influence extended beyond artists. The Symbolists, an intellectual movement mostly of poets, saw an embodiment of their own ideas in his intensification of color and simplification of form as a means of expressing a mystical reality. An experimental avant-garde of the literary world, the Symbolists were also obsessed with the dilemmas of conveying the invisible realities of the inner life through outer visible forms.

Because of his following of young artists and his contacts with the Symbolists, Gauguin had a more immediate impact on art than either Cézanne or Van Gogh. And this impact was instrumental in creating a climate for a new art to develop and for the work of all three of these artists to achieve recognition and acceptance.

Summary   Using the gist of George Kubler's theory of relative time, this chapter examines the relationship between time and art, and provides a framework for explaining the evolution of artistic forms and the sensibilities behind those forms. Kubler's theoretical construct can be used to identify prime objects—innovative artworks that have affected the appearance of works that followed them. Implicitly, it is also a system for attributing aesthetic value or artistic worth. If a painting or sculpture has played a key role in art history, it achieves art-historical status— regardless of its aesthetic appeal.

The modern period, in which change appears almost to have become a permanent condition, has witnessed the most rapid evolution of art forms in the entire history of art. In reviewing the start of that period, we began with Manet and the Impressionists and ended with the Post-Impressionists—by whose time the aesthetic revolution was well underway.

10
The Early Twentieth Century

As we saw in the last chapter, the modern movement, initiated in 1863 by Manet's *Luncheon on the Grass*, continued to evolve throughout the rest of the nineteenth century. The Impressionists developed the ideas that Manet had introduced and the Post-Impressionists carried those ideas another step or two. But the development of the movement was not narrow; it also influenced artists whose work was not directly concerned with those ideas.

Fin de Siècle

The 1890s, known as the *fin de siècle*, or end of the century, were years of great artistic activity but few real advances. The ideas implied in the works of the three principal Post-Impressionists were particularly influential at this time, even though the artists themselves were no longer part of the Parisian art world. Van Gogh was dead, Cézanne was sequestered in Provence, and Gauguin was in self-imposed exile in the South Pacific. Gauguin's ideas, especially, were receiving increased attention. His popularity with the Symbolists—who wrote about him in their magazine—helped provide him an audience. The Nabis, a group of young artists which was an outgrowth of his Pont-Aven following, spread his theories still further. Moreover, his tendencies toward stylized images and decorative patterns were beginning to be reflected in the popular arts of the time—particularly posters and newspaper caricatures.

Georges Seurat, who died in 1891, was another artist whose

ideas continued to receive a great deal of attention in avant-garde circles. Although more closely related to Impressionism, Seurat's work carried an aspect of that style to an extreme that had not been anticipated by the Impressionists themselves. He invented *Pointillism*, a quasi-scientific approach to painting in which an entire picture is made with small strokes or dots of bright color (colorplate 1). When seen from a normal viewing distance, the separate strokes or dots blend in the observer's eye. A very methodical artist, Seurat took great care in composing his paintings while working in a studio from studies he had made outdoors. As a result, his works were not as spontaneous as those of the Impressionists (most of which were painted outdoors), but the luminosity effected by the Pointillist dots implied a degree of abstraction and thus certain possibilities for those artists seeking new approaches.

Another major artist of the period was Henri de Toulouse-Lautrec, whose paintings represent still another variation on Impressionism. In *At the Moulin Rouge* (fig. 10-1), a painting

10-1   Henri de Toulouse-Lautrec, *At the Moulin Rouge*, 1892. Oil on canvas, 47½″ × 55¼″. Courtesy of the Art Institute of Chicago (Helen Birch Bartlett Memorial Collection).

about a bawdy nightclub in Paris, Toulouse-Lautrec's loose brushwork, cropped foreground figure, high eye level, and strong design were clearly influenced by both Impressionism and Japanese prints. But he used this artistic vocabulary not to depict radiant sunlit scenes but to celebrate the artificial lights and shadows of the night. An aristocrat and a cripple with a man's body on a child's legs, he showed a perverse empathy for the "society" of the Parisian brothels and cabarets (fig. 3-12). His paintings and lithographs, which combine sympathy and keen observation with a tinge of satire, reflect something of the cynicism that was symptomatic of the *fin de siècle*.

The intellectual climate of the time also contained a profoundly defeatist attitude about modern life. Anxieties stemming from the unresolved social problems of a new industrial-urban society had a spiritual counterpart in the disturbing questions and self-doubts that surfaced in the writings of poets and philosophers. Much of the art of the generation wallowed in mysticism and eroticism. The most poignant expression of this general climate is found in the art of Edvard Munch, whose painting *The Scream* (fig. 10-2) both signifies and protests against the spiritual crises of the day. Its curvilinear patterns and serpentine lines, traits shared by the works of Van Gogh (fig. 7-16) and Gauguin (colorplate 21), evoke here the sensations of nausea, despair, even paranoia. A Norwegian, Munch spent the most creative part of his life in the cities of Berlin and Paris. And like Van Gogh, another Northerner, he showed sensitivity and a talent for expressing intense psychological experiences.

Art Nouveau, a decorative movement that flourished all over Europe, was the equivalent of Symbolist aesthetics in the realm of applied arts. Its practitioners, rejecting traditional ornamental styles, sought to base Art Nouveau on natural motifs taken from the world of plants (fig. 10-3). The graphics of this style are known for striking patterns reminiscent of Japanese prints; the lurid, "whiplash" lines are almost a caricature of the lyrical forms in the paintings of artists like Gauguin and Van Gogh.

Matisse and the Fauves

The first of the major twentieth-century artists was Henri Matisse, who had begun to paint after completing law studies. He first tried to work in the style of Impressionism and then became acquainted with the work of Cézanne—whose discipline was more suited to his own logical mind. He was also attracted for a

10-2
Edvard Munch, *The Scream,*
1893. Oil on canvas, 36″ ×
29″. Munch-museet, Oslo.

time to Seurat's work, but found that Seurat's tedious technique did not appeal to him—though it did improve his understanding of color. He discovered Van Gogh's work at a retrospective exhibit, where he also met other artists who were under the spell of this emotional use of color. Through his association with them, Matisse came under the same spell—incorporating the audacity of bold color with his analytical temperament.

The public of Paris was given a taste of this explosive mixture at an exhibition in the fall of 1905. The outbreak of color in works like *Window at Collioure* (colorplate 22) so exasperated one critic that, as legend has it, he called the group of painters *fauves* (wild beasts). To critics, this orgy of color—most of it completely unrelated to its subject—was an insult to both art and life. Nevertheless, the colors in *Window at Collioure* do reflect a sense of purpose. The relatively solid areas of pink and blue-green within the room correspond to an exaggerated interpretation of light and shadow; the sky and water outside are indicated with

10-3
Aubrey Beardsley, *The Climax*, 1894. Drawing. Originally published in Oscar Wilde's *Salome, A Tragedy in One Act.*

smaller, isolated strokes that suggest the brightness and the re-flections. Thus the overall effect of this image of a summer day by the Mediterranean shore is all the more expressive because of the vivacious color.

Almost as soon as Matisse had achieved his controversial success with Fauvism, he felt compelled to consolidate his gains as the leading innovative artist of the time. He examined the work of his predecessors—the Impressionists, Cézanne, Seurat, Van Gogh, and even the other Fauves—and developed a style that incorporated their advances while remaining completely his own. The first painting in this new manner was *Joy of Life* (fig. 10-4), a large canvas of rather conventional subject matter—a pastoral setting of naked nymphs and lovers—but treated in a highly unconventional way. Though flat and colorful like Gauguin's, Matisse's figures and forms go far beyond Gauguin's in simplicity and distortion: Figure-ground relationships are more ambiguous and all the traditional methods of making realistic paintings have been subverted to create his new style. The joy in *Joy of Life* is not conveyed by the figures of the dancing nymphs but by the rhythmic line and the ordering of color contained in flat shapes—hallmarks of a style Matisse pursued for the rest of his life.

German Expressionism

Such was the strength of this new spirit in art that the Fauves had counterparts in other European countries, particularly Germany, where a band of young artists calling themselves *Die Brücke* (The Bridge) developed a related style at about the same time the Fauves made their splash in Paris. A few years later, another group called *Der Blaue Reiter* (The Blue Rider), consisting of Germans and expatriates such as the Russian Wassily

10-4   Henri Matisse, *Joy of Life*, 1905–06. Oil on canvas, 68½″ × 93¾″. Copyright 1980 by The Barnes Foundation, Merion, Pennsylvania.

Kandinsky, formed a loosely knit brotherhood dedicated to similar artistic ideals. The work of these groups and other artists in Germany—active from just before World War I until the reign of Adolf Hitler—has come to be known collectively as German Expressionism. Among the many artists involved were Kathe Kollwitz (fig. 2-16) and Oskar Kokoschka (fig. 6-24), two reviewed earlier in this book.

The brief Fauvist movement was a stimulus to the early German Expressionists. Its image-provoking label symbolized their own sense of rebellion, and the liberation of color and shape from the rules of conventional realism corresponded to their own artistic strivings. But there was a crucial difference in approach between the Germans and the French. The themes and subject matter used by the French were essentially unprovocative; color was used for color's sake. Matisse served up a delectable and challenging concoction of color and form as food for the viewer's mind and senses. On the other hand, the Germans' themes were usually provocative,—and the German artists used color and distorted form not for their own ends but for the sake of expressing the artists' deeply felt personal reactions to life. Thus these artists were the true spiritual heirs of the late-nineteenth-century artists Van Gogh and Munch.

Paula Modersohn-Becker, who was not affiliated with Die Brücke or Der Blaue Reiter, is generally regarded as the earliest of the German Expressionists. She was the first German artist to respond to Post-Impressionism and make use of it in an original way, much as the Fauves were at about the same time. The robust shapes in _Old Peasant Woman Praying_ (fig. 10-5) are reminiscent of the vigorous patterns of Gauguin and the Nabis; the strong planes of the face, indicating the structure of the head, reflect the work of Cézanne; and the sympathetic approach to the subject recalls Van Gogh's _Potato Eaters_. Modersohn-Becker emphasized the dignity of the woman by the simplicity and monumentality of the figure, which fills most of the composition. The directness, primitive tendencies, and human concern of her art were much admired by the German Expressionists, and she would no doubt have been a leader in their movement had it not been for her untimely death at the age of 31.

Of all the early Expressionists in Germany, only Kandinsky occupied himself more with the abstract elements of form and color than with human emotions. He was fond of equating the elements of painting with those of music, feeling that they could be treated in much the same way. Abstract painting can be said

10-5
Paula Modersohn-Becker,
Old Peasant Woman Praying, 1906. Oil on canvas, 29¾" × 22¾". The Detroit Institute of Arts (gift of Robert H. Tannahill).

to have been born in 1910, when Kandinsky painted his first completely abstract work. His earliest experiments, consisting of floating colors and lines, were somewhat amorphous (fig. 10-6); his later works were often organized around geometric figures floating in rainbow-colored space. But even his most amorphous works, unlike those by Jackson Pollock (colorplate 15) made around 35 years later, contain a certain number of dominant shapes, colors, and lines to guide the eye. In order to counteract the temptation to seek "real" images in his work and to emphasize the intent to provide a perception of pure form, he often titled his paintings as if they were musical compositions.

Max Beckmann, who did not become involved in the Expressionist movement until after World War I, passed through successive phases before arriving at the disturbing and disjunctive imagery seen in *Departure* (colorplate 23). The painting is in the form of a triptych, a three-section work of the type once used for religious subjects and placed above altars. But instead

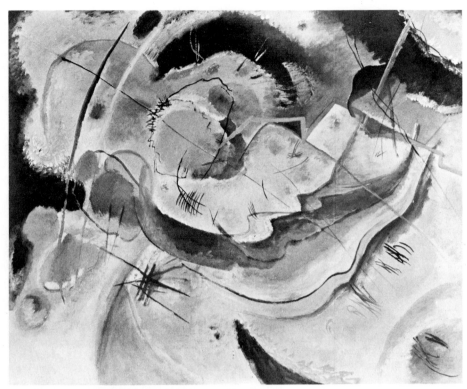

10-6 Wassily Kandinsky, *Improvisation*, 1914. Oil on canvas, 30¾" × 39⅞". Philadelphia Museum of Art (Louise and Walter Arensberg Collection).

of the holy acts of saints, this triptych seems to chronicle the depravity, violence, and fear increasingly common in Germany during the years before World War II. In the two side panels people are being tortured and mutilated; in the center a group of people in classical costume stands in a fishing boat, perhaps departing as the title suggests, perhaps even going into exile (as Beckmann himself was soon to do). His style features abrupt transformations and irrational combinations of images and themes—traits that Beckmann adapted from both Cubism and Surrealism, two art movements reviewed later in this chapter.

German Expressionism included sculpture as well as painting. The rough finish and emotionalism of Rodin's sculptures (fig. 9-12) were the primary inspiration to Wilhelm Lehmbruck, who introduced these qualities into his own work. But the elongation and distortion of his *Standing Youth* (fig. 10-7)—a typical Expressionist method of evoking intense emotion—represent a

10-7
Wilhelm Lehmbruck,
Standing Youth, 1913. Cast
stone, approx. 7'8" high.
The Museum of Modern
Art, New York (gift of Abby
Aldrich Rockefeller).

tampering with proportions that even the bold Rodin would not have dared. Lehmbruck's sculptures convey a depth of concern about human life that was characteristic of German Expressionism in general.

Picasso and Cubism

The Fauves were not the only ones in Paris who responded to the spirit of the new century. Indeed, the excitement they stirred up may have been a direct stimulus for the experimental turn that took place in the work of the Spanish artist Pablo Picasso. There is reason to believe that after he had seen Matisse's *Joy of Life*, Picasso was inspired to produce an innovative painting of his own. Up to this time his work was based on a progres-

10-8
Pablo Picasso, *Self-Portrait,*
1906. Oil on canvas, 36¼″ ×
28¾″. Philadelphia Museum
of Art (A.E. Gallatin
Collection).

sive form of Post-Impressionism (fig. 10-8)—some of it similar to the work of Modersohn-Becker. At any rate, after working for several months Picasso produced his own landmark painting—*Les Demoiselles d'Avignon* (fig. 10-9). (Ironically, Matisse was indignant about the work, calling it an outrage and a mockery of the modern movement.) The paintings of Cézanne and the influence of African sculpture were also important elements in Picasso's breakthrough work. The breaking up of the forms into planes had been learned from Cézanne; the severity of some of these planes—especially those of the faces—was influenced by African art (fig. 1-5). Picasso was the first, but not the only, twentieth-century artist to adapt primitive art to his painting. Ignored for centuries by Europeans who could appreciate only realistic art in the Western tradition, primitive art objects were

10-9   Pablo Picasso, *Les Demoiselles d'Avignon*, 1907. Oil on canvas, 8' ×
7'8". The Museum of Modern Art, New York (acquired through the Lillie P.
Bliss Bequest).

finally being recognized for their aesthetic values. At the same time, their abstract forms and directness of communication provided inspiration for modern artists in search of new artistic solutions. The Fauves rummaged in junk shops for African masks; the members of Die Brücke were attracted to Melanesian art.

Les Demoiselles was the first in a long series of bold experiments with structure in painting. Together with Georges Braque, Picasso launched a major new artistic style called *Cubism*. While the Expressionists and the Fauves charged into color, the Cubists retreated to an art of values alone—painting in grays and browns in order to concentrate on structure. And while Matisse attempted to stress flat patterns, Picasso and Braque resorted to techniques that created the impression of shallow, three-dimensional space.

Braque's *Violin and Palette* (fig. 10-10) is a representative work from the early phase of this style, known as *Analytic Cubism*. The entire picture is a medley of fractured objects transformed into angular, interlocking, translucent planes—recalling the brushwork and the multiple planes in a painting by Cézanne (colorplate 20). But this system goes far beyond Cézanne's by completely ignoring the original shapes of the objects—such as the violin—and remaking them so that one can see their surfaces from several angles simultaneously. The space around the objects becomes part of them, so that the whole composition is suggestive of a multifaceted and complicated gem. The color— more subdued and conservative than any seen since before Manet's breakthrough nearly half a century earlier—does not detract from the shallow but intricate spatial relationships. Thus, while this art roughly parallels Matisse's in its increased abstraction, it disfigures reality with different means and for different reasons. Matisse looked to nature for lyrical harmonies of color and pattern; Picasso and Braque systematically broke nature into abstract volumes and rhythms.

By 1912 Analytic Cubism had been fully developed and had inspired other movements. But Picasso and Braque were ready to move on to something else. They experimented with adding pieces of material—newspaper clippings, cloth, wood veneers, and so forth—to their paintings, and thus invented a new medium known as collage (Chapter 3). These experiments soon led to *Synthetic Cubism* which, unlike Analytic Cubism, tended toward flatness and depended less on real objects as a starting point. Rather than a system of shaded planes, Synthetic Cubism

10-10
Georges Braque, *Violin and Palette*, 1910. Oil on canvas, 36¼″ × 16⅞″. The Solomon R. Guggenheim Museum, New York.

featured flat, overlapping shapes; rather than monochromatic browns and blacks, it specialized, like the art of collage, in color variety and vivid surface textures. In addition, Picasso's *Three Musicians* (fig. 10-11) has a piquant whimsy that is rarely, if ever, found in sober Analytic Cubism. The translucency and multiple viewpoints of the earlier style were sacrificed for a livelier aesthetic surface. About the only thing the two have in common are angularity of shape and line, a trait of Picasso's *First Steps* (fig. 1-3) which, though made more than 20 years later, employs the Cubist idiom.

Elsewhere, the cubist impulse took still other forms. In Italy,

10-11 Pablo Picasso, *Three Musicians*, 1921. Approx. 6'7 " × 7'3¾".
Museum of Modern Art, New York (Mrs. Simon Guggenheim Fund).

a particularly dynamic version was produced under the name of
Futurism that directly influenced the work of the American Joseph Stella (fig. 8-9). In France it launched a multitude of styles
and affected a great many artists, even those who, like Marc
Chagall, were involved in very different pursuits (colorplate 11).
And in Russia, where a generation of avant-garde artists had
appeared on the eve of the Revolution, it was influential in the
drive of the *Constructivists* toward a nearly pure geometry that
reached its ultimate expression in the landmark painting by
Kasimir Malevich, *White on White* (fig. 10-12).

10-12
Kasimir Malevich,
*Suprematist Composition:
White on White*, 1918. Oil
on canvas, 31¼″ × 31¼″. The
Museum of Modern Art,
New York.

Cubism was also responsible for the geometrical abstraction of Piet Mondrian, a Dutchman. Beginning with a variation on Analytic Cubism, Mondrian's work became progressively simpler until he arrived at a basic geometric style that he called *Neoplasticism.* The basic principles of this style can be perceived in *Composition* (colorplate 24), an austere display of rectangles, thin black bars and primary colors. The simplicity of the work belies its variety. No two rectangles are the same size and shape; none of the colors are repeated; the composition is extremely off-center with red, the strongest and largest color, occupying a corner; even the bars vary slightly in thickness. The task of the artist was to achieve a perfect and sublime balance from this variety. According to Mondrian it was a matter of establishing equilibrium " . . . through the balance of unequal but equivalent oppositions." He raised the issue of balance almost to that of a religion— "rising above all suffering and joy is balance"—and hoped that his art would satisfy the spiritual need that people have to discover the universal harmony within them. Whether or not Mondrian ever realized such a lofty goal, his art did influence the applied arts of product design, interior design, and architecture for several years.

Cubist painting naturally had its equivalents in the art of sculpture. The breaking up of the image into exaggerated and

10-13
Pablo Picasso, *Musical Instruments*, 1914. Wood construction, 23⅝" high. Collection the artist.

10-14
Umberto Boccioni, *Development of a Bottle in Space*, 1912. Silvered Bronze, 15" × 12⅞" × 23¾". The Museum of Modern Art, New York (Aristide Maillol Fund).

fragmented planes which tried to re-create the appearance of volume had to lead inevitably to experiments with real space. Picasso and Braque had developed collage which they expanded into assemblages (Chapter 3). Constructions of wood or metal (fig. 10-13), however, appear to have served Picasso largely as studies for his painting. The most impressive sculpture of this type came from Italy, where several of the Futurist painters essayed occasional works. Umberto Boccioni's *Development of a Bottle in Space* (fig. 10-14) is far more dynamic than the works that were done in Paris: In addition to breaking up the forms in order to reveal their structure, he imposed a swirling instability on the composition. Where Picasso's "instruments" are destined to hang against a wall, Boccioni's bottle insists on in-the-round viewing. With its clashing planes and varied perspectives, it seems like a more direct descendant of Cézanne's still lifes than any Cubist painting.

Duchamp and Dada

Up to this time, the battles of the aesthetic revolution had been fought and won mostly on French soil. America had felt only a few of the shock waves coming from the European continent and no city in America had as yet experienced a bombshell comparable to those of Manet's *Luncheon on the Grass* or the Fauves exhibit—until the International Exhibition of Modern Art of 1913. This exhibition, now known as the Armory Show, contained more American works than others—but it was the European collection, especially the recent French works, that created all the stir.

The painting that inspired the most comment of all was Marcel Duchamp's *Nude Descending a Staircase* (fig. 10-15). One wag called it "an explosion in a shingle factory," and Theodore Roosevelt said that it reminded him of a Navajo blanket. Ironically, Americans ridiculed the right artist for the wrong reasons. *Nude Descending a Staircase* was a comparatively tame version of Cubism with a touch of Futurist motion, having neither the raw shock of *Les Demoiselles* nor the novelty of the latest collage inventions.

But many of the artworks created by Duchamp in the years following the *Nude* were radical even by today's standards: for example, a sculpture of 1917 that consisted of a urinal turned on its side and entitled *Fountain* (fig. 10-16). Christened *readymades* by Duchamp, these radical artistic gestures added a confounding feature to an already changing and bewildering art scene. The assumption that the artist controlled the form in some personal manner had never before been challenged. Duchamp seemed to be demonstrating by these acts that the premise of the uniqueness of form did not really matter, that a randomly selected object—even a banal one—could also be thought of as art, and that a mass-produced urinal could rest in a museum alongside a Cézanne.

The works of Duchamp have come to be associated with *Dada*, an intellectual movement characterized by cynicism and buffoonery launched in Zurich in 1916. During World War I, that city had become a haven for refugees of all kinds, including

10-15
Marcel Duchamp, *Nude Descending a Staircase, No. 2,* 1912. Oil on canvas, 58″ × 35″. Philadelphia Museum of Art (Louise and Walter Arensberg Collection).

writers and artists who felt pessimistic about the state of European civilization—an outlook they expressed in actions and works considered preposterous at the time. Poetry was created by drawing words out of a hat, pictures by randomly arranging cut-out shapes. Even the name Dada (French babytalk for "rocking horse") was selected by opening a dictionary and taking the first word that appeared. Implied in these kinds of actions was an attack on the meaning of any cultural endeavor, including art. Although Dada artists were sympathetic to the avant-garde because of its own reputation for recklessness, their contemporaries were not spared their sarcasm. Yet, in spite of the impu-

10-16
Marcel Duchamp (signed R. Mutt), *Fountain*, 1917. Porcelain, 24⅝" high. Arturo Schwarz Collection, Milan, Italy.

dence and madness, the stunts of the Dadaists gave rise to a reassessment of cultural values and to the discovery of new approaches to meaning—especially meaning relating to unconscious associations. "Automatic drawing," a sort of spontaneous doodling, was one of the experiments Dada artists pursued to promote the notion of releasing subconscious forces in the creation of art.

The Dada movement faded away in the early 1920s leaving few, if any, lasting works of art. But the Dada artists, for all their perversities, did leave a legacy. Duchamp's readymades anticipated the art of assemblage, Kurt Schwitters' *Merzbau* (fig. 3-29) was a forerunner of happenings and environments (Chapter 3), and automatic drawing was used by some of the artists of the next art movement—and later by Jackson Pollock. Further, Dada was instrumental in generating the twentieth-century preoccupation with the ironic, the absurd, and the unconscious—notions that frame the foundation of *Surrealism*.

Surrealism

Surrealism, the last major art movement before the end of World War II, was started by a former Dada poet, André Breton. Seeking to establish a brotherhood of poets and artists, he wrote a manifesto in 1924 in which he describes the purpose of Surrealism as resolving ". . . the previously contradictory conditions of dream and reality into an absolute reality, a super-reality." The movement's sources were Symbolist poetry and art, Picasso's Cubist works (which Surrealists said were based on the artist's unconscious), Dada poetry and art, and the writings of Sigmund Freud—especially *Interpretation of Dreams* published in 1900.

The super-reality of Surrealism had been anticipated by Giorgio de Chirico (fig. 10-17), who began painting pictures of hauntingly deserted plazas as early as 1913. The exaggerated open spaces painted in a tense and contradictory perspective, the long shadows, and the ambiguous architecture conspire to create the kind of ominous and mysterious sensation we often experience in our dreams. But they also suggest the magical life of lifeless things—a carryover from childhood, when we might have projected fantasy identities onto inanimate objects. His style, though somewhat unorthodox, is basically realistic. It is the subject matter that is truly original. *Mystery and Melancholy of a Street* includes several things that, ordinarily, one would not find coexisting in the same picture: a girl with a hoop in a deserted square, the shadow of man with a long staff, a gypsy

10-17
Giorgio de Chirico, *The Mystery and Melancholy of a Street*, 1914. Oil on canvas, 34¼″ × 28⅛″. Private collection.

wagon beside an ancient arcade, as well as the multiple eye levels and vanishing points. Such "alien combinations" that assault visual logic are typical of a type of Surrealism that favored, to a greater or lesser degree, the use of pictorial realism. Most importantly, De Chirico's art—which he referred to as *Metaphysical painting*—unearthed possibilities for dealing with unconscious experiences.

The impulse to paint dream phenomena led some artists in a direction that seemed contrary to that of the modern movement. Salvador Dalí (fig. 10-18) dusted off the old methods of chiaroscuro and perspective in order to represent the irrational world of dreams as vividly as possible; hence hallucinatory images and the inhabitants of the dark world of the unconscious assume in his paintings the authority of photographs. Intrigued by the theories of Freud, Dalí was incredibly resourceful in inventing all sorts of dream fantasies that employed not only alien combinations but things made of alien materials and depicted in an alien scale. Witness his enormous limp watches.

René Magritte also painted in a more or less realistic style,

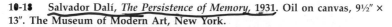

10-18   Salvador Dalí, *The Persistence of Memory,* 1931. Oil on canvas, 9½″ × 13″. The Museum of Modern Art, New York.

but did not choose to dramatize either the style or content of his work. His paintings are evocative rather than provocative. Typically, they pose compact puzzles about what we perceive or think with simple images reminiscent of de Chirico's. For example, we view *The Empire of Light, II* (fig. 10-19) as a nighttime scene and wonder why the sky is blue and the clouds are white, or visualize it as a daytime scene and puzzle over the fact that the street is dark and the windows and street lamp are illuminated. Logic is being mocked to create a new experience out of two opposing realities.

Another branch of Surrealism pursued visions of the unconscious through automatic painting and drawing, a practice that led some of its adherents into forms of abstraction. This frontier had already been pioneered by the Swiss artist Paul Klee, who developed a method he called *psychic improvisation.* Klee would begin a picture in an intuitive, poetic way—without an image or theme in mind—manipulating pictorial elements at random until some distant memory or association began to influence the process. The result was sometimes like a child's drawing, but

10-19 René Magritte, *The Empire of Light, II,* 1950. Oil on canvas, 31″ × 39″. The Museum of Modern Art, New York (gift of D. and J. de Menil).

there was nothing childlike about Klee's talent (fig. 10-20). An influential teacher at the Bauhaus (a famous German art school during the 1920s) who was respected for his intellect, Klee was sophisticated and clever in conjuring up the mysterious life of the subconscious. The principal Surrealist in the abstract vein was Joan Miró (fig. 7-19). He too was playful and humorous and unusually inventive in creating pictorial signs for the same mysterious world.

Summary   Most of the innovations—the prime objects—of early twentieth-century modernism occurred before World War I. These include the breakthrough works of the Fauves, the German Expressionists, the Cubists, the first completely abstract paintings of Kandinsky, and even the metaphysical pictures of de Chirico.

The brief Dada movement started during the war, and Surrealism emerged during the 1920s. Other than the liberation of the subconscious produced by these two movements, no significant breakthroughs took place between the two world wars. The aesthetic revolution had not come to a stop, but it seemed to have slowed—concentrating more on consolidating the advances made earlier than on making new ones.

10-20   Paul Klee, *Tropical Gardening*, 1923. Watercolor and oil on paper, 7⅞″ × 19¼″. The Solomon R. Guggenheim Museum, New York.

11
The Late Twentieth Century

The next important stage of the modern movement occurred in the United States with major breakthroughs occurring just after World War II. Even though these breakthroughs took place on American soil, they were essentially an outgrowth of ideas and approaches initiated in Europe. But before looking at this phase of the aesthetic revolution, a review of the status of American art prior to the end of the war and a consideration of the major factors that would prove influential in these later developments should be helpful.

Prelude   Even before the 1913 Armory Show, the work of such artists as Matisse and Picasso had been exhibited in New York in the gallery of photographer-art dealer Alfred Stieglitz. In addition to dealing in modern art, Stieglitz published an avant-garde magazine that printed articles by American artists and writers who were followers of the new developments in Europe. But with relatively few American artists experimenting with newer approaches, the growth of an indigenous modern movement was meager. Further, their work had little influence outside this country and was not popular in this country—not even among American collectors interested in modern art, most of whom preferred to collect the works of Matisse and Picasso.

In the 1930s the development of modern art in America almost stopped. The mood of the time did not favor either experimentation or European influences. American artists concentrated instead on American themes and worked in rather conservative styles. The dominant movement of the time was Regionalism, exemplified by the works of Benton (fig. 7-18) and Hopper (fig. 8-10 and colorplate 16). Benton's work, however, is more typical of the movement. Most Regionalists romanticized rural America, creating populist myths about life in the small towns and on the farms of their part of the country. For example, Grant Wood of Iowa often endowed a country scene in his state with magical enchantment and bucolic charm (fig. 11-1). While this kind of art was popular in America, it received little recognition in other countries.

Europeans persisted in thinking of American culture, especially its painting, as provincial—an opinion shared by the American artists and intellectuals themselves, especially the younger ones. But in New York, various forces were already at

11-1   Grant Wood, *Stone City, Iowa,* 1930. Oil on canvas, 30″ × 40″. Joslyn Art Museum, Omaha, Nebraska.

work to counteract this provincialism. European modernist painting and sculpture were appearing in greater and greater numbers in that city's collections, particularly that of the up and coming Museum of Modern Art. At the same time, European artists were fleeing to the United States because of the political crises on their own continent. These artists—including Chagall, Dalí, Duchamp, Gabo, Masson, and Mondrian—settled mostly in New York. And among the various groups, it was the Surrealists who made the biggest impression on young American artists.

During the forties, a new form of abstract painting began to emerge in New York. It was based in large part on the Surrealists' idea of automatic drawing (or psychic automatism), but at the same time it broke with their tendency to base forms on images—even the vaguely recognizable images reminiscent of children's art. The new painting was also influenced by other intellectual currents. The war had contributed to a somber vision of human existence, and the writings of Jean-Paul Sartre—a leader in the Existentialist movement—were extremely influential during the postwar period. Sartre and other Existential thinkers argued that existence came before essence and that life was not necessarily a part of a greater scheme of things under the protection and guidance of a supreme being. On the positive side, this meant that people were free to choose and shape their own destinies. But such freedom came with a high price: According to the Existentialists, humankind was physically and spiritually abandoned on earth and ultimately vulnerable. At the same time, Existentialism attributed a great deal of importance to the subjective aspects of the individual personality. The abstract painters, who had reached similar conclusions on their own, were already searching deeply within themselves to liberate this source of expression. But many, influenced by the theories of the psychologist Carl Gustav Jung, also believed that there was a universal dimension to this source. According to Jung, everyone shares certain experiences—part of a collective unconscious inherited as a part of the brain. Although the contents of this experience are not consciously remembered, they show up in the dreams and myths of all the cultures of the world. The artists—in addition to Pollock, such artists as Arshile Gorky and Adolph Gottlieb—who subscribed to this view felt, therefore, that they could find abstract symbols that would be both intensely personal and universal. And from these efforts the first major American art movement was born—*Abstract Expressionism.*

Plate 25   Mark Rothko, *Untitled*, 1956. Oil on canvas, 79⅜″ x 69″.
Collection Mr. and Mrs. Lee V. Eastman.

Plate 26   Willem de Kooning, *Door to the River*, 1960. Oil on canvas, 6′ 8″ x 5′ 10″.
Whitney Museum of American Art, New York (gift of the Friends
of the Whitney Museum of American Art [and purchase]).

Plate 27 Roy Lichtenstein, *Little Big Painting*, 1965. Oil on canvas, 5′ 8″ x 6′ 8″.
Whitney Museum of American Art (gift of the Friends
of the Whitney Museum of American Art).

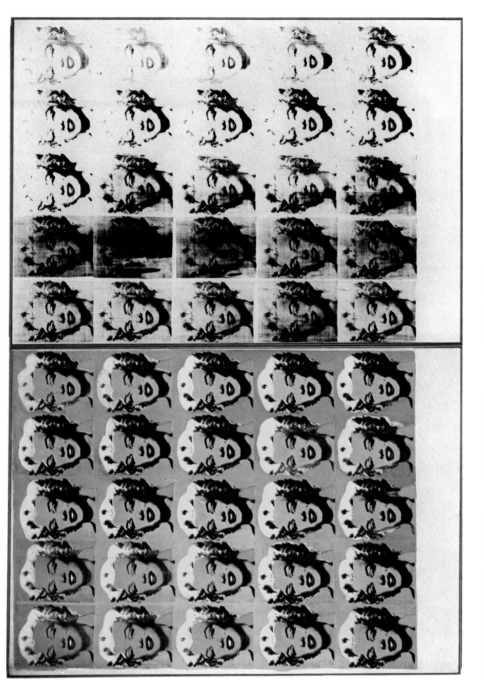

Plate 28 Andy Warhol, *Marilyn Monroe Diptych*, 1962. Oil on canvas, 6' 10'' x 9' 6''. Collection Mr. and Mrs. Burton Tremaine, Meriden, Connecticut. Photo courtesy of Leo Castelli Gallery, New York.

Plate 29   Helen Frankenthaler, *Cravat*, 1973. Acrylic on canvas,
5' 2½'' x 4' 10¾''. Collection Mr. and Mrs. Gilbert H. Kinney.
Courtesy of Andre Emmerich Gallery.

Plate 30 Victor Vasarely, *Orion Bleu*, 1965. Tempera on wood,
32½″ x 32⅝″. Private collection. Courtesy Gallerie Denise René.

Plate 31   Sam Gilliam, *Seahorses*, 1975. Acrylic on canvas, largest piece 30' x 90'.
As exhibited at the Philadelphia Museum of Art. Courtesy of the artist.

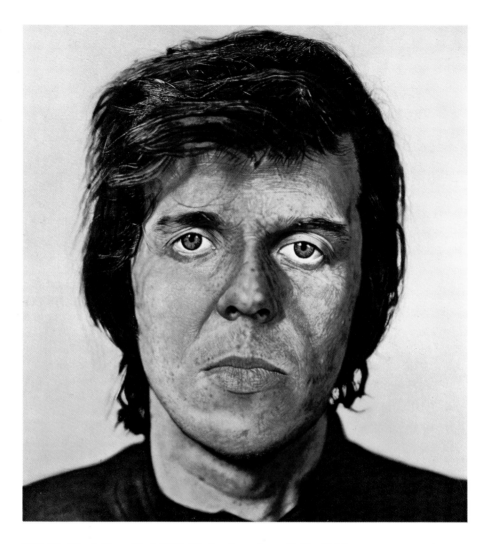

Plate 32 Chuck Close, *Kent*, 1970–71. Acrylic on linen, 8' 4'' x 7' 6''.
Art Gallery of Ontario, Toronto. Photo courtesy Bykert Gallery.

Abstract Painting

The painters of one branch of the new art, often called *Chromatic Abstraction*, emphasized color in a new way. Typically, these painters filled huge canvases with large areas of color that tend to monopolize the visual space of anyone standing within the normal viewing distance. Like Pollock, these painters eliminated all intentional images, yet many also severely limited the number of details of any kind that might distract the viewer's perception of a huge, engulfing field of color. Mark Rothko made a specialty of luminous, blurred rectangles that seem to float in space (colorplate 25). The delicate color transitions around the edges of each shape provide a hazy, almost spectral, effect similar to that of the misty atmosphere in a Chinese landscape (colorplate 8). And, like Chinese art, Rothko's paintings seem intended to provide a sensation of boundless space and encourage a feeling of revery.

Barnett Newman's canvases were usually divided vertically by one or more stripes set in an expansive sea of flat, unmodulated color. In *First Station* (fig. 11-2), Newman has embedded a thin sharp-edged stripe in a narrow field of loosely-brushed color which in turn is surrounded by the color of the background—an ambiguous treatment that confuses the usual relationship between figure and ground. Some of Newman's canvases are so enormous that the effect of the bright color is almost overwhelming. One critic said of this color that it was used to "shock the mind," but Newman held that his works were meant to inspire religious feelings. The paintings of both Rothko and Newman appeal to the viewer's visual sense in a most direct way, but both are ultimately intended to move us to contemplation.

The other branch of Abstract Expressionism—usually known as *Action Painting*—consisted largely of what Pollock called "energized marks of paint." It was believed that these paintings were created out of some inner necessity on the part of the artist and were capable of conveying the artist's inner feelings without the aid of symbols. Action painters seemed to revel in surface variety; their paintings are covered with bold, freely shaped forms, agitated textures, and rapid shifts of color and value. Within this style a variety of approaches emerged. Franz Kline's muscular, broad slashes of black on white (fig 11-3) contrast with Pollock's nervous, weblike lines (colorplate 15). The pronounced figure-ground relationship of black/white in Kline's canvases seems to symbolize a fundamental principle of antithesis—male/female, life/death, and so on. But his crisscrossing

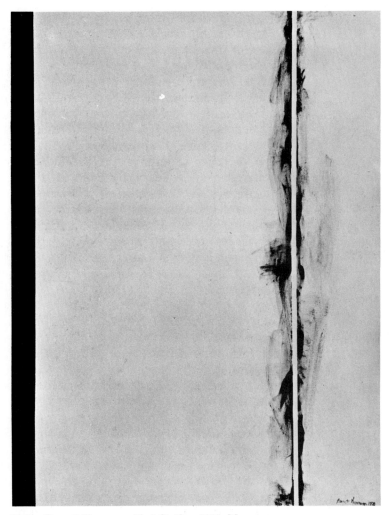

11-2 Barnett Newman, *First Station*, 1958. Magna on raw canvas,
78" × 60". From the series *The Stations of the Cross: Lema Sabachthani*.
Collection Annalee Newman.

bars could also be a kind of reference to the urban landscape,
alluding to bridges and buildings under construction.

Willem de Kooning's highly agitated paintings represent yet
another approach to Action Painting (colorplate 26). The violence of de Kooning's brushwork is all the more unsettling because of his tendency to use soft colors—warm yellows, fleshy
pinks, and so on. Yet this combination of elements often lends
itself to figurative and sexual interpretations. His paintings, in

11-3   Franz Kline, *Mahoning*, 1956. Oil on canvas, 80" × 100". Whitney
Museum of American Art, New York (gift of the Friends of the Whitney
Museum of American Art).

which broad brushstrokes go in all directions, best epitomize the
gestural style.

In addition to Pollock, Kline, and de Kooning, other notable
artists involved in Action Painting were Philip Guston, Hans
Hofmann, Robert Motherwell, and Clifford Still.

The year 1947, when Pollock began "drip painting," was an
important time in Europe, too. There a number of gallery show-
ings revealed that several artists—many working separately—
shared similar goals. Under a number of different labels—such
as *Art Informel, Abstraction Lyrique,* and *Tachisme*—this painting
featured freely brushed abstract forms, usually thick with paint.
What is all the more interesting about this phenomenon is that
the art world in Europe was largely unaware of the Abstract
Expressionists until 1950, when these painters' works were
shown there rather extensively. A major exhibition held in Paris
that year featured representatives of both the European and
American avant-garde. In general the American abstract art was

bolder and more dramatic, the European more lyrical and stressing a greater sensitivity to the subtle possibilities of the new style. One European branch emphasized texture above all else, relying on the evocative power of the material itself. The French artist Jean Dubuffet (fig. 2-19) sometimes created working surfaces out of cut-up pieces of canvas, thick glue, and asphalt. He would knead, trowel, and scrape them, allowing the material itself to suggest the way in which it should be manipulated. The work of the Spaniard Antonio Tàpies also focused on textures, but in combination with strong, often almost geometric structures. *Gray with Two Black Stains* resembles an American Chromatic Abstraction in that it features delicate transitions of hue and value as well as texture (fig. 11-4). And, like a painting by Rothko, its subtle relationships of abstract form are capable of putting one in a meditative frame of mind.

In retrospect, the most important consequences of Abstract

11-4   Antoni Tàpies, *Gray with Two Black Stains,* 1959. Mixed media on canvas, 38½″ × 51¼″. Albright-Knox Art Gallery, Buffalo, N.Y., The Martha Jackson Collection, 1974.

Expressionism appear to have been more cultural than aesthetic. For one thing, the relationship between European and American art had changed; for the first time in history the latter was looked upon as a vital force in the art world. Now European artists had to run to keep pace with a vigorous new American competition. And, ironically, even as American art broke out of provincialism, its new avant-garde began to acquire a strong (sometimes arrogant) sense of national identity. Abstract Expressionism had a romantic quality and a distinctly American accent. Its raw style and defiance of conventions fit the image Americans had of themselves as being boldly individualistic.

Abstract Sculpture

During the fifties, developments in sculpture were generally overshadowed by the exuberant world of abstract painting. Although the aesthetic advances immediately after World War II were pioneered by painters, sculptors were attuned to the new thinking and skillfully expressed it in their own way.

In the late forties, a number of sculptors developed techniques for working with metal that corresponded roughly to the spontaneous methods of Abstract Expressionist painters. Their dramatic works often equalled those of Kline or de Kooning in boldness. Some, following the lead of Julio González (fig. 3-20), shaped their works by welding successive layers of metal, capitalizing on the naturally rough residues and the oxides resulting from the welding process. However, unlike most Abstract Expressionists, these sculptors were addicted to biological forms, their works often resembling such things as animal skeletons, spiny plants, seed pods, and thorns. Many were influenced by the work of Henry Moore in England (fig. 6-18) and were reacting against what they considered to be the arid impersonality of geometrical abstraction in sculpture (represented by Naum Gabo, fig. 3-21).

The closest tie between the abstract sculpture and the abstract painting of the 1950s is found in the work of David Smith. Trained as a painter, he first came under the influence of the work of such artists as Kandinksy, Miró, and Mondrian. But a summer job in a car factory—where he learned to cut and weld metal—together with his discovery of the welded sculptures of Picasso and González, stimulated him to pursue the art of steel sculpture. Throughout his career he saw the aims of sculpture and painting as being essentially the same, saying that they were separated by only one dimension. He was not averse to painting on his sculptures, sometimes covering a piece with layers of epoxy, zinc, or auto enamel. But the most basic relationship between a painting and Smith's early sculpture, such as *Hudson River Landscape,* was the sculpture's frontality (fig. 11-5). Rather than being intended for in-the-round viewing, most of his works were designed to be seen from only one angle.

In his later work Smith concentrated on simpler shapes, like those of the *Cubi* series—compositions of stainless steel geometric forms that look as though they are about to fall apart (fig. 11-6). Most of these are also relatively frontal works, and their novel construction and precarious balance are mindful of the impromptu nature of an Abstract Expressionist painting. Even the random buffing swirls on the surfaces have the character of brushstrokes. However, the most influential elements of the *Cubi* sculptures for later art were the reduction of their forms to a simple, straightforward geometry and their similarity—both in form and manufacture—to industrial objects.

Assemblage

The technique of assemblage became relatively popular in the late 1950s. Pollock had already experimented with the addition of pebbles and other small objects to the painting surface, much as Dubuffet and Tàpies had done. To the younger American artists, this direction seemed particularly promising. If personal expression could be accomplished by the spontaneous spread-

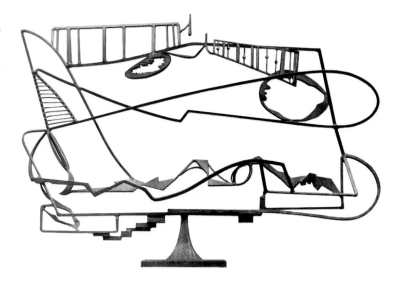

11-5
David Smith, *Hudson River Landscape,* 1951. Welded steel, 75" × 49½" × 16¾". Whitney Museum of American Art, New York.

ing of paint or other materials, it could also be accomplished—
with perhaps richer possibilities—by the spontaneous assembling of objects.

Robert Rauschenberg and Jasper Johns—the two artists
who experimented most radically and most successfully with
assemblage in the fifties—were experienced painters who grew
out of Abstract Expressionism. Rauschenberg would attach objects such as torn photographs, neckties, broken umbrellas,
clocks, old trousers, or pillows to a vigorously painted surface.
Although he called these works ''combine-paintings,'' some of
them developed into rather substantial three-dimensional ob-

11-6
David Smith, *Cubi XVII*,
1963. Stainless steel, 107¾"
high. Dallas Museum of
Fine Arts (The Eugene and
Margaret McDermott Fund).

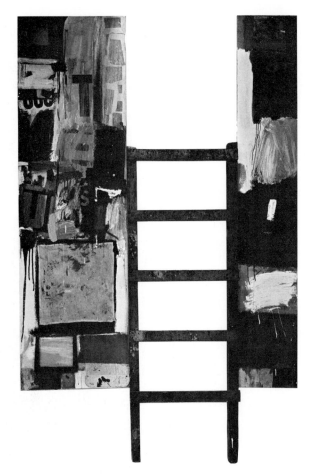

11-7
Robert Rauschenberg,
Winterpool, 1959.
Combine painting, 88½″ ×
58½″. Collection Mr. and
Mrs. Victor W. Ganz,
New York.

jects (fig. 11-7). Rauschenberg's use of objects ran counter to the basic methods of Abstract Expressionism, but his bravura use of paint revealed a profound understanding of those methods. The rich coating of drips and smears that permeates and surrounds everything in a Rauschenberg work surprisingly creates unity out of what might otherwise be a meaningless collection of items.

Jasper Johns's assemblages generally employ less variety— their paint surfaces emphasizing Abstract Expressionism's heavy textures more than its brushstrokes. Johns is known mainly for his elaboration of such flat images as targets or flags which he would form with thick paint, wax, and bits of paper. One such painting, *Target with Plaster Casts* (fig. 11-8), combined a large target with a series of plaster casts of parts of the human

11-8
Jasper Johns, *Target with Plaster Casts*, 1955. Encaustic collage on canvas, with wood construction and plaster casts, 51″ × 44″ × 3½″. Collection Mr. and Mrs. Leo Castelli, New York.

body set in tiny boxes above the bull's-eye—a mildly unsettling juxtaposition reminiscent of those found in the paintings of Magritte (fig. 10-19).

In discussing their work, Rauschenberg and Johns have tended to discourage the search for special meanings for their objects and images. Yet their inspired combinations do breed interpretations: Rauschenberg's rapid flux of images and surface effects can easily be seen as an expression of hectic times or a junk-filled, modern industrial culture. Johns's ironic images, which include American flags and maps as well as targets, explore the relationships between sign and art and essay the possibilities of incorporating popular myths in art. In the context of the late 1950s, their works are provocative—an avant-garde assault on the Abstract Expressionist establishment. Although they were berated for their "impurity" and lack of seriousness, today they are looked upon as transitional between Abstract

Expressionism and some of the major developments of the next decade.

Not all assemblages of the late 1950s were hectic, disturbing, or provocative. Louise Nevelson's works, like those of Rothko and Tàpies, tended to emphasize order and calm. Although she utilized discarded objects, Nevelson imposed order on an otherwise random assortment by restricting her materials mostly to wood, painting them a single color, and structuring the assemblage with repeated forms (usually the rectangular shapes of boxes). These primarily frontal works are open to the viewer and filled with simple shapes and fragments such as chair legs, knobs, and scrap lumber (fig. 11-9). The series of niches often creates a subtle interplay between surface and depth, positive and negative. By themselves, neither the niches nor the objects have any particular meaning, but together in the assemblage they generate images suggesting cluttered cupboards or medieval altarpieces.

Pop Art

The sixties, one of the most tumultuous decades in American history, were also the scene of tumultuous changes in art. The rather sudden success of *Pop Art* in the early part of that decade had a profound impact on the art world. Simply stated, Pop Art celebrated and satirized popular culture—particularly the most banal and debased aspects of that culture. Because of America's prominence as an originator of popular artifacts—from soft drinks to Hollywood movies—it was only natural that American artists were the most successful of the Pop Art movement. But England had also become an important source of popular culture, and English artists figured strongly as well—especially in the area of music. In fact the earliest works of Pop Art were created by a London-based avant-garde of artists who expressed a particular interest in the connections between popular culture and art. Many of the hallmarks of Pop Art—humor, parody, imitation of advertising art—were already present in their experimental works of the fifties.

Many works of Pop Art appear to be so different from those of Abstract Expressionism that Pop Art is often thought of as a total break with the past. But there is an ambiguous continuity between the two. Pop Art is certainly a part of the total modern movement, for many of its traits—ready-made images and irony, to mention two—have precedents in earlier art movements, especially Dada and Surrealism. Furthermore, many Pop

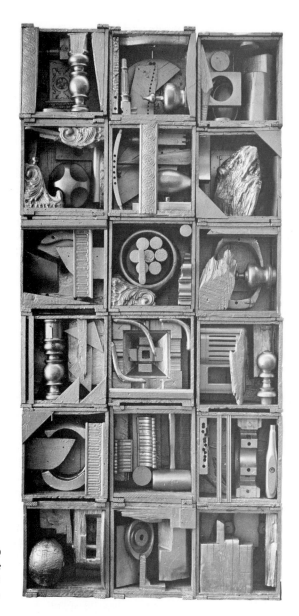

11-9
Louise Nevelson, *Royal Tide I,* 1960. Gilded wood, 96″ × 40″ × 8″. Private collection.

artists had begun as Abstract Expressionists, and—even though they were reacting against the older school—their vision of the world was at least somewhat affected by it.

The striking differences between Pop Art and Abstract Expressionism are demonstrated by the American artist Roy Lichtenstein's series of paintings of brushstrokes. *Little Big Painting* (colorplate 27) is an image of the marks that a painter like de Kooning (colorplate 26) would make with a few sweeps of his large brush, right down to the "accidental" drips. But in Lichtenstein's smooth-surfaced, hard-edged product, such personal touches as drips or spills are completely eliminated. He even used enlarged Ben Day dots—a mechanical method for indicating tones—as the background. To an Abstract Expressionist, a brushstroke was the spontaneous mark of an artist's feelings, the stamp of a personality. To Lichtenstein, it was another shape to be transformed by huge scale and the mechanical means of commercial art. And by his deadpan use of comic-strip methods to *represent* (rather than to create spontaneously) the Abstract Expressionist brushstroke, Lichtenstein was making a mockery of the cherished Expressionist belief that art can be a direct and true revelation of inner feeling.

Abstract Expressionism is a relatively closed aesthetic system that rejects all references to everyday culture, preferring instead to pontificate about the human condition with emotional brushmarks. The Pop artists turned all of this inside out. Their painting methods are deliberately cool and their themes are often taken without modification from the familiar commercial culture that previously had not been considered worthy enough for art. Lichtenstein himself openly imitated comic strips (fig. 11-10). In an interview titled "What is Pop Art?" he stated:

> Well, it *is* an involvement with what I think to be the most brazen and threatening characteristics of our culture, things we hate, but which are also powerful in their impingement on us. I think art since Cézanne has become extremely romantic and unrealistic, feeding on art; it is utopian. It has had less and less to do with the world, it looks inward. . . . Pop Art looks out into the world; it appears to accept its environment, which is not good or bad, but different—another state of mind.

Pop Art's vision of the world was not so cool that it precluded any judgment of what it saw. It is full of implied social

11-10   Roy Lichtenstein, *Whaam!*, 1963. Acrylic on canvas, 68″ × 160″. Tate Gallery, London.

commentary in its choice and its treatment of subject matter. The whole question of American themes that had been a major problem for earlier generations of artists (Chapter 8) never even arose for the Pop artists, who plunged gleefully into the consumer society around them for their material. Just as Lichtenstein expanded the comic-book look into an art form that accurately reflected the emotional and intellectual level of the nation, Andy Warhol used serial imagery and mass-production techniques to emphasize the shallowness of American sexual myths (colorplate 28). Tom Wesselmann echoed Warhol's theme by presenting the Great American Nude in the context of commercial advertising (fig. 6-19). Continuing this trend, George Segal drew attention to the boredom and anomie that so often accompany such commercialism through his rough-plaster cast of a real woman (cover). Finally, Larry Rivers did not parody Napoleon so much as he did the myths of history and art history in his fragmented and impudent adaptation of a renowned portrait of the French Emperor (Part III opening photograph).

The implied commentary of Claes Oldenburg's *Yale Lipstick* (fig. 11-11) touches on art, education, and the military in addition to commercialism and sex. The twenty-four-foot-high sculpture is intended to mock those sculptures that are large in scale and noble in theme and are constructed in public squares to inspire a sense of grandeur and tradition. Although the lipstick sculpture is large, it is hardly noble and inspires only a sense of the absurd. Instead of a public figure or commemorative obelisk, Oldenburg created a gigantic version of a very com-

11-11
Claes Oldenburg, *Yale Lipstick*, 1969. Steel, aluminum, fiberglass, and paint, 24' high. Yale University Art Gallery (gift of the Colossal Keepsake Corporation).

mon object. And instead of building a solid base, he mounted the form on bulldozer treads that suggest the sculpture may be moved from one place to another. The monumental treatment of the commonplace and the mobility of the public work are only the beginning of this work's contradictions, however. Viewing it, we become aware that this object designed for women has a suggestively masculine shape. Yet, set on treads, it also bears a close resemblance to a cannon. These simple variations on the traditional object lead us to interpret a symbol of sexual desire as a symbol of aggression.

Oldenburg's visual games were well suited to the confusion of the times. The lipstick piece was such a focal point of controversy on the Yale campus in 1969—at the height of the Vietnam War—that it became a victim of graffiti and radical posters, and was eventually moved to a less conspicuous location.

Pop Art may have established closer relations between art and the ordinary world, but at the same time it raised questions about the nature of art. If Roy Lichtenstein could copy a frame from a comic strip and call it art, then what was the original? Were the Sunday papers full of little works of art? If Warhol could reproduce a Campbell's tomato soup label, was a supermarket a kind of art gallery? The distinction between art and nonart had become less and less meaningful.

Color-Field Art

At about the same time that Rauschenberg, Johns, and the English Pop artists were restoring subject matter to painting and sculpture, others were continuing to explore the potentialities of abstract art. But unlike the Action Painters, they did not work in bold gestures. Even at the height of Abstract Expressionism, the desire to express one's inner feelings spontaneously was not universal among those painters. Many had chosen less dramatic ways to work, preferring to concentrate on the investigation of problems of color and space.

The luminous and atmospheric qualities of Helen Frankenthaler's stained canvases (colorplate 29) have much in common with the paintings of the Chromatic Abstractionists, particularly Rothko. But the shapes in Frankenthaler are far more irregular and tend to suggest natural forms. Frankenthaler's methods were supposedly influenced by the staining techniques of Pollock, but unlike him she used fast-drying, water-based acrylic paints on raw canvas rather than slower-drying oil paints on sized canvas. Frankenthaler was the first to concentrate on staining, allowing the fluid color to soak into the fabric and sometimes to run and form unexpected shapes. She has since expanded her range of working methods to include practically every way that paint can be spread on canvas—pouring, sponging, even brushing—and has discovered numerous approaches to the creation of the sensation of depth through staining. Over the years, her work has been in the forefront of the advances of *color-field painting.*

Morris Louis discovered the staining technique when he met Frankenthaler. He then went on to develop a style of his own that involved pouring acrylics in broad, smooth floods to create overlapping "veils" of color (fig. 11-12). Later, he poured the paint to form separate stripes of color that stood out against the bare canvas. Although they were somewhat irregular, these stripes did introduce to his style a certain amount of simplicity, repetition, and symmetry—qualities not usually found in color-field paintings. Meanwhile, the shift in sensibility away from

11-12   Morris Louis, *Dalet Kaf,* 1958. Acrylic on canvas, 100¼″ × 142½″.
Estate of the artist. Courtesy André Emmerich Gallery.

the subjective and gestural painting style of the Abstract Expressionists was beginning to be reflected in the work of more and more artists.

Minimal Art

Minimal Art was the major branch of abstract art in the sixties. In painting it was a continuation of the work begun by artists like Rothko and Newman, but the focus was on form and structure with an emphasis on simple, geometrical shapes. Although it seemed to hark back to the paintings of Mondrian (colorplate 24), Minimal Art reflected a very different approach to geometrical abstraction. Minimal artists, like Frank Stella (below) and Ellsworth Kelly (fig. 2-4), did not share Mondrian's mystical ideas about order and harmony and were not at all opposed to making straightforward, symmetrical compositions. The dry and simple patterns of Stella's painting *Itata* (fig. 11-13) resemble

11-13   Frank Stella, *Itata,* 1964. Metallic powder in polymer emulsion on canvas, 77″ × 122″. Private collection.

the cool, unemotional images of Pop more closely than those of other abstract art—whether by Mondrian or the Abstract Expressionists. Just as the previous generation had been influenced by the subjective views of Existentialism, the new generation of abstract painters was influenced by the objectivism of analytical philosophy—especially the branch led by Ludwig Wittgenstein, who championed a common-sense view of the world through a disciplined analysis of language. This approach was reflected in the matter-of-fact, disciplined character of Minimal art.

Stella aimed at consolidating a painting into a single, indivisible image and employed several devices to accomplish this: His works were usually symmetrical, limited to two unmodulated colors, painted on raw canvas to increase the flattening effect, and structured in narrow bands that ran parallel to the edges of the frame to echo the overall shape. His intention was to make paintings that would not refer to anything else. They were only about themselves—an ultimate step in the exclusion of content. As Stella once put it, "only what can be seen there is there." In its metamorphosis from window-on-the-world to self-referring object, painting had sought to divest itself of content and the ability to trigger emotional reactions.

Minimal sculpture was based on essentially the same sensibility and philosophy as Minimal painting, rejecting dynamic compositional effects and preferring the most elementary arrangements of forms. The extra dimension of sculpture, however, greatly multiplied the number of relationships between elements that the artist might work with and helped to reinforce the sense that the artwork was an object. Some Minimalist sculptors attempted to develop these aspects by creating works of several elements in which the space between parts became almost as important as the solid structures. The fluorescent-light sculptures of Dan Flavin (colorplate 7) were among the first and most radical experiments in changing the space and making the viewer more aware of it. Donald Judd's wall sculptures—sets of metal boxes attached to the wall one above the other—presented a similar idea on a smaller scale, stressing a single form through a persistent repetition of the form and equal intervals of the same dimensions (fig. 11-14). Other artists carried the spatial-relationship aspect even further, exhibiting their work in ways that made the viewer aware of relationships between the individual sculptures or between the sculpture and the shape of the exhibition space. Carl Andre specializes in laying simple industrial materials, such as bricks, on a gallery floor as if they were kitchen tiles. His "floor pieces" are completely dependent upon the physical and symbolic context of a gallery for their status as art. Ouside of this context, *8th Reversed Steel Corner* (fig. 11-15) would be just a collection of metal plates. Just as Minimal painting was far removed from the idea of the painting as window, Minimal sculpture aimed at playing a role quite different from that of the traditional statue isolated on top of a pedestal.

Op and Kinetic Art

Technology pervades all of art—whether the work is a polyester resin and fiberglass sculpture or a fifteenth-century oil painting. Some artistic products, however, make particular use of recent scientific and postindustrial technology.

Op Art, derived from the word *optical*, enjoyed the public limelight just after Pop Art (hence the linguistic alliteration between the names). While using the traditional medium of paint on canvas, the Op artists were notably skillful in applying a scientific understanding of optics. Like Minimal Art, Op Art was abstract, geometric, and hard-edged—yet differed markedly in

11-14
Donald Judd, *Untitled,* 1965.
Galvanized iron and
aluminum, seven boxes
measuring 9″ × 40″ × 31″
with 9″ intervals. Private
collection.

that it presented an active rather than a passive visual field.

Op Art grew directly out of the works of Mondrian and the artists and designers of the German Bauhaus and was influenced by the studies of visual perception that were being carried out by many psychologists and scientists from the 1920s onward. The recognized pioneer of this style was the Hungarian-born Victor Vasarely, whose work in Paris in the forties and fifties set an example for many other artists. It was a movement dominated by Europeans and South Americans living in Europe, although a few artists from the United States such as Richard Anuszkiewicz (colorplate 3) did develop related styles. Vasarely's experiments have covered all of the visual elements

11-15 Carl Andre, *8th Reversed Steel Corner,* 1978. Hot rolled steel, each piece 19⅝" square. Courtesy Sperone Westwater Fischer Gallery, New York.

from color to line and tend to apply the principles discovered to the creation of illusions of space. He is skilled in the art of making a flat surface appear to advance or retreat, or establishing a number of levels within a picture with simple, rhythmic abstract patterns and color variations that establish their own nonlinear systems of perspective (colorplate 30). Vasarely has also been a leader in the search for a more useful social context for art. Like the American Minimalists, he has rejected the idea of art as an expressionistic gesture of the individual. Going a step further, he has attempted to find ways to place this art at the service of the public—through murals, industrial design, and mass production. For a time in the midsixties—while Op Art was considered fashionable—some designs were adopted, converted, or invented for the decoration of clothing. Other than that, the movement and its social ideas have had little impact in America.

Bridget Riley, a British Op artist, has been the most successful in creating the sensation of motion, which she achieves with compact patterns spread over large areas (fig. 11-16). Systems of curving lines or other related shapes will not permit the eye to rest, an effect that is both tantalizing and annoying. Riley has experimented extensively with color as well and is unique in her

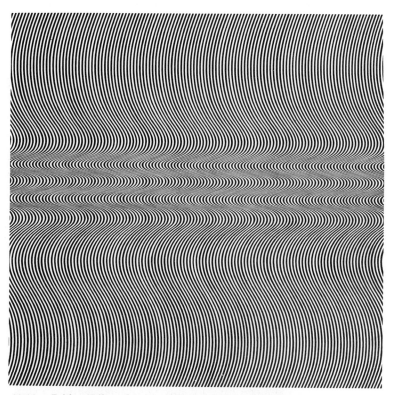

11-16   Bridget Riley, *Current*, 1964. Synthetic polymer paint on composition board, 58⅜″ × 58⅞″. The Museum of Modern Art, New York (Philip C. Johnson Fund).

studies of graduated tone variations (with which she can add effects of depth to those of motion).

Kinetic art, discussed in Chapter 3, underwent an interesting new period of development during the fifties and sixties as well, its aims being closely linked to those of the Op artists. Many of the most impressive of these artists did work in Paris with Vasarely, or at least were acutely aware of what he had done. The Argentinian Julio Le Parc's dazzling murals of light (fig. 11-17) were typical of the approach of the European-based artists of the 1960s, who favored extremely simple means and tended to shy away from mechanical devices. Le Parc's Continual Mobiles were descendants, as the name suggests, of the works of Alexander Calder (fig. 3-23) and were constructed of nothing more than pieces of polished metal hung on nylon threads. Ironically, in spite of their simplicity and geometric elements, the reflections these mobiles cast on walls and ceiling recalled the slashing brushwork of the Abstract Expressionists.

More advanced kinetic sculpture has not been as common as one might expect in this modern era, and what has been done is not as respectful of the machine as was the painting, sculpture, and architecture of the early part of the century. The impudent contraptions of Jean Tinguely (fig. 3-24) offer more to laugh about than to think about—pumping away and achieving absolutely nothing or performing such tasks as drawing "abstract" pictures.

Art as Activity and Idea

One of the more interesting developments of recent years—an important element in the general "opening up" of art—has been the revival of live performances by artists. This phenomenon began with the Futurists in the early years of the century and

11-17   Julio Le Parc, *Continual Mobile, Continual Light,* 1963. Steel and nylon, 63″ high. The Tate Gallery, London.

first attracted interest in the United States with Happenings (Chapter 3). In the late sixties and seventies, new forms evolved that attracted a great many artists. The range of these activities can be extraordinarily broad, from an intensely individual work to monumental operations involving hundreds of people. One example of such an event was the wrapping of one million square feet of Australian coastline by hundreds of volunteers in 1969 (fig. 11-18). The project was the idea of the Bulgarian-born American artist Christo, who began wrapping objects in cloth in the early sixties. He slowly worked his way up, covering public monuments and buildings, until he reached the super scale of the Australian enterprise. His two major projects in the seventies were a 200,000-square-foot curtain suspended over a Colorado canyon and a 24½-mile white fence erected in northern California—both of which, for all their materials, labor, and impressive results, were temporary.

11-18   Christo, *Wrapped Coast,* Little Bay, Australia, 1969. Cloth and rope, 1,000,000 square feet.

Performances   *Performances* are the principal result of art's expansion into theater. They usually involve only the artist (perhaps an assistant) who presents a scripted activity or carries out some form of experiment. One of the most prominent performers is Joseph Beuys of Germany, who bridges the gaps between art and life, the visual and the theatrical by becoming a sort of living, walking work of art (fig. 11-19). Beuys became an avid promoter of Happenings in the early 1960s. His own *Actions*, as he calls them, are usually performed alone and often involve a wide assortment of materials—wood, metal, rope, tape recorders, skeletons, dead or live animals, and cooking fat. They are rich in symbolism and invented ritual, and many have political overtones as well—sometimes rather provocative ones. One performance in Aachen literally caused a riot.

Another type of performance, sometimes referred to as *Body Art*, makes use of the artist's own body as the medium. This form of art differs from theatrical performance largely in terms

**11-19   Joseph Beuys, *I Like America and America Likes Me*, 1974.
Performance, three days long. Courtesy of the René Block Gallery and
Ronald Feldman Fine Arts, Inc., New York.**

11-20   Chris Burden, *White Light/White Heat,* 1975. As exhibited at Ronald Feldman Fine Arts, Inc., New York.

of its focus. If any kind of story is represented, it is usually autobiographical; more often, the concerns are conceptual. Perhaps the most extreme—possibly the most fascinating—of the Body Artists is Californian Chris Burden, who has risked death a number of times and has subjected himself to a great deal of pain. One of his less spectacular works, *White Light/White Heat,* reflects just how personal an experience Body Art can often be (fig. 11-20). It consisted of the artist's lying hidden from view in a shallow space close to the ceiling of an art gallery for a period of three weeks. During this time he did not eat, exercise, or speak with anyone. Burden designed the piece largely as an experiment in the effects of isolation and fasting. Thus the arrival of each visitor was important to him as an escape from the boredom and pain and as an examination of the variety of sensations (heightened by the effects of fasting) he experienced. The encounter with the visitor was not a one-sided affair, Burden claimed, for a kind of "energy" existed between them that both could sense. But even if this were not the case, such works certainly do leave the visitor with a number of unusual thoughts and issues to ponder.

Conceptual Art

Conceptual Art is another major approach to art as idea that developed in the late sixties. Indeed, Conceptual artists have argued that the creation of art is possible without the use of objects or events. Just as Duchamp has challenged the definition of art by designating certain random, manufactured objects as artworks (fig. 10-16), these artists were prepared to challenge the need for anything but the idea itself.

Conceptual Art was partly an outgrowth of the expansion of art into events and performances. Some projects took up such a large geographical area that the participants were able only to communicate by letter or phone, so the object itself—or any kind of contiguous visual form—no longer existed. Other projects, like some of Burden's, were reduced so far that the idea seemed to overshadow the visual form and the event. In still other projects, because the expense or other considerations made the work impossible to create or perform, the whole thing remained in the proposal stage.

Yet in spite of their emphasis on the idea, Conceptual artists have made concessions to the physical world—since it is impossible, short of telepathy, to communicate an idea without some kind of a medium. They therefore provide a document of some kind for each piece—usually something as simple as a photograph, a tape recording, or even a postcard. John Baldessari's *Cremation Piece*, for example, is documented by a printed statement (fig. 11-21) that describes the process of the work and even some of its ramifications, by photographs of the studio, by the paintings that were burned and the act of cremation, by the ashes themselves, and by a plaque that reads *John Anthony Baldessari, May 1953–March 1966*.

The ways in which art has been practiced as idea or as activity have helped to expand the range of artistic possibilities and, of course, make definitions even more impossible to establish. Some forms rely on performance as the medium, others on writing, still others on normally undetectable means such as radio waves passing through a room—and the objectives of such art are nearly as numerous as the artists. Rather than leading to a dead end, the de-emphasis of the art object has produced a seemingly endless number of possibilities.

Entering the Eighties

Trying to understand the immediate past is like trying to make sense out of the blur of sights from the rear of a fast-moving train. Everything is passing by too rapidly to see clearly and is

"One of several proposals to rid my life of accumulated art. With this project I will have all of my accumulated paintings cremated by a mortuary. The container of ashes will be interred inside a wall of the Jewish Museum. For the length of the show, there will be a commemorative plaque on the wall behind which the ashes are located. It is a reductive, recycling piece. I consider all these paintings a body of work in the real sense of the word. Will I save my life by losing it? Will a Phoenix arise from the ashes? Will the paintings having become dust become art materials again? I don't know, but I feel better."

11-21   John Baldessari, *Cremation Piece,* 1969. As shown at The Jewish Museum in the exhibition *Software,* 1970.

too close in time and space to determine which object is important enough to focus on. This analogy is especially true for recent art: Our present train of thought seems to be passing through an unusually profuse and exotic landscape—picking up speed as it goes.

Yet in spite of—perhaps because of—this incredible variety and speed, no significant new schools of art have appeared on the scene since the decade of the sixties. Pop, Color-field, Minimalism, and other styles have not continued as movements into the seventies—although many of the artists who developed them have continued to work in those styles. Apparently the developments of the sixties left artists with enough ideas to create and explore for some time to come.

Since there are no longer any constraints about the materials that may be used in an artwork—dirt, garbage, animals, fat, ashes, radio waves, even the artist's body—there seem to be few significantly original materials left for an artist to employ. But one can always find new ways to look at the old materials. Alice Aycock's sculptures are as new as Earth Art and as old as architecture. Using traditional construction materials such as wood and concrete, she builds untraditional structures. Typically, they invite the viewer to enter a space that is inaccessible or uninhabitable. Some are quite low and partly built into the ground; some are set high above the ground; others are merely

11-22   Alice Aycock, *The Beginnings of a Complex . . .* , 1977. Wood and
concrete. Tallest tower approximately 30' high. Documenta VI, Kassel, Germany.

facades. Because of its interesting spatial relationships, its clean
lines, and even its freshly milled lumber, *The Beginnings of a
Complex . . .* (fig. 11-22) appeals to us as an abstract sculpture.
But as a shelter, it challenges the imagination. In this latter context we tend to associate it with our own bodies, comparing it to
other shelters. Where do the steps lead? Can we sit in it? Stand
in it?

Sam Gilliam's material—paint and canvas—are about as traditional as any an artist can use, and even some of his more
unusual techniques were anticipated by painters and sculptors
working in other styles. But if Gilliam began with traditions, he
soon revised them to the point where they seemed to be radical
innovations. In a long and intriguing series of works through
the late sixties and most of the seventies, he combined the stain
and spatter techniques of acrylic painting with the free shaping
of soft sculpture (colorplate 31). His canvases are rarely framed;
most often they are tacked to the wall, hang from the ceiling, or

drape across corners. While other artists argued about the relative importance of the picture plane, Gilliam resolved the problem by doing away with it altogether.

Other kinds of recent art involve neither new materials nor particularly novel ways of using old materials. Instead, their novelty concerns the radicalness of the idea behind them— meaning that a Conceptual Art sensibility is involved even though a traditional medium is used to make a relatively conventional painting or sculpture. One type of sculpture, like traditional realistic sculpture, entails making objects that represent things in the real world. But it goes so far in its imitation of the appearances of things that it manages to challenge reality itself. The creators of these "false objects" tend to reproduce everyday articles in their original size, shape, and color, but in an alien material—strawberries of painted bronze or a motorcycle of carved wood. Among the most fascinating examples of this type of art are the "leather goods" of Marilyn Levine. A viewer is almost forced to touch *Trent's Jacket* (fig. 11-23) to realize that the material hanging limply on the coat rack is hard ceramic and not supple leather.

Closely related to Levine's false objects are the paintings of the Photo-Realists, whose work often resembles photographs. *Kent* (colorplate 32) by Chuck Close even simulates photographic focus, blurring the subject's nose—which is too near— and his neck and shoulders—which are too far away. While Close prefers to make large blowups of his friends with acrylic paints and an airbrush (fig. 3-4), others, like Ralph Goings, prefer to reproduce banal scenes of modern life (fig. 8-13) with oil paints and ordinary brushes. Photo-Realist paintings became popular in the early seventies, when the art world finally realized that they were not simply another wave of traditional realist painting but an attempt to make use of the unique characteristics of the camera. By prodigiously copying photographs in paint, artists like Close and Goings are calling attention to the surface effects of pattern and color peculiar to the camera's special way of seeing. In the wake of Photo-Realism came two developments: photography (Chapter 3) coming into its own as an art form and the revival of traditional realism, even including realistic landscapes. In the 1980s, both of these kinds of art have been featured in major shows.

Along with a revival of realism, subject matter—almost abandoned during the modern period—is now slowly beginning to attract attention again. In an age in which the bounda-

11-23 Marilyn Levine, *Trent's Jacket*, 1976. Ceramic, wood, and metal hooks, 35″ × 18″ × 8″. Private collection. Courtesy of the O.K. Harris Gallery.

ries between the arts have been erased and anything goes, the only rules left to break are those that Modernism itself established. Most of the avant-garde artists who turned to subject matter seem to have felt a bit self-conscious, concerned perhaps that they would be rejected by their peers. But in the end they have realized it was the only way they could say what they felt they had to say.

Sculptor Luis Jimenez attempted to work without images when he was a student, but found that they were the only adequate means to express the ideas that interested him. Divided between two cultures, he has found ample material to work with: the clash of the old and the new, the Mexican and the American, tradition and technology. Working with polyester resin and fiberglass, coloring his works with garish sparkle-paints and exaggerated hues, Jimenez produces "contemporary icons" that record and rework traditional images of the South-

11-24   Luis Jimenez, *Progress, Part I,* 1973. Fiberglass and epoxy, 7'7" ×
8'8" × 9'9". Collection the artist. Courtesy of the O.K. Harris Gallery.

west. Some of their sources are to be found in both pre-Columbian and popular Mexican art, others in the vulgarity of plastic dime-store souvenirs. In *Progress I* (fig. 11-24), he created a monument to the spirit of the Old West—a huge pyramid of a sculpture that joins hunter, horse, and buffalo in a single dynamic swirl of mass and color. It is both heroic and satiric, a work that nudges our emotions in two directions at once. It is a post-Pop vision of the cowboy-and-Indian sculptures that Frederic Remington and other artists once created to record the myths that progress was rapidly destroying.

On the other side of the country, New York-based artist Dottie Attie has experimented with the restoration of content in a more direct and literary way. Her love of drawing and of the great art of the past—particularly that of the period from about 1600 to the early 1800s—inspired her to develop an unusual form of *Narrative Art*. Attie begins by meticulously drawing a miniature version of an Old Master painting, usually isolating such details as a face, a pair of hands, or some form of contact between two people. She then frames each of these tiny sketches and alternates them with brief fragments of stories she invents or borrows from books. Mounted on a wall, these miniature narratives sometimes stretch more than 40 feet (fig. 11-25). Typically, the events they suggest are vaguely erotic or perverse. Yet she never openly represents such activities in the pictures or explicitly states them in the texts—but leaves it up to the viewer to draw conclusions. Attie's droll stories are crisp and elegant understatements that stimulate curiosity and imagination.

Related to the apparent acceptance (or "re-acceptance") of subject matter occurring in the eighties is the emergence of a renewed interest in expressionism. Critics are divided over the importance of the phenomenon and the quality of the work associated with it. Is it a significant new wave or simply a ripple in late modern art history?

However, all writers agree that—for the first time since Abstract Expressionism—there occurred at approximately the beginning of the decade an unusual volume of art in both Europe and America exhibiting thick, vigorously applied paint. Although varying from abstract to realistic, the majority of "Neo-Expressionism" is pictorial—apparently satisfying a public hunger for images—following three decades or so of abstractionism, minimalism, and conceptualism. Like the drawings of Attie, this art is often narrative, the story content evoked by images or by the title of the work. And like both Jimenez and Attie, Neo-Expressionist artists freely delve into the realms of allegory, myth, art history, and history for their sources. Their content, like that of the German Expressionists 70 years earlier, is often angst-ridden. But instead of epic statements about the human condition, their messages often refer to the problems of late-modern art and their own self-conscious roles as artists.

The Idleness of Sisyphus (fig. 11-26) by Italian artist Sandro Chia is a case in point. In Greek myth Sisyphus was condemned eternally to push up the side of a mountain a huge stone that rolls down every time it nears the top. The myth is easily interpreted as an allegory on the absurdity and frustrations of modern life. But some critics believe it is about modern art—Chia's

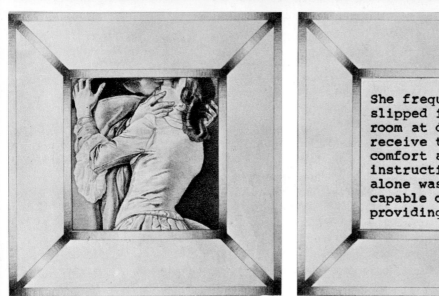

11-25   Dottie Attie, *Carolina and Her Father,* 1978. Pencil on paper, each drawing 2″ square. Installation and details at the A.I.R. Gallery, New York. Collection the artist.

11-26　Sandro Chia. *The Idleness of Sisyphus,* 1981. Oil on canvas, 122″ ×
152″. **Museum of Modern Art.**

personal debunking of modernism, reflecting doubts about its
validity. Despite such ambiguous attitudes, the works of Chia
and other Neo-Expressionists do well in the art market. Unlike
the German and the Abstract Expressionists, they have not yet
had to starve while fighting heroic avant-garde battles.

　Social commentary—content referring to social injustice and
so forth—though arguably present in the works of Neo-Expressionists as well as in the works of Jimenez, Oldenburg, and Warhol, is at most implied. Since the 1940s, when the modern movement gained momentum in this country, strong social
commentary in art has been rare. As we have seen, much of
modern art is completely detached from the concerns of the
world at large—and many in the art world have advocated this
precise position. Accordingly, art with explicit social/political
content has regularly been repudiated. But, again, about the
only rules left to break are those established by modernism itself. So, some dialogue about the relationship between art and

society has occurred in the eighties—and some art reflecting this dialogue has appeared, but not enough yet to be termed a movement.

Perhaps the most significant artwork with political content made since World War II, certainly the most ambitious, is Judy Chicago's *Dinner Party* (fig. 11-27). Three tables, arranged in a 48' × 48' × 48' triangle, have been prepared for 39 "guests"— famous women of history going back to prehistoric times. (Among those invited: Egyptian Queen Hatshepsut, American Indian Sacajawea, feminist Susan B. Anthony, and artist Georgia O'Keeffe.) Inscribed on the 1,000-square-foot triangular floor under and between the tables are the names of 999 additional famous women. Overwhelming in its color and pomp, to say

11-27   Judy Chicago, *The Dinner Party*, © Judy Chicago, 1979. Photograph by Michael Alexander. As installed at the San Francisco Museum of Modern Art.

nothing of its scale, *Dinner Party* is a stunning banner for the feminist cause. According to art critic Lucy Lippard, "Chicago recognizes women's 'deep cultural hunger' for affirmative symbols." The decoration for each of the guests' "plates"—sculpted in various degrees of relief and colored in various hues of china painting—features a central oval form, directly or indirectly representing a vagina, surrounded by other visual metaphors traditionally appropriate to the woman's life and role in history. Queen Hatshepsut's plate, painted in gold, is like an Egyptian shield; poet Emily Dickinson's is adorned with delicately sculpted pink ruffles (fig. 11-28). Each place setting has a chalice, tableware, and an elaborately decorated runner. A multimedia

11-28   Judy Chicago, detail of *The Dinner Party* (fig. 11-27). Emily Dickinson Place Setting, © Judy Chicago, 1979. Photograph by Michael Alexander.

piece involving sculpture, ceramics, needlework, and years of labor, *Dinner Party* has much to commend it. Ironically, it is more controversial as a piece of art than it is as a political statement. While the ensemble has exhibited in many places and received more public attention than most artworks, some art critics—because of the bias discussed earlier—do not agree that it deserves to be called art.

The recent paintings of Leon Golub constitute a further example of explicit social commentary. However, here the issue is political terror—not sexual politics. And Golub's medium—acrylic on canvas—is surely more conventional than Chicago's.

Golub's career began during the time of Abstract Expressionism, and remnants of that movement's style—particularly the large scale and rough textures—are present even in his newest work. Yet Golub was never enthusiastic about the principles of Abstract Expressionism, especially its emphasis on the artist's inner world of subjective feelings. Instead, he preferred to emphasize the outer world by symbolizing the human condition—predominately suffering—through large images of roughly-painted, semiabstract giants. Recently, though, Golub has grown impatient with symbolizing abstract notions, preferring to deal directly with concrete situations. And these situations concern kidnapping, imprisonment, torture, death—the entire range of twentieth-century political violence. He begins his images by painting them with acrylic and then scraping them down to the bare canvas—leaving only residues of color. In *Interrogation II* (fig. 11-29), the terrifying vulnerability of a political victim is starkly revealed. As critic Carter Ratcliff explains: " . . . Leon Golub confronts us with the grisly reality of domination, drawing us out of ourselves, rubbing our sensitivity—like his paint—raw."

Fin de Siècle

Entering our own *fin de siècle,* end of the century, we should pause to see where we have been—then try to imagine where we are going.

Though the modern movement was never a unified orderly progression, certain general patterns, or streams of influence, can be identified. One stream, centering on an interest in form, began with Cezanne and linked the Cubists, Constructivists, and Mondrian with the recent geometric art of Minimalism and Op. Another stream, concentrating on color, began with the Impressionists and connected Seurat, Matisse, and Kandinsky—

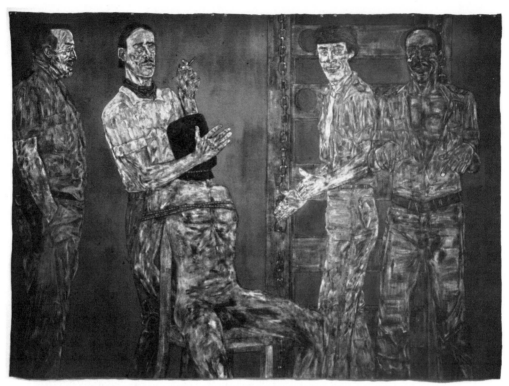

11-29 Leon Golub, *Interrogation II*, 1981. Acrylic on canvas, 120″ × 168″.
Art Institute of Chicago.

as well as such color-oriented abstract artists of our own day as
Newman, Louis, and Frankenthaler. The expressionist tradition
of Van Gogh and Munch, flowing through the German and the
Abstract Expressionists, extended to recent manifestations of
Neo-Expressionism. The radical experimentation and ironies of
Dada reemerged in Happenings and Pop Art and were contin-
ued by events, performances, and Conceptual Art. These
streams are interdependent, often overlapping one another.
And many works as well as artists belong to more than one
tradition.

Today the terms "post-modern" and "post-modernism"—
implying that the modern movement is coming to an end—are
being voiced more and more by those who write on art. The fact
that the modern movement is ending may be debatable; the fact
that the perception of its ending exists is not debatable and is
significant. Such a perception did not exist, let alone enjoy prev-
alence, before the late 1960s.

The presence of extreme pluralism coupled with a dearth of new ideas suggests that modernism is exhausted. Yet another indication is the changed position of the avant-garde. The French public was offended by the relatively minor liberties taken by Manet in the 1860s; later it heaped scorn on the Impressionists. In 1905, it was outraged by the artistic lawlessness of the Fauves. In 1913, the American public was shocked by the Armory Show. Both the public and the art world were initially close-minded toward Abstract Expressionism. Today, however, anything short of crime can be done in the name of art, including suicide. And the public—European or American—hardly seems to notice. (A German body-artist died the result of dismembering, piece by piece, parts of his body.) Does the lack of reaction mean the public is more tolerant? Perhaps. Does it mean that modern art is more acceptable? Perhaps—the market for modern art today is stronger than ever. What it surely does mean, however, is that modern art has lost its power to shock people and therefore its power to move minds.

Whether or not the perception is correct, the ending of a major movement is never abrupt or definite. As art historian and critic Robert Hughes explains:

> Histories do not break off clean, like a glass rod; they fray, stretch, and come undone, like rope. There was no specific year in which the Renaissance ended; but it did end, although culture is still permeated with the active remnants of Renaissance thought. So it is with modernism, only more so, because we are much closer to it . . . The modernist achievement will continue to affect culture for another century at least, because it was large, so imposing, and so irrefutably convincing. But its dynamic is gone, and our relationship to it is becoming archaeological.

It is futile to speculate about the twenty-first century, except to say that new centuries have a unique way of reinvigorating culture. We witnessed the explosive developments in art that occurred during the first three decades of this century; the same striking events took place in music, literature, and science. Perhaps today some relatively unknown artist, like Cezanne 100 years ago, is quietly producing work that will be extolled in the next century as the harbinger of a new art.

Suggestions for Further Study

Chapter 1 Arnheim, Rudolf. *Art and Visual Perception: A Psychology of the Creative Eye*. Berkeley and Los Angeles: University of California Press, 1954.

Barr, Alfred. *Picasso—Fifty Years of His Art*. New York: Museum of Modern Art, 1955.

Fast, Julius. *Body Language*. New York: Simon & Schuster, Pocket Books, 1971.

Goodman, Nelson. *Languages of Art: An Approach to a Theory of Symbols*. Indianapolis, Ind.: Bobbs-Merrill Co., 1968.

Kubler, George A. *The Shape of Time: Remarks on the History of Things*. New Haven: Yale University Press, 1962.

Langer, Susanne K. *Philosophy in a New Key; A Study in the Symbolism of Reason, Rite, and Art*. 3rd ed. Cambridge, Mass.: Harvard University Press, 1976.

Segall, M. H., Campbell, D. T., and Herskovits, M. J. *The Influence of Culture on Visual Perception*. Indianapolis: Bobbs-Merrill Co., 1966.

Chapter 2 Arnheim, Rudolf. *Visual Thinking*. Berkeley and Los Angeles: University of California Press, 1969.

Bloomer, Carolyn M. *Principles of Visual Perception*. New York: Van Nostrand Reinhold Co., 1976.

Clark, Kenneth. *Looking at Pictures*. Boston: Beacon Press, 1968.

Eitner, Lorenz. *Introduction to Art*. Minneapolis: Burgess Publishing Co., 1961.

Ehrenzweig, Anton. *The Hidden Order of Art: A Study in the Psychology of Artistic Imagination*. Berkeley and Los Angeles: University of California Press, 1967.

Gibson, James J. *The Perception of the Visual World*. Boston: Houghton Mifflin Co., 1950.

————. *The Senses Considered as Perceptual Systems*. Boston: Houghton Mifflin Co., 1966.

Gombrich, Ernst H. *Art and Illusion: A Study in the Psychology of Pictorial Presentation*. 2nd ed. Princeton: Princeton University Press, 1961.

Gombrich, E. H., Hochberg, J., and Black, M. *Art, Perception and Reality*. Baltimore: Johns Hopkins University Press, 1972.

Gregory, R. L. *Eye and Brain*. New York: McGraw-Hill, 1966.

Hogg, James, ed. *Psychology and the Visual Arts*. Baltimore: Penguin Books, 1970.

Kepes, Gyorgy. *Language of Vision*. Chicago: Paul Theobald & Co., 1945.

Kohler, Wolfgang. *Gestalt Psychology*. New ed. New York: Liveright, 1970.

Russell, John. *Seurat*. New York: Praeger Publishers, 1965.

Chapter 3 Celant, Germano. *Art Povera*. New York: Praeger Publishers, 1969.

Craven, George M. *Object and Image*. Englewood Cliffs, N.J.: Prentice-Hall, 1975.

de la Croix, Horst, and Tansey, Richard G. *Gardner's Art Through the Ages*. 7th ed. New York: Harcourt Brace Jovanovich, 1980.

Dyckes, William, *Contemporary Spanish Art*. New York: Art Digest, 1975.
Encyclopedia of World Art, 15 Vols. New York: McGraw-Hill, 1959–68.

Ivins, William M., Jr. *Prints and Visual Communiction*. Cambridge, Mass.: M.I.T. Press, 1969.

Kirby, Michael, ed. *Happenings: An Illustrated Anthology*. New York: E. P. Dutton & Co., 1965.

Martindale, Andrew. *Gothic Art*. New York: Praeger Publishers, 1967.

Mayer, Ralph. *The Painter's Craft*. New York: D. Van Nostrand Co., Inc., 1948.

Mendelowitz, Daniel M. *Drawing*. New York: Holt, Rinehart & Winston, 1967.

Popper, Frank. *Origins and Development of Kinetic Art*. Greenwich, Conn.: New York Graphic Society, 1969.

Read, Herbert. *The Art of Sculpture*. 2nd ed. Princeton: Princeton University Press, 1961.

Seitz, William. *The Art of Assemblage*. New York: Museum of Modern Art, 1961.

Sontag, Susan. *On Photography*. New York: Farrar, Straus & Giroux, 1977.

Wollheim, Richard. *Art and Its Objects: An Introduction to Aesthetics*. New York: Harper & Row, 1968.

Chapter 4 Engel, Heinrich. *The Japanese House: A Tradition for Contemporary Architecture*. Rutland, Vt. and Tokyo: Charles E. Tuttle Co., 1964.

Evenson, Norma. *Le Corbusier: The Machine and the Grand Design.* New York: George Braziller, 1969.

Furneaux Jordan, Robert. *A Concise History of Western Architecture.* New York: Harcourt Brace Jovanovich, 1970.

Giedion, Sigfried. *Space, Time and Architecture: The Growth of a New Tradition.* 5th rev. ed. Cambridge, Mass.: Harvard University Press, 1967.

Huxtable, Ada L. *Will They Ever Finish Bruckner Boulevard?* New York: Macmillan, 1970.

Jacobs, J., ed. *The Great Cathedrals.* New York: American Heritage, 1968.

Jencks, Charles, and Baird, George, eds. *Meaning in Architecture.* New York: George Braziller, 1970.

Nishihara, Kiyoyuki. *Japanese Houses: Patterns for Living.* Tokyo: Japan Publications, 1967.

Norberg-Schulz, Christian. *Existence, Space and Architecture.* New York: Praeger Publishers, 1971.

————. *Meaning in Western Architecture.* New York: Praeger Publishers, 1975.

Rudofsky, Bernard. *Architecture Without Architects: A Short Introduction to Non-Pedigreed Architecture.* Garden City, New York: Doubleday & Co., 1969.

————. *Streets for People.* Garden City, New York: Doubleday & Co., 1969.

Scully, Vincent. *American Architecture and Urbanism: A Historical Essay.* New York: Praeger Publishers, 1969.

————. *Modern Architecture.* Rev. ed. New York: George Braziller, 1974.

Wright, Frank Lloyd. *When Democracy Builds.* Chicago: University of Chicago Press, 1945.

Zucker, Paul. *Town and Square: From the Agora to the Village Green.* New York: Columbia University Press, 1959.

Chapter 5

Carter, Dagny. *Four Thousand Years of China's Art.* New York: Ronald Press, 1948.

Clark, Kenneth. *Landscape Into Art.* London: John Murray, 1966.

————. *Leonardo da Vinci.* Baltimore: Penguin Books, Pelican Books, 1968.

Giedion, Sigfried. *The Eternal Present: The Beginning of Art.* Princeton, N.J.: Princeton University Press, 1964.

Hartt, Frederick. *History of Italian Renaissance Art.* New York: Harry N. Abrams, 1969.

Kahler, Heinz. *The Art of Rome and Her Empire.* New York: Crown Publishers, 1963.

Klingender, Francis D. *Animals in Art and Thought to the End of the Middle Ages.* Ed. by Evelyn Antal and John Harthan. Cambridge, Mass.: M.I.T. Press, 1971.

Michalowski, Kazimierz. *The Art of Ancient Egypt*. New York: Harry N. Abrams, 1969.

Peacock, Carlos. *John Constable: The Man and His Work*. Rev. ed. Greenwich, Conn.: New York Graphic Society, 1972.

Richter, Gisela M. A. *Perspective in Greek and Roman Art*. London: Phaidon, 1971.

Shepard, Paul. *Man in the Landscape*. New York: Alfred A. Knopf, 1967.

Willets, William. *Foundations of Chinese Art*. New York: McGraw-Hill, 1965.

Chapter 6   Berger, John. *Ways of Seeing*. New York: Penguin Books, 1977.

Clark, Kenneth. *The Nude: A Study of Ideal Form*. Garden City, New York: Doubleday & Co., Anchor Books, 1956.

Crespelle, Jean-Paul. *Chagall*. New York: Coward, McCann & Geoghegan, 1970.

Hodin, J. P. *Oskar Kokoschka*. Greenwich, Conn.: New York Graphic Society, 1966.

Honour, Hugh. *Neo-Classicism*. Harmondsworth, England: Penguin Books, 1968.

Lal, Kanwar. *Immortal Khajuraho*. Delhi: Asia Press, 1965.

Powell, Ann. *The Origins of Western Art*. New York: Harcourt Brace Jovanovich, 1973.

Richter, G. M. A. *A Handbook of Greek Art: A Survey of the Visual Arts of Ancient Greece*. 6th rev. ed. London: Phaidon Press, 1969.

Schefold, Karl. *Myth and Legend in Early Greek Art*. New York: Harry N. Abrams, 1966.

Sewter, A. C. *Baroque and Rococo*. New York: Harcourt Brace Jovanovich, 1972.

White, Christopher. *Rubens and His World*. New York: Viking Press, 1968.

Chapter 7   Clements, Robert J. *Michelangelo: A Self-Portrait*. New York: New York University Press, 1968.

De Tolnay, Charles. *The Art and Thought of Michelangelo*. New York: Pantheon, 1964.

Friedman, B. H. *Jackson Pollock: Energy Made Visible*. New York: McGraw-Hill, 1972.

Hauser, Arnold. *The Social History of Art*. New York: Alfred A. Knopf, 1961.

Hibbard, Howard. *Michelangelo*. New York: Harper & Row, 1974.

Lubin, Albert J. *Stranger on the Earth: A Psychological Biography of Van Gogh*. New York: Holt, Rinehart & Winston, 1972.

Muller, Joseph-Emile. *Rembrandt*. Trans. by Brian Hooley. New York: Harry N. Abrams, 1969.

O'Connor, Francis V. *Jackson Pollock*. New York: The Museum of Modern Art, 1969.

O'Hara, Frank. *Jackson Pollock*. New York: George Braziller, 1959.

Ramsden, E. H. *Michelangelo*. New York: Praeger Publishers, 1971.

Rosenberg, Jacob. *Rembrandt: Life and Work*. New York: Phaidon Press, 1964.

Schapiro, Meyer. *Vincent Van Gogh*. New York: Harry N. Abrams, 1970.

Tralbaut, Marc E. *Van Gogh*. New York: Viking Press, 1969.

Van Gogh, Vincent. *Letters of Vincent Van Gogh*. Ed. Mark Roskill. New York: Atheneum, 1963.

Chapter 8

Driskell, David C. *Two Centuries of Black American Art*. New York: Alfred A. Knopf, 1976.

Fine, Elsa H. *The Afro-American Artist: A Search for Identity*. New York: Holt, Rinehart & Winston, 1973.

Goodrich, Lloyd. *Edward Hopper*. New York: Harry N. Abrams, 1971.

McCoubrey, John W., ed. *American Art 1700–1960: Sources and Documents*. Englewood Cliffs, N.J.: Prentice-Hall, 1965.

McLanathan, Richard. *The American Tradition in the Arts*. New York: Harcourt Brace Jovanovich, 1968.

Owings, Nathaniel A. *The American Aesthetic*. New York: Harper & Row, 1969.

Rose, Barbara. *American Art Since 1900*. New York: Praeger Publishers, 1967.

Taylor, Joshua. *America as Art*. Washington, D.C.: National Collection of Fine Arts, 1976.

Tighe, Mary Ann, and Lang, Elizabeth E. *Art America*. New York: McGraw-Hill, 1977.

Whitney Museum. *200 Years of American Sculpture*. Boston: David R. Godine, 1976.

Wilmerding, John. *American Art*. New York: Penguin Books, 1976.

Chapter 9

Arnason, H. H. *History of Modern Art: Painting, Sculpture and Architecture*. Englewood Cliffs, N.J.: Prentice-Hall; New York: Harry N. Abrams, 1968.

Badt, Kurt. *The Art of Cézanne*. Trans. by Sheila A. Ogilvie. Berkeley and Los Angeles: University of California Press, 1965.

Balakian, Anna. *The Symbolist Movement: A Critical Approach*. New York: New York University Press, 1977.

Bell, Clive. *Art*. New York: G. P. Putnam's Sons, Capricorn, 1959.

Boudaille, Georges. *Gauguin*. Trans. Elisa Jaffa. New York: Tudor, 1964.

Champigneulle, Bernard. *Rodin*. Trans. by J. Maxwell Brownjohn. New York: Harry N. Abrams, 1967.

Duret, Theodore. *Manet and the French Impressionists*. Trans. J. E. Crawford Fitch. Freeport, N.Y.: Books for Libraries Press, 1971.

Hamilton, George H. *Manet and His Critics*. New York: W. W. Norton & Co., 1969.

Harris, A. S., and Nochlin, L. *Women Artists, 1550–1950*. New York: Alfred A. Knopf, 1977.

Hess, Thomas B., and Ashbery, John, eds. *Avant-Garde Art*. New York: Macmillan, 1971.

Kubler, George A. *The Shape of Time: Remarks on the History of Things*. New Haven: Yale University Press, 1962.

Loengren, Sven. *The Genesis of Modernism*. Indianapolis: Indiana University Press, 1971.

Rewald, John. *Post Impressionism: From Van Gogh to Gauguin*. New York: Museum of Modern Art, 1962.

Slocombe, George. *Rebels of Art*. Port Washington, N.Y.: Kennikat Press Corp., 1969.

Chapter 10

Barr, Alfred. *Matisse: His Art and His Public*. New York: Museum of Modern Art, 1951.

Bowness, Alan. *Modern European Art*. New York: Harcourt Brace Jovanovich, 1972.

Chipp, Herschel B. *Theories of Modern Art: A Source Book by Artists and Critics*. Berkeley and Los Angeles: University of California Press, 1968.

de la Croix, Horst, and Tansey, Richard G. *Gardner's Art Through the Ages*. 7th ed. New York: Harcourt Brace Jovanovich, 1980.

Diehl, Gaston. *The Fauves*. New York: Harry N. Abrams, 1975.

Douval, Bernard. *The School of Paris*. Trans. Cornelia Brookfield and Ellen Hart. New York: Alfred A. Knopf, 1977.

Haftmann, Werner. *Painting in the Twentieth Century*. Vol. 1, *An Analysis of the Artists and Their Work*. New York: Praeger Publishers, 1965.

Jean, Marcel, and Mezei, Arpad. *The History of Surrealist Painting*. Trans. by Simon Watson Taylor. New York: Grove Press, 1960.

Madsen, Stephan T. *Sources of Art Nouveau*. Trans. R. I. Christopherson. New York: McGraw-Hill, 1967.

Mondrian, Pieter Cornelis. *Plastic Art and Pure Plastic Art*. New York: George Wittenborn, 1945.

Neumeyer, Alfred. *The Search for Meaning in Modern Art: Die Kunst in Unserer Zeit*. Trans. by R. Angress. Englewood Cliffs, N.J.: Prentice-Hall, 1965.

Penrose, Roland. *Picasso: His Life and Work*. Rev. ed. New York: Harper & Row, 1973.

Read, Herbert. *The Art of Sculpture*. 2nd ed. Princeton: Princeton University Press, 1961.

Rickey, George. *Constructivism*. New York: George Braziller, 1967.

Rosenblum, Robert. *Cubism and Twentieth-Century Art*. New York: Harry N. Abrams, 1968.

Rubin, William S. *Dada, Surrealism and Their Heritage*. New York: Museum of Modern Art, 1968.

Selz, Peter. *German Expressionist Painting*. Berkeley and Los Angeles: University of California Press, 1974.

Chapter 11 Amaya, Mario. *Pop Art . . . and After*. New York: Viking Press, 1972.

Ashton, Dore. *A Reading of Modern Art*. Cleveland: Press of Case Western Reserve University, 1969.

————. *The New York School: A Cultural Reckoning*. New York: Viking Press, 1973.

Battcock, Gregory, ed. *Idea Art: A Critique*. New York: E. P. Dutton & Co., 1973.

————, ed. *Minimal Art: A Critical Anthology*. New York: E. P. Dutton & Co., 1968.

————, ed. *The New Art: A Critical Anthology*. Rev. ed. New York: E. P. Dutton & Co., 1973.

————. *Super Realism: A Critical Anthology*. New York: E. P. Dutton & Co., 1975.

Burnham, Jack. *Beyond Modern Sculpture*. New York: George Braziller, 1968.

Gottlieb, Carla. *Beyond Modern Art*. New York: E. P. Dutton & Co., 1976.

Hughes, Robert. *The Shock of the New*. New York: Alfred A. Knopf, 1981.

Hunter, Sam, and Jacobus, John. *American Art of the Twentieth Century*. New York: Harry N. Abrams, 1973.

Leymarie, Jean, ed. *Art Since Mid-Century*. Greenwich, Conn.: New York Graphic Society, 1971.

Meyer, Ursula. *Conceptual Art*. New York: E. P. Dutton & Co., 1972.

Muller, Gregoire. *The New Avant Garde*. New York: Praeger Publishers, 1972.

Popper, Frank. *Origins and Development of Kinetic Art*. Greenwich, Conn.: New York Graphic Society, 1969.

Rose, Barbara. *American Art Since 1900*. Rev. ed. New York: Praeger Publishers, 1967.

Russell, John. *The Meanings of Modern Art*. New York: Harper & Row, Publishers, Inc., 1981.

Sandler, Irving. *The Triumph of American Painting: A History of Abstract Expressionism*. New York: Praeger Publishers, 1973.

Sontag, Susan. *Against Interpretation and Other Essays*. New York: Farrar, Straus & Giroux, 1966.

PART II
CHRONOLOGY

(* = works in Part I or Part III related in time to those in Part II)

ERA/DATE	TITLE	ARTIST	FIGURE/PLATE
Ice Age			
15000 B.C.	Hall of Bulls, Lascaux cave		(5-1)
15000 B.C.	Bellowing Bison, Altamira		(5-2)
Egyptian			
2500 B.C.	Hippopotamus Hunt		(5-4)
2500 B.C.	Mycerinus and Queen		(6-2)
230 B.C.	Temple of Horus		(4-2)*
Greek			
600 B.C.	Kouros		(6-1)
480 B.C.	Kritios Boy		(6-3)
460 B.C.	Temple of Hera		(9-5)*
450 B.C.	Doryphoros	Polykleitos	(6-4)
448 B.C.	Parthenon		(4-3)*
400s B.C.	Acropolis, Athens		(4-20)*
300s B.C.	Plan of Priene		(4-24)*
330 B.C.	Apollo Belvedere		(6-5)
330 B.C.	Cnidian Aphrodite	after Praxiteles	(6-10)
Roman			
100–0 B.C.	Wall painting, Villa of A. Postumus		(5-5)
100–0 B.C.	Wall painting, Villa Boscoreale		(5-6)

ERA/DATE	TITLE	ARTIST	FIGURE/ PLATE
A.D. 10	Roman Aqueduct, Segovia		(4-5)*
A.D. 100s	Trajan's Market		(4-29)*

Medieval

ERA/DATE	TITLE	ARTIST	FIGURE/PLATE
1000	Christ Entry into Jerusalem, Gospel Book of Otto III		(5-8)
1100s	Detail of Royal Portals, Chartres Cathedral		(6-21)
1194	Chartres nave		(3-28)*
1194	view of Chartres Cathedral		(4-10)*
1194	Wine Merchant, window of Chartres		(plate 6)*
1300s	Virgin of Paris, Cathedral of Notre Dame, Paris		(6-11)

Renaissance–Modern

ERA/DATE	TITLE	ARTIST	FIGURE/PLATE
1310	Madonna Enthroned	Giotto	(3-1)*
1300s	Meeting at the Golden Gate	Giotto	(plate 4)*
1425	Meeting of Solomon and Sheba	Ghiberti	(3-18)*
1430	Expulsion from Garden of Eden	della Quercia	(6-23)
1432	God the Father, Ghent Altarpiece	van Eyck	(3-2)*
1436	Florence Cathedral Dome	Brunelleschi	(4-11)*
1437	Madonna and Child	Lippi	(1-4)*
1450	St. John in the Wilderness	di Paolo	(5-10)
1480	Birth of Venus	Botticelli	(plate 10)
1496	Four Horsemen of the Apocalypse	Dürer	(2-3)*
1498	Virgin and Child with St. Anne	Leonardo	(7-2)
1498	Pietà	Michelangelo	(7-1)
1501	David	Michelangelo	(6-6)
1503	Mona Lisa	Leonardo	(5-9)
1508	Sistine Ceiling	Michelangelo	(7-4)
1508	Creation of the Sun and the Moon	Michelangelo	(plate 12)
1514	Barbara Dürer	Dürer	(2-14)*
1534	The Last Judgement	Michelangelo	(7-5)

ERA/DATE	TITLE	ARTIST	FIGURE/PLATE
1534	detail with "self-portrait"	Michelangelo	(7-6)
1538	Venus of Urbino	Titian	(6-12)
1555	Pieta Rondanini	Michelangelo	(7-7)
1619	St. Ignatius Exorcising Demons	Rubens	(7-8)
1623	David	Bernini	(3-17)*
1636	Judgement of Paris	Rubens	(6-13)
1636	Blinding of Samson	Rembrandt	(7-9)
1642	The Night Watch	Rembrandt	(plate 13)
1648	The Burial of Phocion	Poussin	(5-12)
1649	Christ Healing the Sick	Rembrandt	(3-9)*
1652	Self-Portrait	Rembrandt	(7-10)
1665	Return of the Prodigal Son	Rembrandt	(7-11)
1800	Portrait of a Negress	Benoist	(6-14)
1816	Willy Lott's House	Constable	(5-13)
1821	The Hay Wain	Constable	(plate 9)
1826	The Death of Sardanapoulus	Delacroix	(plate 5)*
1832	George Washington	Greenough	(6-7)
1846	The Oxbow	Cole	(8-1)
1849	Watching the Cargo	Bingham	(8-3)
1851	Blue Hole, Flood Waters	Duncanson	(8-2)
1871	The Country School	Homer	(8-5)
1873	The Berry Pickers	Homer	(3-3)*
1876	The Age of Bronze	Rodin	(6-8)
1879	Birth of Venus	Bouguereau	(6-15)
1882	Daughters of Edward D. Boit	Sargent	(8-4)
1885	The Potato Eaters	van Gogh	(7-12)
1888	View of Arles with Irises	van Gogh	(7-14)
1888	The Night Cafe	van Gogh	(plate 14)
1888	Self-Portrait	van Gogh	(7-15)
1889	The Starry Night	van Gogh	(7-16)
1907	Dancer	Picasso	(6-16)
1907	Le Luxe II	Matisse	(6-17)
1907	Stag at Sharkey's	Bellows	(8-7)
1912	McSorley's Bar	Sloan	(8-6)

ERA/DATE	TITLE	ARTIST	FIGURE/ PLATE
1914	The Tempest	Kokoschka	(6-24)
1917	Double Portrait with Wineglass	Chagall	(plate 11)
1920	Skyscrapers	Stella	(8-9)
1924	The Harlequin's Carnival	Miró	(7-19)
1925	House by the Railroad	Hopper	(plate 16)
1929	Black Cross, New Mexico	O'Keeffe	(8-8)
1930	Stone City, Iowa	Wood	(11-1)*
1932	Arts of the West	Benton	(7-18)
1934	Seascape	Pollock	(7-17)
1938	Recumbent Figure	Moore	(6-18)
1942	Nighthawks	Hopper	(8-10)
1942	Tombstones	Lawrence	(8-11)
1943	Pasiphae	Pollock	(7-20)
1947	Cathedral	Pollock	(7-21)
1950	One (Number 31)	Pollock	(plate 15)
1957	Man and Woman in Large Room	Diebenkorn	(8-12)
1962	Marilyn Monroe Diptych	Warhol	(plate 28)*
1967	Indian #16	Scholder	(8-14)
1968	Great American Nude No. 99	Wesselmann	(6-19)
1971	Super Indian #2	Scholder	(plate 17)
1973	Kentucky Fried Chicken	Goings	(8-13)
1976	Walter Finley	Sleigh	(6-9)

Nonwestern

ERA/DATE	TITLE	ARTIST	FIGURE/ PLATE
1000s	Clearing Autumn Skies	Kuo Hsi	(5-7)
1100s	Clear Day in the Valley	Tung Yuan	(plate 8)
1000s	Walls of Kandarya Mahadeva Temple		(6-20)
1000s	Detail of Kandarya Mahadeva Temple		(6-22)
—	Bushmen Defending Herds		(5-3)
1800s	The Great Wave	Hokusai	(7-13)

Chronology of Certain Works in Parts I and II as Discussed in Part III

These works in Parts I and II are either mentioned in Part III or are particularly relevant to the developments of the modern movement.

ERA/DATE	TITLE	ARTIST	FIGURE/ PLATE
Chapter 9	**Art and Change**		
1885	The Potato Eaters	van Gogh	(7-12)
1888	View of Arles with Irises	van Gogh	(7-14)
1888	The Night Cafe	van Gogh	(plate 14)
1888	Self-Portrait	van Gogh	(7-15)
1889	The Starry Night	van Gogh	(7-16)
1890	After the Bath	Degas	(3-5)
Chapter 10	**The Early Twentieth Century**		
Fin de Siècle:			
1883	Bathing at Asnières	Seurat	(plate 1)
1893	Jane Avril	Toulouse-Lautrec	(3-12)
1900–1943:			
1909	Head of a Woman	Picasso	(1-4)
1914	The Tempest	Kokoschka	(6-24)
1917	Double Portrait with Wineglass	Chagall	(plate 11)
1920	Skyscrapers	Stella	(8-9)
1924	The Harlequin's Carnival	Miró	(7-19)
1924	Merzbau	Schwitters	(3-29)
1934	Death Seizing a Woman	Kollwitz	(2-16)
1936	Head	González	(3-20)
1943	First Steps	Picasso	(1-3)
Nonwestern:			
1775	African Negro Mask		(1-5)

ERA/DATE	TITLE	ARTIST	FIGURE/ PLATE
Chapter 11	**The Late Twentieth Century**		

American Modernism before World War II:

ERA/DATE	TITLE	ARTIST	FIGURE/PLATE
1920	Skyscrapers	Stella	(8-9)
1929	Black Cross, New Mexico	O'Keeffe	(8-8)

Regionalism:

1932	Arts of the West	Benton	(7-18)
1934	Seascape	Pollock	(7-17)
1942	Nighthawks	Hopper	(8-10)

Post World War II:

1943	Pasiphae	Pollock	(7-20)
1947	Cathedral	Pollock	(7-21)
1950	One (Number 31)	Pollock	(plate 15)
1950	Tree of Fluids	Dubuffet	(2-19)
1951	No. 3	Pollock	(2-15)
1959	18 Happenings in 6 Parts	Kaprow	(3-30)
1960	Untitled	Kelly	(2-4)
1962	Marilyn Monroe Diptych	Warhol	(plate 28)
1963	All Things Do Live in the Three	Anuskiewicz	(plate 3)
1968	Great American Nude No. 99	Wesselmann	(6-19)
1969	Double Negative	Heizer	(3-31)
1971	Untitled (to Donna) 5A	Flavin	(plate 7)
1973	Kentucky Fried Chicken	Goings	(8-13)
1973	Triond	Vasarely	(3-13)
1983	Untitled,	Sherman	(3-15)

Glossary

abstract   Pertaining to art consisting of patterns or shapes not necessarily resembling anything in the real or imaginary world. Of any art in which subject matter and images are either entirely absent or deemphasized.

Abstract Expressionism   An American abstract art movement beginning in the 1940s and flourishing during the 1950s. It consists of two types of paintings: (1) *Chromatic Abstraction* characterized by large broadly-painted, soft-edged shapes and (2) *Action Painting* characterized by multiple colors and shapes highly agitated in appearance—as if painted rapidly and spontaneously. Both types are considered highly subjective, created out of the inner necessity of the artist.

academic   Pertaining to academies. Artwork overly committed to rules, unoriginal, and/or pedantic.

academy   A school for artists.

acrylic   A synthetic painting medium. A technique of painting in which pigments are mixed with acrylic. A painting made by this technique.

aerial perspective   Suggesting depth in a picture by the use of progressively cooler hues, more subdued color contrasts, and softer edges for distant things. A method of simulating atmospheric conditions. See *sfumato*.

aesthetic   Pertaining to art. Of a sensitivity to art or things beautiful.

aesthetics   The study of art and/or theories of beauty.

airbrush   An atomizer, or miniature spray gun, used for applying paint to a support. See *support*. A painting technique in which an airbrush rather than a brush is used.

analogous colors	Colors similar in hue such as blue, blue-green, and green. See *hue, color wheel*.
anecdote	A brief story about an event of human interest, usually amusing or sentimental. Typically employed in genre art. See *genre art*.
arch	A principle of construction in which an open space is bridged by a series of wedge-shaped masonry blocks that form a semicircular curve. Characterized by *load-carrying* walls. A structure made by this method. See fig. 4-4.
architectonic	Of artwork that manifests the qualities of architecture: structure, order, monumentality, and so forth.
architecture	The process of designing and constructing buildings. A building or buildings.
artifact	Any made object.
Art Nouveau	An applied-arts movement in the late nineteenth and early twentieth centuries. The Art Nouveau style is known for ornate patterns, curvilinear lines and shapes, and plant motifs. Its graphic arts are similar in certain respects to the works of the Post-Impressionists—especially Gauguin, Van Gogh, and Toulouse-Lautrec.
art world	Collectively, the people (artists, critics, dealers, patrons) and the institutions (studios, galleries, museums, publishing houses) who produce or deal with contemporary art.
assemblage	Artwork in which a variety of three-dimensional objects and materials, often unrelated to one another, are combined to form a work of mixed media. See *mixed media, found object*.
assimilation effect	A pattern of small units of one color superimposed over a different background color that causes the color underneath to shift its value and hue somewhat toward that of the pattern. See *optical mixing*.
automatic drawing	Freely executed lines, shapes, or colors based primarily on the artist's unconscious thoughts and feelings. Sometimes called "automatic writing" or "automatism."
avant-garde	Literally "forward guard." A group of artists whose work and philosophy are perceived by the art establishment and general public as nonconformist or experimental. The leaders of an art movement. See *modern movement*.
balance	A perception that opposing parts—right and left, top and bottom, foreground and background—of an artwork are in balance, that the various *visual weights* and *psychological weights* have been equalized. See *composition*.
balloon frame	The nineteenth-century name for wood-frame construction.
Baroque	Pertaining to a style of art and architecture flourishing in western Eu-

rope during the seventeenth century and characterized by grand-scale (or the appearance of such) drama, exuberance, and richness of detail.

baroque Having the qualities of Baroque art. See *Baroque*.

barrel vault See *vault*.

Body Art Related to Performance and Conceptual Art—where the artist's own body is the focus. See *Performance, Conceptual Art*.

camera A lightproof box with lens used for capturing the image of a subject on light-sensitive film. See *photography, film negative*.

carving Producing a sculpture by cutting, chipping, or hewing wood or stone. A sculpture produced by this method.

casting The process of producing a sculpture by pouring a liquid material that later hardens—such as molten bronze or polyester resin—into a mold. A sculpture made by this process.

ceramic Pertaining to clay that has been changed into a hard substance through baking at a high temperature.

chiaroscuro Literally "light-dark." Representing the changing effects (particularly the changes in value) of reflected light as it falls on a three-dimensional object or any uneven surface. Often referred to as *shading*. See *value*.

cire perdue See *lost wax*.

Classical Of the period of Greek art from 480 to 323 B.C.

classical Pertaining to the art and culture of ancient Greece and Rome. Pertaining to classicism. See *classicism*.

classicism Resembling, imitating, or referring to the art and culture of ancient Greece or Rome. Having the qualities of restraint, order, harmony, and balance. The opposite of romantic art.

closure The tendency to perceive an incomplete shape as complete; for example, seeing a number of unconnected dots as a single pattern or shape, or perceiving a person sitting behind a desk as a whole person (rather than as just the visible portion of that person).

collage An artwork in which fragments of things—paper, photographs, news clippings, cloth, odds and ends, and so forth—are pasted to a flat surface. See *mixed media*.

color Technically a sensation in the retina of the eye resulting from light waves of varying lengths—but normally a perceived quality of an object. Color is affected by the amount and nature of light falling on an object. Color can be analyzed in terms of its three properties: *hue* (the quality that distinguishes one color from another), *value* (lightness or darkness), and *saturation* (brightness or dullness). Color is considered the most basic of the visual elements because it is through its variations of hue, value, and saturation that we perceive shapes, lines, textures, and space.

color constancy
The tendency to perceive the color of an object as unchanging regardless of variations in the amount of light falling on the object.

colored light
An environment affected by reflected light of different colors produced naturally (as with sunlight filtered through stained glass) or artificially (as with fluorescent light fixtures). See *environment*.

Color Field
An abstract style of painting involving the method of dripping paint invented by Jackson Pollock. However, in Color Field painting acrylics are poured on unprimed canvas (rather than oils on primed canvas) to allow the paints to penetrate and stain the canvas.

color wheel
A circular chart used to display the relationships among the different colors (particularly the hues of those colors). The primaries—red, yellow, and blue—are located at three equidistant points on the circle (forming a triangle). Midway between the primaries are the three secondaries: *green* between yellow and blue, *purple* between blue and red, and *orange* between red and yellow. Large color wheels contain hues between the primaries and secondaries that are related to their neighbors. For example, *blue-green* is between blue and green, *yellow-orange* between yellow and orange, and so forth.

column
A cylindrical vertical support, especially in Egyptian and Greek temple architecture.

commission
To hire or contract an artist to do a work of art, such as a mural or portrait (verb); a contract or agreement between an artist and a patron (noun). See *patron*.

complementary colors
Colors opposite in hue, such as red and green or yellow and purple. Complementaries are on opposite sides of a color wheel. See *hue, color wheel*.

composition
The organization of all the parts of an artwork. The arrangement of the visual elements and other ingredients—images, subject matter, symbols, and so forth—that constitute an artwork. See *unity*.

Conceptual Art
A theory and practice of art that rejects the use of art objects, maintaining that the essential aspect of an artwork is the idea behind it. Conceptual artists, nevertheless, use objects—photographs, printed matter, audio tapes, and so forth—to document their ideas.

cool colors
Blues, blue-greens, blue-purples—any analogous colors (hues) in which blue predominates. The opposite of *warm colors*. See *analogous colors*.

content
The essential meaning of an artwork as distinguished from its form or subject matter. See *theme*.

continuity
A single feature or a series of features that extends throughout a large part of a composition. An aid to unity. See *unity*.

cross vault	A structure consisting of the intersection of two vaults at right angles. See *vault*, fig. 4-7.
Cubism	A semiabstract style of art invented by Pablo Picasso and Georges Braque consisting of two types: (1) *Analytic* (*c.* 1907–1911) in which a subject—typically a still life—is freely represented in monochromatic color by a number of fragmented semitransparent shapes, and (2) *Synthetic* (*c.* 1912–1913) in which bright colors, vivid textures, and flat jagged shapes vaguely suggest images.
Cubists	An early twentieth-century avant-garde that developed and practiced the style of Cubism—especially Picasso and Braque. See *Cubism*.
Dada	Literally "hobbyhorse." A short-lived arts movement during World War I that began as a protest against the war. Emphasizing parody, anarchy, nihilism, and absurdity (as symbolized by the name), Dada artists customarily expressed themselves through experimental, witty, or outrageous actions—rather than in permanent art objects such as paintings or sculptures.
dominant feature	A feature in a picture that stands out most because of its large size, central location, bright color, and/or strong contrast with its surroundings. An aid to unity. See *unity*.
Doric	Pertaining to a style of temple architecture developed by the ancient Greeks.
drawing	Producing an artwork by making marks—usually of a single color—on a support—usually paper—and including the color of the support as part of the work. An artwork produced by this method. See *medium*.
drypoint	A print made from an image scratched by needle into a copper plate. See *intaglio*.
Earth Art	An artwork in which the physical landscape has been altered to create holes, mounds, trenches, and so forth. See *environment*.
engraving	A print made from an image cut by a hard tool into a copper plate. See *intaglio*.
environment	An artwork that surrounds the viewer on all, or nearly all, sides. See *medium*.
epic	See *heroic, the*.
etching	A print made from an image cut into a copper plate by means of acid. See *intaglio*.
Existentialism	A popular philosophy among intellectuals, including Abstract Expressionists, during and immediately following World War II. Believing that existence precedes essence, Existentialists extol human freedom and reject thought systems that would limit human choice and potential. According to them, however, this freedom tends to breed a sense of loss which in turn leads to loneliness and despair—a pervasive condition of modern life.

express	Literally "press out." To communicate ideas or feelings through art.
expression	An idea or feeling communicated by a work of art. See *content*.
expressionism	The artist's personal feelings expressed primarily through distortion of images and vividness of form rather then through realistic depiction of subject matter. Certain art movements of the twentieth century. See *German Expressionism, Abstract Expressionism*.
expressionistic	Pertaining to expressionism.
expressive	Pertaining to expression. Full of feeling.
eye-level line	An imaginary horizontal line in a picture that corresponds to the height of an imaginary viewer of the scene. See *linear perspective*.
Fauves	Literally "wild beasts." An early twentieth-century avant-garde (led by Henri Matisse) whose major contribution to the development of the modern movement was a controversial exhibit of their work at the Salon d'Automne in 1905. In general, Fauve painting consists of bright arbitrary colors, flat patterns, and distorted stylized images.
ferroconcrete	A principle of construction employing concrete reinforced with steel rods or mesh to increase its tensile strength. Reinforced concrete.
figure	An image of the human body. A shape. See *shape, figure-ground*.
figure-ground/ figure-ground principle	In perception, the tendency to divide a visual pattern into two kinds of shapes—figure and ground—with the figure(s) appearing to be on top of and surrounded by the ground. In art, figure and ground are often referred to, respectively, as *positive* shape(s) and *negative* shape(s). See *shape*.
film negative	A light-sensitive sheet of celluloid which—after being exposed to light in a camera and developed in a darkroom—bears a translucent, negative image of the subject. See *photography*.
fine art	Paintings, drawings, sculpture, and like art, typically found in museums and galleries and/or discussed in art books and art magazines. Distinguished from *popular art*.
flying buttress	An exterior wall support for a Gothic building consisting of a buttress (in this case a tall, narrow masonry pier) connected with a wall at some distance from it by a half arch. See *arch, Gothic*, fig. 4-9.
foreshortening	Shortening the depth dimension (lines withdrawing in depth) in a picture to create a three-dimensional illusion.
form	The particular characteristics of an artwork's visual elements (colors, shapes, lines, textures, and space) as distinguished from its subject matter or content. See *style, composition*.
found image	A picture—usually a photograph or reproduction—removed from one context, such as a newspaper or magazine, and placed in a new context, such as a collage. See *collage*.

found object	A nonart object removed from its original context and placed in an art context—such as an art gallery—or combined with other objects to form an assemblage. See *assemblage*.
frame construction	A principle of construction in which narrow lightweight members of wood and/or metal are joined to form a framework that will support the walls and roof. Characterized by *nonload-carrying* walls. A building made by such a method.
fresco	A technique of painting on wet plaster with pigments mixed with water. A painting made by this technique.
geodesic dome	A principle of construction in which hollow lightweight metal rods are joined to form a series of triangles or hexagonal pyramids that in turn forms a dome or shell. A geodesic dome can be covered with a thin sheet of metal, plywood, clear plastic, or like material.
geometric shapes	Shapes having uniformly straight or curved edges and surfaces. These can be either two-dimensional forms such as rectangles, triangles, polygons, and circles (or combinations thereof) or three-dimensional forms such as cubes, pyramids, spheres, and hemispheres (or combinations thereof). Geometric shapes are distinguished from *organic shapes*.
genre art	Art in which the subject matter is of everyday, ordinary life.
German Expressionism	An early twentieth-century art movement consisting of small avant-garde groups and other progressive artists of central and northern Europe. The paintings of the German Expressionists, like those of the Fauves, are characterized by arbitrary colors, flatness, and distortions. But unlike the latter, the German Expressionists emphasize serious content—especially that of an intensely personal point of view.
gestural	Of paint or drawing strokes apparently made by a broad gesture of the hand and arm, and usually of thick paint.
Gothic	A style or system of architecture developed in western Europe during the twelfth century characterized by *cross vaults, pointed arches,* and *flying buttresses.* Pertaining to such a style.
gradient of texture	In a picture, units of texture or detail (such as blades of grass) becoming progressively smaller as they withdraw in depth.
grouping	Bringing unity to an artwork by clustering things in groups. See *unity*.
Happening	An artwork involving actions of performers, objects, and sometimes viewer(s). A form of improvisational theatre. See *environment, Performance*.
harmony	A condition in which colors and/or shapes of a work appear to go well together. The opposite of clashing.
hatching	Close-spaced parallel lines to suggest, depending on their thickness and density, different shades of gray. In a line drawing, used for chiaroscuro. See *optical mixing, chiaroscuro*.

heroic	Pertaining to the heroic. See *heroic, the*.
heroic, the	An expression of the qualities of manliness, bravery, and/or power on a superhuman scale.
highlight	That portion of an object where the reflected light is brightest. See *chiaroscuro*.
horizon	See *eye-level line*.
hue	The quality of a color that distinguishes it from others: as red is distinguished from blue, yellow, or green—and so forth. Scientifically, a hue is identified precisely by measuring its light wave and assigning it a position in the color spectrum. For artistic purposes, a hue is identified by name and by assigning it a position on a color wheel. See *color, color wheel*.
hue contrast	Adjacent colors having opposite hues, such as red and green or yellow and purple. See *complementary colors*.
humanism	Devotion to human concerns.
ideal	Of architecture that manifests excellence in its proportions, balance and harmony of its parts, and so forth. Of painting, sculpture, or any image—particularly that of the human figure—that represents or fulfills a concept of perfection.
idealism	Manifesting or expressing a concept of perfection, particularly in the treatment of the human figure. Typical of classical art. See *classicism*.
idealistic	See *ideal*.
idealization	See *idealism*.
idealized	See *ideal*.
idiom	See *style*.
image	A representation of a person or object.
Impressionism	An art movement during the 1870s and 1880s of mostly Parisian artists who stressed the effects of light through freely executed paintings—usually on the site rather than in a studio—with short strokes of bright color. A style characterized by this technique of painting.
ink wash	A transparent or semitransparent layer of ink applied by brush to a support such as paper. See *drawing*.
Italian Futurism	An Italian art movement of the early twentieth century that sought to express the dynamism of modern life and technology through a style based on Cubism. See *Cubism*.
intensity	See *saturation*.
in-the-round sculpture	Sculpture that is independent, freestanding, and normally can be viewed from any direction.

intaglio Making a print from a plate whose depressed surfaces only—incised lines and gouges—receive the ink which will be transferred to the print after the raised surfaces are wiped clean. See *engraving, etching,* illustration 3-8.

kinesthetic sense Awareness of one's own body movements. See *space.*

kinetic sculpture A sculpture with movable parts set in motion by a mechanical and/or natural power source. See *mobiles.*

line In terms of figure-ground, a narrow elongated figure. In art, a long thin mark ordinarily made by pencil, chalk, brush, and so forth. An outline around a shape. The edge or boundary of a shape. See *visual elements.*

linear perspective A systematic method for representing three-dimensional shapes in a picture—as seen by the eye from a given viewpoint. The size and shape of each object and the relationships between objects are determined by the locations of one or more *vanishing points* and an *eye-level line* (horizon). See figs. 2-25, 2-26, 2-27.

lithograph A print made by the process of lithography. See *lithography.*

lithography A printmaking technique in which the image is drawn on a flat stone or metal plate with a greasy pencil or liquid. The image is then chemically treated so that the image only receives ink—the remaining surface resisting ink. See *planography.*

load carrying Of a wall or post that supports a roof, as distinguished from a nonload-carrying wall or post. In the case of masonry roofs, ordinarily such walls or posts must be thick and/or numerous. See *arch, masonry, post and lintel.*

lost wax A method of hollow-bronze casting in which a mold is lined with a 3/8″ layer of wax, filled with a solid core of plaster, and heated to melt the wax, leaving a 3/8″ cavity between mold and core into which molten bronze is poured. Sometimes called *cire perdue.* See *casting.*

masonry The use of stone, brick, or cement blocks to build a structure. Characterized by *load-carrying* walls. That part of a structure, such as "stonework" or "brickwork," made with masonry materials. See *principle of construction.*

mass Three-dimensional shape. See *shape.*

medieval Pertaining to the Middle Ages. See *Middle Ages.*

medium The materials and techniques used to make an artwork. A particular category of art such as painting, sculpture, environment, and so forth.

metal frame See *frame construction.*

Middle Ages The period of western European history from the decline of the Roman Empire to the beginning of the Renaissance (A.D. 476 to *c.* A.D. 1400).

middle value	A value (or color) that is neither particularly light nor particularly dark. Gray. See *value*.
Minimal Art	An abstract style that flourished in the late 1960s characterized by the use of simple geometric shapes, straightforward symmetrical compositions, and extreme parsimony.
mixed media	Artworks in which two or more media are combined—often in an incongruous way. Artworks in which two-dimensional approaches are combined with sculptural approaches.
mobile	An abstract sculpture with movable parts—rods and thin forms connected by swivels—set in motion by air currents. See *kinetic sculpture*.
modeling	Producing a sculpture from a pliable material such as clay or wax and by manipulating the material with the hands or with shaping tools such as paddles or knives.
modern art	The various kinds of art made since the 1860s and associated with the modern movement. See *modern movement*.
modern movement	The series of changes in art and in events related to those changes in art that began in the 1860s. For the most part, the changes were away from realism and toward greater use of abstract modes.
multiple-point perspective	A picture drawn in linear perspective that uses more than one vanishing point—usually two. See *linear perspective*, fig. 2-26.
mold	A hollow plaster form the cavity of which is the negative image into which a substance, such as molten bronze, is poured to form a positive image or casting. See *casting*.
monochromatic	Of an artwork having only one color. Typically the color exhibits varieties in its value and saturation but not in its basic hue. See *color*.
monumental	Larger-than-life or appearing to be larger-than-life.
mural	Literally "wall." A picture painted directly onto a wall. See *fresco*.
negative shape	See *figure-ground*.
Neoclassical	Pertaining to Neoclassicism. See *Neoclassicism*.
Neoclassicism	Literally "new" classicism. A movement in the visual arts of the late eighteenth and early nineteenth centuries in which artists and critics sought inspiration from the art of ancient Greece and Rome (particularly early Rome) and emphasized in their own artwork the qualities of simplicity, order, and balance. See *classicism*.
Neoplatonism	A revival of the writings and ideas of Plato (fifth-century B.C. Greek philosopher) that flourished in Renaissance Italy, particularly in Florence.
neutral color/ neutral	A color so low in saturation that it lacks an identifiable hue: gray, brown, white, and black. See *saturation*.

nonload-carrying	Of a wall attached to a frame structure. A wall that does not support a roof. As distinguished from a load-carrying wall. See *frame construction*.
oil	A technique of painting in which pigments are mixed with oil, usually linseed oil. A painting made by this technique.
oil on canvas	The technique of oil applied to a canvas support.
oil painting	See *oil, oil on canvas*.
one-point perspective	See *single-point perspective*.
open sculpture	A sculptural form penetrated by one or more openings. Sculpture, such as a welded sculpture, in which the parts are pieced together around empty space(s).
Op Art	An abstract style of art popular in the early 1960s that emphasizes optical effects through the use of geometric patterns.
optical mixing	Perceiving a single color yet looking at numerous small, close-together, different colors. For example, from a distance side-by-side dots of red and yellow appear orange; dots of black and white appear gray—and so forth.
organic shapes	Shapes having irregular edges or surfaces as distinguished from *geometric shapes*. Shapes resembling things existing in nature (whether animate or inanimate).
pagan	Not Christian or Jewish—particularly in reference to the art and mythology of ancient Greece and Rome.
painting	Producing an artwork by applying *pigments* mixed with a *vehicle* (a liquid such as water or oil) to a *support* (a surface of some kind, such as canvas or wood). An artwork produced by this method. See *medium*.
Paleolithic	Literally "old stone." Of a hunter-gatherer culture that existed from 30,000 to 10,000 years ago.
patron	A person, usually of wealth and high social station, who purchases art or provides financial support for an artist in exchange for his or her work.
patronage	The function of a patron. A system of financial support for artists through commissioning their services or buying their works on the open market. Patrons collectively. See *patron, commission*.
Performance	An artwork involving an act or stunt by the artist rather than a tangible object such as a painting or sculpture. See *Happening*.
photograph	An artwork produced by means of photography. Light-sensitive paper (called contact paper) exposed in a darkroom to light passed through a film negative and then developed. See *photograpy*.

photography	Producing an artwork by capturing the image of a subject on light-sensitive materials by means of a camera and a chemical process termed developing. See *medium*.
pictorial convention	A customary manner of representing people or objects in an artwork.
Pietà	Literally "pity." An image of the dead Christ mourned by Mary.
pigment	Coloring matter. A substance of a particular color that when mixed with a vehicle can be used to make a painting. See *painting*.
planography	Making prints from a plane-surface plate. Ink is retained by portions of the surface because of their chemical variations (lithography) or their physical variations (serigraphy or silkscreen). See *lithograph, lithography, serigraphy, silkscreen*, fig. 3-11.
plate	A wooden block, metal sheet, flat stone, or silkscreen used in printmaking. See *printmaking, woodcut, engraving, etching, lithograph, silkscreen*.
Pointillism	A painting method, favored by Georges Seurat, that consists of applying paint in tiny dots of pure color.
Pop Art	An art movement of the 1960s that satirized popular culture (sometimes, high culture) through deadpan imitations of advertisements, signs, illustrations, and so forth. Because of its blatant use of subject matter as well as hard-edged shapes and *bright* colors, Pop Art was perceived as a reaction against Abstract Expressionism.
popular art	Chiefly products of the entertainment, advertising, and news industries: television shows, movies, commercials, billboards, illustrations, comic strips, news photography, and so forth. Distinguished from *fine art*.
positive shape	See *figure-ground*.
post and lintel	A principle of construction in which the horizontal members—lintels or beams—that span an open space are supported by vertical members—posts, columns, walls, piers, and so forth. Characterized by *load-carrying* walls.
Post-Impressionists	A late nineteenth-century avant-garde consisting chiefly of Cézanne, Gauguin, and Van Gogh—whose paintings resemble those of the Impressionists in their use of bright color. However, rather than emphasizing the effects of light, these artists aimed at exploring the formal structure of art or expressing their personal feelings.
principle of construction	The particular materials and technology used to build a structure. See *architecture*.
primary colors	The hues of yellow, red, and blue. Theoretically, all other hues are produced from these three. Combining equal amounts of any two will

produce a secondary color: *orange* from yellow and red, *green* from yellow and blue, and *purple* from red and blue. See *color wheel, hue.*

print
(1) A woodcut, etching, engraving, lithograph, silkscreen, or the like. One of several impressions made from an inked plate. See *printmaking.* (2) A photograph. One of several copies of a single film negative. See *photograph.*

printmaking
Producing a number of identical artworks, *prints,* by impressing paper against an inked *plate* on which an image has been carved, drawn, or stenciled. See *medium.*

proportion
The comparative relationships between a whole and its parts or between only the parts themselves—with respect to size, height, length, or width.

psychic improvisation
See *automatic drawing.*

psychological weight
The relative symbolic or emotional importance of a feature in an artwork. See *balance.*

realism
A relatively high degree of resemblance between the form of a painting or sculpture and what the eye sees. Also the use of "true-to-life" subject matter rather than fantastic or idealized subject matter.

relief printing
Making prints from a plate whose raised surfaces only receive the ink that will be transferred to the print. See *woodcut,* fig. 3-7.

relief sculpture
Sculpture whose images or forms protrude from a flat background.

Renaissance
Literally "rebirth." A cultural surge in the arts founded largely on a revival of classical art that began in fifteenth-century Italy and eventually spread to all of western Europe.

rhythm
A repetition of similar elements or features. See *grouping, similarity, continuity.*

Romantic
Pertaining to Romanticism. See *Romanticism.*

romantic
Of any thought, deed, or artistic expression that is dramatic, emotional, visionary, and/or exotic.

Romanticism
A nineteenth-century arts movement that emphasized the values of subjectivity, passionate emotion, and artistic freedom—all tending toward visionary, dramatic, or exotic themes. A reaction against Neoclassicism.

salon
A distinguished cultural event, usually held annually or on some regular basis. An art exhibit of this type. The place where such an event is held.

saturation
The relative purity of a color from bright to dull. Sometimes referred to as intensity. See *color.*

sculpture	The process of producing three-dimensional art. A three-dimensional artwork. See *medium*.
secondary colors	See *primary colors*.
sensibility	A cultivated sensitivity, especially to art and intellectual pursuits.
serigraphy	A stencil method of printmaking using a silkscreen as a plate. See *planography, silkscreen*.
sfumato	Literally "smoke." In a picture, the effect of hazy atmosphere produced by blurring or softening the outlines of objects and figures.
shading	See *chiaroscuro*.
shape	That quality of a thing pertaining to the limits of its external edge or surface. Shape is either *two-dimensional* (having height and width) or *three-dimensional* (having height, width, and depth). See *visual elements, figure-ground*.
shape constancy	The tendency to perceive the shape of a three-dimensional object as unchanging regardless of any change in the position of the object with respect to the viewer.
silkscreen	(1) A plate used in the silkscreen or serigraphy process consisting of a frame of mesh material through which ink passes and an attached stencil(s) that blocks the passage of ink. (2) A print made by the silkscreen or serigraphy process. See *serigraphy, printmaking*.
similarity	The resemblance between two or more things in an artwork, usually with respect to one of the visual elements—color, shape, and so forth. An aid to unity. See *unity*.
simulated texture	Texture(s) represented in a picture or realistic sculpture as distinguished from the texture of the artwork itself.
single-point perspective	A picture drawn in linear perspective with only one vanishing point. See *linear perspective*, fig. 2-25.
size constancy	The tendency to perceive the size of an object as unchanging regardless of any change in the distance between the object and the viewer. See *shape constancy*.
size/sizing	A viscous substance applied in a thin layer(s) to a porous surface such as canvas. Used on canvas before the application of oil paints. See *oil*.
space	The area between and around three-dimensional objects or shapes; the area within open or hollow shapes. Although space is experienced by moving within it (using our kinesthetic sense), its boundaries and limits—as defined by the shapes it touches—can be perceived visually. See *visual elements*.
still life	A picture of small objects—typically things found in a home or studio.

style	The distinguishing traits of an artwork that identify it as having been produced by a particular artist, school of art, period, or culture. The way in which an artwork is made, designed, or composed as distinguished from its subject matter or content. See *form*.
stylize	In an artwork, emphasis on the manner in which a thing is represented rather than the way it appears to the eye. To make an image conform to the rules of a particular style. To imbue an artifact or an artwork with a particular style. See *style, pictorial convention*.
subject/ subject matter	The people or objects represented in an artwork. See *image, theme*.
support	Any surface—canvas, wood, paper, wall, and so forth—on which a painting or drawing can be made.
Surrealism	A theory and practice of art that seeks to portray subconscious experiences or dream phenomena. An art and literary movement of the 1920s. Surrealistic paintings vary from realistic styles—often depicting dreams or other exotic subjects—to semiabstract styles containing primitive or childlike images
symbol	A feature in an artwork that signifies something else—as the cypress tree in "The Starry Night" symbolizes death (fig. 7-16).
Symbolists	A literary avant-garde of the late nineteenth century whose theories and approach paralleled those of the Post-Impressionists—especially Gauguin. See *Post-Impressionists*.
tactile	Concerning the sense of touch. See *texture*.
tempera	A technique of painting in which pigments are mixed with water and casein, glue, or egg yolk (traditionally the latter). A painting made by this technique.
tensile strength	The ability of a construction member (such as a lintel), when spanning a given area, to withstand the stress of its own weight or the weight of something resting on it.
texture	The surface quality of things: smooth, rough, soft, glossy, matte, and so forth. Although generally perceived through the sense of touch, texture can also be seen. See *visual elements*.
theme	The subject and/or underlying idea of an artwork. Subject matter is ordinarily less general and less abstract than theme. For example, the subject matter of Toulouse-Lautrec's painting (fig. 10-1) is "people at a cabaret"; the theme is "decadence." See *content*.
three-dimensional shape	See *shape*.
two-dimensional shape	See *shape, figure-ground*.

two-point perspective	See *multiple-point perspective*.
unity	Literally the state of being one. In a work of art, a perception that each thing fits, harmonizes, and functions well with everything else in the work. As opposed to a perception that one or more things do not fit, harmonize, or work well—in the extreme, a perception of chaos. The means for providing unity include the use of *grouping, similarity, continuity,* and *dominant feature.* See *composition*.
value	The relative lightness or darkness of a color. Values of a color (with an unchanging hue and saturation) can be located on a scale from white to black. See *color*.
value contrast	Adjacent colors with opposite values such as dark blue and light blue or black and white. See *value*.
vanishing point	The point in a picture at which all parallel lines that withdraw in depth converge. See *linear perspective*.
vault	A continuous arch resembling a tunnel or half barrel used to span a rectangular space. See *arch*, fig. 4-4.
vehicle	A liquid such as water or oil with which pigments can be mixed. See *painting*.
visual elements	Colors, shapes, lines, textures, and space.
visual weight	In an artwork, a feature's relative size, color brightness, and degree of contrast compared to its surroundings. See *balance*.
volume	See *space*.
warm colors	Red, yellow, orange, red-orange, yellow-orange, red-purple, and yellow-orange. Any analogous colors (hues) in which red and/or yellow predominate. The opposite of *cool colors*. See *analogous colors*.
welding	Producing sculpture by joining pieces of molten metal.
Western	Pertaining to the history and civilization of western Europe from the Middle Ages to the present and of the American continent from colonial times to the present.
woodcut	A print made from an image carved in a wooden block. See *relief printing*.
wood frame	See *frame construction*.

Index

A

46–47
Volkswagen, 232, *233*

W

Wall painting, Roman, 125–28, *126, 127*
Walter Finley Seated Nude (Sleigh), 150, *151*
Warhol, Andy, 162, 289, 291
  Marilyn Monroe Diptych, colorplate 28
Warm colors, 21
Wash, 52
Watching the Cargo (Bingham), 209–11, *210*
Watercolor, 52
Weight shift, 145, 152
Welding, 67
Wesselmann, Tom, 162–63, 289
  Great American Nude No. 99, 162–63, *163*
Whaam! (Lichtenstein), 288, *289*

White Light, White Heat (Burden), 301, *301*
Willy Lott's House Near Flatford Mill, Suffolk (Constable), 137, *138*
Window at Collioure (Matisse), 253–54, *colorplate 22*
Wine Merchant, Chartres Cathedral, *colorplate 6*
Winterpool (Rauschenberg), 283–84, *284*
Wittgenstein, Ludwig, 293
Women, portrayal of
  in Greek art, 150–52, *152*
  in Italian Renaissance, 153–56, *156*
  late nineteenth century, 159, *160*
  during Middle Ages, 153, *154*
  Neoclassical, 158–59, *158*
  seventeenth century, 156–58, *157*

twentieth century, 159–64, *161, 162, 163*
  Victorian, 159, *160*
Wood, Grant, *Stone City, Iowa,* 275, *275*
Woodcut, 56
Woodfield Shopping Center, Schaumburg, Illinois, 105, *107*
Wrapped Coast (Christo), 299, *299*
Wright, Frank Lloyd
  Broadacre City plan, 101–102
  Guggenheim Museum, 40, *40*
  Robie House, Chicago, 111, *111*

Y

Yale Lipstick (Oldenburg), 289–90, *290*

Picture Credits

bottom, Photo Draeger, Paris; **86,** Art Resource; **87,** HBJ photo; **88,** British Architectural Library, RIBA, London; **89,** photo Wayne Andrews; **90,** Ezra Stoller, ©ESTO; **91,** ©SPADEM, 1986; **92,** Australian Information Service; **93,** Canadian Consulate General, New York; **95,** American Airlines; **96,** Alison Frantz; **97,** The Public Archives of Canada; **98,** Wendy V. Watriss, Woodfin Camp and Associates; **99,** from "The Dogon People" by Fritz Morgenthaler, ©1969 Barrie and Jenkins, LTD., London. Reprinted from *Meaning in Architecture,* Charles Jencks and George Baird, editors, George Braziller, Inc., New York, 1970; **100,** from *Art Through the Ages,* 6th Edition, by Helen Gardner, ©1975 by Harcourt Brace Jovanovich, Inc. Reproduced by permission of the publisher; **101, 102,** the Art and Architecture Division of The New York Library, Astor, Lenox, and Tilden Foundations; **103,** New York Housing Authority; **105, 106,** Art Resource; **107,** Robert Stefl; **108,** Doug Long, Photocraft; **109,** from *The Japanese House* by Heinrich Engel, Charles E. Tuttle Co., Inc., Tokyo, Japan. Reproduced with permission of the publisher; **110,** Shashinka Photo, Scienceland, Inc., **111,** Chicago Architectural Photography, Chicago; **113,** Hedrich-Blessing Photography, Chicago; **114,** Colorado Office of Tourism; **115,** Atelier 5, Bern, Switzerland.

Chapter 5   **p. 119,** Colorphoto Hans Hinz, Allschwil-Basel; **120, 122,** American Museum of Natural History; **124,** Hirmer Fotoarchiv, Munich; **126,** Deutsches Archaeologisches Institut, Rome; **129,** Hirmer Fotoarchiv, Munich; **133, 135, 136,** Art Resource.

Chapter 6   **p. 143,** TAP Service; **144, 146, 147,** Art Resource; **150,** Gary Mortenson; **151,** Geoffry Clements Photography; **152, 154, 156,** Art Resource; **158,** ©SPADEM, 1986; **160,** Studio MADEC; **161,** left and right, ©SPADEM, 1986; **163, 165,** Geoffry Clements Photography; **166,** left, Art Resource; right, Raghubir Singh, Woodfin Camp and Associates; **168,** Art Resource.

Chapter 7   **p. 173, 175, 176–77, 179, 181,** left and right, **182, 184, 187,** Art Resource; **197,** the Estate of Lee Krasner Pollock; **198,** E. Irving Blomstrann; **200,** Rudolph Burckhardt; **204,** Hans Namuth.

Chapter 8   **p. 222,** Geoffry Clements Photography; **225,** photo courtesy O. K. Harris Works of Art.

Chapter 9   **p. 231, 232, 233,** bottom, Chrysler Motors Corporation Historical Collection; **233,** top, Ben Kocivar, Air Pixies; **234, 236, 237,** Art Resource; **239,** ©SPADEM, 1986.

Chapter 10   **p. 266,** top, **269,** ©SPADEM, 1986; **270,** photo courtesy the Museum of Modern Art; **273,** Robert E. Mates.

Chapter 11   **p. 279, 282,** Geoffry Clements Photography; **284, 285,** photo courtesy Leo Castelli Gallery, **287,** Rudolph Burckhardt; **290,** William Dyckes;

293, 295, photo courtesy Leo Castelli Gallery; **296,** Bevan Davies; **299,** Harry Shunk; **300,** Caroline Tisdall; **304,** photo courtesy John Weber Gallery; **311, 312,** photo courtesy Through the Flower, Benicia, CA.

Colorplates   **Plate 3,** Geoffry Clements Photography; **4, 5, 6, 10, 11, 12, 18,** Art Resource; **21,** photo Tom Scott; **22,** ©SPADEM, 1986; **25,** photo courtesy the Solomon R. Guggenheim Museum; **28,** photo courtesy Leo Castelli Gallery; **29,** photo courtesy Andre Emmerich Gallery.

B6
C7
D8
E9
F0
G1
H2
I3
J4